CHORAL TECHNIQUE

AND

INTERPRETATION.

HANDBOOKS FOR MUSICIANS

EDITED BY ERNEST NEWMAN.

To my Old Friend

DR. W. G. McNAUGHT, F.R.A.M.

CHORAL TECHNIQUE

AND

INTERPRETATION

BY

HENRY COWARD

MUS. DOC. OXON.

LONDON: NOVELLO AND COMPANY, LIMITED.

NEW YORK: THE H. W. GRAY CO., SOLE AGENTS FOR THE U.S.A.

MADE IN ENGLAND.

PREFACE.

THIS book has been written to assist Choral Conductors and Choirmasters, though its scope is not limited to these, as many of the principles embodied in the text are applicable to Soloists as well as to Orchestral and Military Conductors.

There is no padding or mere theorizing in the book. Everything written is the outcome of living experience, and has stood the test of many years' trial.

Other methods may be equally good, or better ; but because I have found what is herein stated to be, in my judgment, the most effective, I have, without reserve, placed my plans and experience at the disposal of all who are seeking to develop Choral music and Choral singing, either in the small Choir or in the large Festival Chorus.

H. C.

2, MOORGATE AVENUE,
        SHEFFIELD.

MODERN
CHORAL TECHNIQUE AND
INTERPRETATION.

WHEN journeying round the world during 1911 with the Sheffield World Tour Choir, to realise Dr. Charles Harriss's great imperial idea of musical reciprocity in the British Empire, amongst my pleasantest experiences I count the meetings and friendly discussions with the conductors of the numerous choral societies in Canada, America, Australia, New Zealand, and South Africa. In every case a spirit of enthusiasm for choral singing was manifested, coupled with a keen desire to reach a high standard. Therefore it was only natural that these conversations almost invariably drifted into a series of inquiries as to the management of the voice, the problem of maintaining the pitch, how to secure *pianissimo*, the secret of clear diction, and other topics connected with Choral Technique in its most modern development.

All these points of inquiry, which are also exercising the minds of hundreds of choral conductors in the British Isles, I carefully noted, and I propose in the following pages to give such hints, advice, and instruction that no single problem connected with choral singing, shall, if possible, remain unsolved.

This may seem a presumptuous remark, but to vindicate the statement I propose to press into service the crystallized essence of forty years' experience as conductor of all sorts and conditions of choirs, which I trust will enable me to justify the assertion.

This extended practical knowledge has been gained from bodies of singers ranging from the raw, rough material of village singers to the polished select choir; from small bodies of twenty-four voices to masses of over fifty thousand.

From the above foreshadowing of the scheme of the book, it will be gathered that its object is intensely practical—in fact, to assist in every possible way the hosts of choral conductors and choir-masters to become effective participators in that tremendous and wonderful forward movement in choral singing, splendid examples of which are now to be heard at many of our Musical Festivals, advanced choral societies' concerts, and choral contests, whether known as Eisteddfodau or Competitive Festivals.

DEFINITION OF THE NEW TECHNIQUE, AND INTERPRETATIVE AIM.

To the question, What is the New Choral Technique? the answer may be given that it embraces all the splendid qualities, grand, rich tone, broad effects, and thrilling climaxes of the old style of choral singing, as exemplified at the Leeds and Birmingham Musical Festivals of the 'eighties and 'nineties, plus the more refined expression and greater dramatic import demanded by the more advanced and much more critical audiences of to-day.

These added attributes of progressive choral training may be briefly summarized as follows:—

(*a*) Greater vocal control on the part of the singers. This must be shown in homogeneity of tone, so that each vocal part, however numerous, sounds like one huge voice and not like a congeries of conflicting voices.

Further, the voices must be able to produce different qualities of tone. No longer will one tone-quality satisfy the claims of interpretation of even such works as *The Messiah* and *Elijah*, whilst in modern choral works variety of tone-quality is absolutely necessary. Therefore numerous tone tints—the white, the impersonal, the ethereal, the dull and the dark, the breathy, and many other colourings—must be available.

There must be also characterization of tone to exemplify the sob, the exclamation, the snarl, the laugh—playful, mocking, derisive, or fiendish—the shout of triumph, &c. In fact, the whole gamut of dramatic emotion has now to be portrayed by the subtle shadings of the tone-quality of the voices.

(*b*) Expression of a more refined and artistic character must be shown.

In addition to the sudden contrasts from *pp* to *ff* and *vice versa*—dearly beloved of old—the fine *cres.* and *dim.*, the melting and merging of one phrase into another, the definite prominence or subordination of any part or parts, as in artistic string quartets, and the due attention to contrasts of force, all need incorporation in the modern scheme of expression.

(*c*) Words and their articulation call for supreme attention. The new technique predicates greater care in securing correct vowel quantity and clear definition of consonants, whether they be initial, middle, or final.

In addition to this technical perfection, vitalising of the words and sentences by proper tone and emphasis is demanded, so that the dramatic sense is never in doubt, the result being the attainment of good diction—that pearl of great price.

(*d*) In phrasing, it exacts careful marking of the breathing places so as to secure a natural grouping of the words.   Further, the musical phrasing, when not controlled by the text, is not left to haphazard treatment, as has been too often the case.

(*e*) Rhythm is exalted to a high position.   Means are adopted to secure such a control of accents and stresses—regular and irregular—that each distinctive phrase maintains its individuality while not interfering with the other parts, thus avoiding the muddiness and jumble which one often hears, say, in Bach's music when badly rendered.

The sense of the composition must be faithfully reflected in the performance.   It will not suffice to sing " He trusted in God " in the same manner as " Glory to God "; or the " Wraith of Odin " (*King Olaf*) with the same atmosphere as the succeeding chorus, " A little bird in the air "; or a madrigal in part-song fashion.   A recognition of diversity of styles of composition and adaptation of means to end is now exacted.

(*f*) Breathing must be dealt with systematically, not only to secure power to phrase, but to get control of breath pressure, so as to produce those extraordinary *fortissimo* effects which suggest illimitable power of voice.

The new training also demands a wider outlook and a greater range of composition than

existed in the past. It will not do to confine the
performances to a few well-known works, or even a
wider range of old works, to the exclusion of
modern compositions. Up to a few years ago
there was a strong disposition on the part of both
conductors and societies to treat with scant courtesy
any work which presented anything out of the
current idiom, and which was therefore rather
difficult to perform. I am of opinion that the
many failures in the rendering of works at our
leading Musical Festivals have been due to the
inertia of the performers rather than to the
demerits of the compositions. The way difficulties
were shirked used to make my blood boil, because
many new, strange effects were never realised, and
the works were consequently damned. A conspicuous example of putting new wine into old
bottles was the first performance of *Gerontius*.
We can now look back and smile at the fiasco,
because we properly attribute the failure to the
fact that the new spirit of progress—so well
vindicated since at the same festival—had not
entered into either the officials or the singers. This
spirit of tackling and mastering difficulties for an
artistic purpose must be paramount in all who
wish to march under the banner of the newest
choralism.

The foregoing demands of modern choral
singing may seem appalling to many, but experience
has shown that they can all be met. When, from
1875 to 1895, I attended all the chief festivals as
musical critic, the limitations of the old style of
choralism were often very evident to me. Though
there were very many things to praise—and I never
had occasion to write an adverse criticism of the

choral singing—the lack of delicacy, the absence of
clearness in the words, the few attempts (generally
failures) at characterization, the lack of spring and
alertness, &c., produced such a feeling of dis-
satisfaction in me that I had often to lecture
myself in some such manner as the following: " You
are unreasonable to expect a large body of singers
to be as smart and agile as a small select choir or
the principals. Is it fair to expect four hundred
voices to give a real *pianissimo;* or to demand
perfection in chromatic chords; or to exact individuality in involved polyphony ? You might as
well expect an omnibus to go noiselessly along the
road, or railway engines to skip like rams, or an
elephant to say ' See me dance the polka.' In the
nature of things it is impossible. Be reasonable.
Praise the things that are worthy of praise, and
leave the irremediable faults alone."

Happily I had a choral society—the Sheffield
Musical Union—which enabled me by frequent
experiment to put to practical test whether it
was possible for a large choir to equal a smaller
body in the matters of responsiveness, alertness,
quality of tone, expression, and diction. The ever-
faithful singers enthusiastically pursued the ideal
of their leader, and fearlessly trod strange paths,
traversed many unknown vocal regions, and scaled
choral heights which had hitherto not been
attempted. The success and the great local
reputation of the Sheffield Musical Union chorus
led to the choir of the first Sheffield Festival being
placed under my sole control.

It is not presumption to say that the singing of
these three hundred and twenty voices was a
genuine revelation to the visiting critics, and

proved that all the attributes of artistic singing—
good vocal tone, power without roughness, delicate
nuances without weakness, true intonation, perfect
chording and blend, clearness of attack, clearness
of words together with perfection of mobility and
discipline—could be attained as well by a large
body of vocalists as by a small select choir.

The possibilities of higher achievements being
shown, the path thus opened out has been successfully followed by highly talented and enthusiastic
conductors, with the result that we hear to-day at
most Musical Festivals, Eisteddfodau, and other
competitive meetings, performances of compositions
which, in respect of their difficulty and the
excellence of their rendering, would have been
thought impossible a dozen years ago.

Herein lies the reason for the writing of this book.
It is to set forth the *underlying* principles of artistic
choral attainment, so that the ordinary well-
informed enthusiastic choral conductor may
approximate in result to the excellent renderings
of the select souls to whose conducting reference
has been made above, and thus raise the artistic
standard of singing throughout the world.

THE REHEARSAL.

The choral society exists, or should exist, primarily for the realisation of an ideal, the flower and fruit of this being a performance, as perfect as possible, of the work undertaken.

In this ideal there should be faultless technique and artistic expression — the former to give intellectual satisfaction, the latter to stir the emotions,—the whole to transport the hearer to that exaltation of spirit, free from baser passions, which it is the glory of music to produce.

While this end should always be kept in mind, we must never lose sight of the means to the end. Hence the importance of giving attention to the supreme factor in musical achievement — *the rehearsal*.

There is a hoary fiction that a final bad rehearsal ensures a good performance. It may be granted that a poor final effort may have its value by making the performers careful at the concert, but it is a mistake to think that a poor or bad rehearsal is anything but a calamity to a society of amateurs. Artistic ideality soon droops in the chilly atmosphere of incompetent dulness ; shrivels up in the air of strenuous misdirection of effort; withers and expires in the sultry blasts of querulous irritability.

Therefore the subject *How to conduct rehearsals* is of vital importance to the artistic, and incidentally to the commercial success of the choral society.

In the main there are three methods of taking rehearsals. These I name:—

    1st. The Conventional Generalizing ;

    2nd. The Critical (or hypercritical)—
        Particularizing ; and

    3rd. The Compartmental Specializing.

These methods may be used at both full and sectional rehearsals.

Generally all three varieties are used consciously or unconsciously by all conductors, but as "Method is the secret of success," if conductors are able to realise the distinctive features and differences of the three plans of conducting rehearsals, and also know the best stage at which to use each style— whether singly or in combination—rehearsals will be made much more effective and enjoyable. The enjoyment aspect is to my mind of such importance that it swallows up every other consideration, for pleasurable choral rehearsals mean profitable social reunions.

I will now consider this trinity of plans, with a view of obtaining unity of effects, namely, getting as much good work done as possible in the limited time for rehearsal.

THE CONVENTIONAL GENERALIZING METHOD.

The Conventional Generalizing Method is the one to be followed chiefly as the foundation of all rehearsals. It consists of going through the music time after time until the general outline of it is mastered, and the spirit of the composition fully grasped by the singers. Theoretically this is quite correct, and, as such, this useful and necessary process is followed by the great majority of conductors. Most of them, however, fail to achieve success, or at least distinction, because of the limitations of the method. It needs that element of ideality which the Particularizing and Specializing Methods presuppose. At a recent Three Choirs Festival an enthusiastic gentleman amateur asked a very well-known composer—who is generally regarded as a great genius in composition—What is genius? He replied, "Two per cent. of inspiration, and ninety-eight per cent. of perspiration." In artistic matters, as in the Sheffield high-grade steel, it is the two per cent. of inspiration which makes all the difference between the ordinary and the really good. Those who follow the Generalizing Method exclusively, just miss this two per cent. —the "vital spark"—and the oft-heard remark of conductors, "That will do," when really the fine edge of polish and attainment has never been attempted or even thought of, shows that thousands of choirmasters regard this conventional treatment as a terminus, not merely a thoroughfare which has to be traversed in the search for artistic perfection.

THE CRITICAL PARTICULARIZING METHOD.

The Particularizing Method consists in striving for perfection in each detail—music, words, expression, &c.—to attain which the method is absolutely necessary. Strangely enough this method, as carried out by some conductors, produces disastrous results—by exciting irritation instead of giving irradiation or illumination, and thus killing all pleasure in the rehearsals.

Let us follow, in a matter-of-fact way, the common usage of a conductor who adopts this method.

Full of zeal, with a lofty ideal, and familiar with the score, he begins the rehearsal with high hopes and a firm determination to achieve something good. In the first few bars he hears some wrong notes. Instead of allowing these to pass and " blundering through " somehow, he stops the choir to try over, say, the bass and contralto parts separately. He starts again, and finds the sopranos and tenors are wrong, therefore he stops again to put them right. If he let that suffice all would be well, because choirs rather like short explanatory stoppages ; but presently he stops because a phrase has been sung *forte* instead of *piano*, and says, with a growl, that it is surprising that they should not observe expression marks, &c. A harsh voice and a mispronounced word call for stoppage and reproof ; and by the end of the rehearsal one chorus, perhaps, has been got through. The choir meanwhile are invariably annoyed and " fretted " at being stopped so often—like a spirited horse that is being constantly " pulled " by a tactless driver—and sore at having to sit, for a seemingly long part of the evening, listening to the other " parts " correcting their mistakes. The feeling running through it all is " much cry and little wool." This kind of thing is repeated at subsequent rehearsals, because of the avowed determination of the conductor to "make everything perfect as we go along," with the result that at the concert the last chorus, or perhaps two choruses, have to be sung practically at sight; and as the earlier choruses are not sung too well through not being heard frequently as a whole, the final impression on the mind of the audience is one of disappointment.

This is not a fancy picture, as I know societies which have undergone this treatment from well-meaning, clever men for season after season, until a rebellion of the long-suffering members has led to a change of conductors.

The mistake is to expect artistic results too soon. They forget the old saw " Rome was not built in a day." Singers as a rule are aware of mistakes, and when they have got a kind of subconscious grasp of harmonies they master the errors privately. In this matter of note-perfection, after pointing out errors or very difficult phrases, it is good policy to leave it to the members and "wait and see." This is better than doing as some conductors do, viz., keep three-quarters of the society doing nothing for half the night while one of the parts is mastering a knotty point.

Equally wasteful and unsatisfactory is it to try to get a body of players or singers to render a phrase with expression before the phrase itself and the words have become familiar, or rather burnt into the mind. Every artistic effect must have its antecedent of preparatory work. Taking it as a whole, long experience of myself and others has shown me that more harm is done by the too early application of the Particularizing hypercritical wanting-to-do-too-many-things-at-a-time Method, than by the apparently slower—even stodgy—conventional "non-stop" manner, where at least the choir does get a full night's singing and thereby makes some progress, whereas the " fretting " system irritates the singers.

THE COMPARTMENTAL SPECIALIZING METHOD.

The little known and little practised Compartmental Specializing Method consists in taking some special point or topic, and concentrating all attention on it, and, for the time being, ignoring everything else. For instance, if note-perfection of a difficult phrase be the object sought, all faults of tone-quality, words, breathing, or expression are passed over. The same rule is observed if the topic of study be the development of a fugal subject, or obtaining fluency in runs, divisions, or roulades, as in " His yoke is easy," or " For unto us."

Amongst the many features that call for specialization we may include the working up to a climax ; the polishing of a *pianissimo* phrase ; the obtaining of perfect attack ; the management of the *crescendo* and the *diminuendo ;* the realising of the dynamic and emotional *sforzandos* and pressure notes ; the clarifying—to the listener—of close imitations ; the development of marked entries ; the perfecting of vowels and consonants ; the marking of breathing places ; the unifying of tone-quality ; and the developing of characteristic tonal effects, as in the " Demons' Chorus," " He trusted in God," the " Amen " in *Faust*, &c.

The above list is not exhaustive, as each composition presents its own problems. This specializing method may be described as the Napoleonic " Divide and Conquer " policy : or perhaps it more nearly follows the plan of

Mr. Maskelyne and other famous jugglers and plate-spinners, who get one plate spinning before they attempt to set going the next.

Of course care must be taken not to give too large doses of this method at one time, or it would become as wearisome as the Particularizing Method. Fortunately experience has shown that it takes only a seemingly short time to enforce one or two points during an evening, because when the object aimed at is explained to the singers they generally enter into the spirit of the quest, and when they become interested the time is pleasurably and profitably spent.

THE UNION OF THE THREE METHODS.

It will be seen from the above that by no one of the three methods alone can the highest results be achieved, and as the success of the rehearsals depends upon the conductor's mental grasp of the three methods, and his power to blend the trinity into a unity, it is necessary to consider how and when to use the methods singly and in combination.

First in order comes the General Conventional Method. This should be used almost exclusively for the first two or three rehearsals, and, combined with the other methods, should continue to the final rehearsal. When the music and words have been roughly but firmly outlined, and the "hang" of the piece fairly grasped, then Specializing or Particularizing treatment should supplement the general coaching.

The specializing should be introduced at the very earliest moment, but in the early stages should be applied in homœopathic doses. It is the opportunist's method. It gives the smart conductor the chance of putting right a particularly knotty point, and, while relieving for five minutes the decorous general method, it also gives the conductor credit for alertness.

For instance, a good method of specializing is to take one or two difficult intervals or phrases in a piece, and, before the music is sung over, to pattern the phrase by voice or pianoforte, showing how it should be sung. By this means pitfalls are made comparatively easy to circumvent, and much time is saved. As examples of the kind of phrase here meant, I would refer to bar 11 of Elgar's "Go, song of mine," where the sudden transition from B minor to E flat minor is very disconcerting unless the mind of the singer has been prepared for it. Similarly the sopranos must be prepared for the high G natural, bar 14, in F minor, which comes abruptly after G flat in the bass and contralto parts in bar 13. It will not be necessary to multiply examples to which this principle can be applied, because almost every modern piece contains one or more phrases in which it is necessary. This specializing should not be undertaken without previous preparation on the part of the conductor. He should know what he wants and how to go about getting it.

During the early general rehearsals he should notice any errors of notes, time, rhythm, attack, release, phrasing and what not, marking in blue pencil the places that want special attention. He is then able to form his plan of operations, and having decided upon his special subject for the next rehearsal, he should not be diverted from the one point by the appearance of other errors, but

c

carry it through, while noting the faults which require attention at a future rehearsal.

It is well known that in nearly every piece there are certain parts which require much more rehearsal than, say, the other nine-tenths, but owing to the inconvenience of stopping a choir in full swing, the difficulties are allowed to pass unnoticed. By applying this method the desirable extra rehearsal is met with conspicuous success and usually in a pleasant form. A feature of this specializing is *to keep all the choir engaged.* For instance, in the mastering of a fugue—especially if the subject be difficult or unusual, as in Brahms's *Requiem*—I ask all the choir to sing both the subject and the answer in unison until each is practically learned by heart, the result being brilliant attack in performance. If the subject be florid, as in "For unto us," or "Let Zion's children" (in Bach's Motet, *Sing ye*), the whole choir sing each part in unison softly, the object being to give fluency to the runs, divisions, or roulades, and agility to the voice, the emphasis in these cases being placed on the improvement of the voice.

It is said that the great artist Turner, the day before the Royal Academy was open to the public, used to touch up his pictures by means of a brush at the end of a long stick. This was done to accommodate the picture to the distance from the spectator and the surroundings. This plan of "final touching up" I strongly approve, and it should be carried out whenever it happens that the work is practically finished by the time of the penultimate rehearsal. At the final rehearsal I find it a good plan to specialise, to impress upon the minds of singers all those details over which great pains have been taken—such as *pianissimos*, the balancing of tone so that each entry is heard and each inner melody is duly prominent, the maintenance of pitch at critical points, &c., &c. There is no doubt that this last effort produces maximum results.

When, with great saving of time and temper, the choir has been prepared, by the Conventional and Compartmental Methods, for the consummation of the rehearsals, then the Critical Particularizing Method can be introduced with advantage both to the conductor and the conducted. It is easy to see how it can now be successfully applied, because each section—voice, music, words, expression—having been dealt with separately, all that is needed is to combine the various constituents in a well-balanced whole. It is as though an artist had made finished sketches of each object, figure and background, and then had merely to harmonize them on a single canvas into an artistic whole—the picture.

The conductor will find that the worry to himself and the fretting to the choir have now disappeared, because the singers, being in a state of preparedness, can give full attention and practical effect to any new demand of interpretation. Further, at this stage they become by their responsiveness fellow helpers, almost anticipating every wish; and furthermore, they enjoy the polishing process when they feel that they can realise the conductor's ideas. There is now no irritation at being stopped again and again; in fact they like it, because they feel every interruption means improvement in one point or another, and this makes them feel the joy of successful conquest, and they leave the rehearsal room shaking hands with themselves at what has been attempted and accomplished.

As to the conductor, he will go home delighted, and refreshed in spirit though perhaps tired in body. For has he not had the joy of seeing—or rather hearing—his ideals of beauty materialise? Like another Aladdin, he has only had to call, and lo! an artistic edifice has sprung to life at his bidding—happy man!

In conclusion of this topic, I would strongly urge highly-strung, anxious-souled conductors not to "put the cart before the horse"—*i.e.*, try to force the pace by neglecting the so-called inartistic preliminary grinding. If they do, they will find, as I have found, that it is a case of more haste less speed. I have small faith in the "make-perfect-as-you-go-along" plan, but prefer the system of arriving at perfection concurrently with the grasping of the atmosphere of the composition as a whole. Like the man who said he knew honesty was the best policy because he had tried both, I say I have tried every method of conducting, and the plans I recommend above are the best—best for the music, best for the choir, and best for the conductor. I may say that now I never go away disappointed from a rehearsal, because I always get from the choir as much as I expected. The first rehearsal gives satisfaction, the next more satisfaction, and at each following rehearsal there is generally a *crescendo* of pleasurable feeling till, after a final hypercritical Particularizing rehearsal, I feel jubilant at the splendid responsiveness of the choir, and look forward with confidence to the thrills which will be experienced at the concert by the conductor, the performers, and the audience.

VOICE.

It has been assumed in the foregoing remarks that reading ability, vocal power and control, and temperament were all possessed by the choralist, and at hand for the conductor, who had only to fit these constituents into his preconceived plan in order to realise all that was in his mind. Alas, this is seldom the case. The conductor has often to create, or develop from a feeble germ, the elements which make good singing possible. With respect to the voice this is frequently so. In most choral societies, even in those where the voices are tested, there are a great majority of untrained voices, which may be roughly classified as follows :—weak and quavery, worn and tinny, harsh and shrill, strident, metallic, shouty, throaty, cavernous, hooty, scoopy, and nondescript. I have been blessed with voices answering to each of the above classes for thirty or forty years, and have not wholly got rid of them to the present day—and yet I have survived! With such singers as a general vocal asset, is there any wonder that the most frequent question I have had to answer at home and abroad has been : " What would you do if you had to conduct a choir of poor, faulty voices ?" The questioners imagined that my choirs were composed of trained singers, which is not and has not been the case. The obvious answer has always been : " Make the best of the material you have— as I have to do ; keep on pegging away on right lines, and good results will accrue ; be not too impatient, but ' learn to labour and to *wait*.' " To the inevitable question which followed : " How would you bring about the improvement ? " I will now endeavour to give an answer in detail.

First let us see what qualities of voice the members of a choral society should possess :—

1. They should have a fair amount of power.
2. The voices should be properly produced.
3. They should have some agility and flexibility.
4. They should be under good control.
5. When used collectively they should be homo-geneous ; that is, each part should sound like one full, glorified voice, and not as an assortment of voices. It is the possibility of getting this unity of voice—with well-directed effort and a little trouble—that is the bright spot and salvation of choral-voice equipment.

Conductors, in their despair at not having an army of Pattis, Butts, Lloyds, and Santleys, may think that they are the victims of a specially hard fate, but really they have no need to be down-hearted.

Every society is made up of average voices, and my experience is that there is not nearly so much difference as some would have us believe in the average voices, such as are to be found all through the English - speaking countries. I make this statement with the special object of inspiring conductors with hope, and of assuring them that they have great potentialities at hand in their choirs if they will only make up their minds to expend the requisite labour.

To quote only one instance, out of many, of what can be done with a set of average voices—and that a low average,—I would say that the fifty singers who established the reputation of the Sheffield Musical Union were all young and untrained, and not one was tested for voice in any form, the sole qualification being the possession of the elementary certificate of the Tonic Sol-fa College, or, in later years, the alternative of a similar certificate in the staff notation.

The fact is, really good results can be obtained from a choir of average voices if the following hints and instructions are carried out, and the conductor is willing to " labour and to wait," instead of, like most inefficient workmen, grumbling at his tools.

HOW TO SECURE HOMOGENEITY OF VOICE.

The problem of how to blend the harsh, dull, and twangy voices of untrained singers into an agreeable unity is not so difficult as it appears at first sight. The defects enumerated above (page 19) nearly all arise from one source—the wrong placing of the voice, which, stated in simple language, means that the air current after it has passed over the vocal chords (the larynx) when producing sound is allowed to proceed in the wrong direction, or lacks control. Therefore all that is necessary is to get the choralist to control the breath, and direct the sounding air current to one approved spot or region in the mouth where the sound seems to float on the breath. This spot or region lies between the front of the mouth—just where the teeth join the palate—and the lips, according to the kind and quality of tone required. Of course it is more difficult to get a large body of singers to do this than a single individual, but there is always a good percentage who follow instructions and can successfully imitate a pattern, and this is the leaven which permeates the whole choir in time, though not as quickly as some conductors desire.

In my scheme of choral voice-building I start with the three axioms :—

1. The exercises, and the time spent in voice exercises, must be short.

2. The exercises must be very easy, so that they can be memorized and sung automatically, and thus prevent the mind from being diverted from the object to be attained.

3. The exercises must unfailingly lead to the desired result.

Long experience and uniform success have shown the wisdom of these axioms, the practical application of which now follows.

On a blackboard I write this exercise :

" Write and memorize the following :—

Ex. 1.

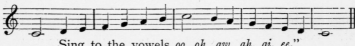

Sing to the vowels *oo, oh, aw, ah, ai, ee.*"

Before giving the pattern for the choir to imitate I explain the particular point they are to aim at—unity of tone—remarking that the

singers themselves have shown how necessary it is
to have some exercises for this purpose, as there
are so many conflicting tone - qualities—harsh,
strident, raucous, dull, hooty, throaty, twangy—
amongst them.

I explain that the disagreeable effect of some of
these tone - qualities (the strident, the nasal, the
guttural, the throaty, &c.) is due to the harsh
harmonics which are developed by their faulty
voice-production, which harmonics refuse to blend
with any other sound ; hence the heterogeneity of
tone. The remedy for this is to direct the voice, or
in other words the air column, as they sing, to the
front of the mouth, when, the harmonics being
fewer, more consonant, and approximately the
same, they will blend sufficiently well to produce
an agreeable compound tone; thus all throatiness,
twang, hooting, &c., will disappear. This I
show by giving specimens of each fault and
its remedy, driving home the fact that a person's
natural voice is not unalterable, like the colour of
his eyes, but is subject to control by the will of the
singer. This preliminary explanation over, I then
sing Ex. 1 very softly in key B♭, to the vowel *oo*,
with the sound at my lips. The choir then
imitate the pattern. Many fail to do it, but there
are a good number who imitate well, and these act
as a stimulus to the unsuccessful. We try again,
with better results. Having secured good blending
tone on *oo*, I then pattern *ee*, calling attention to
a better quality of tone. The singers are also
urged to observe their own physical sensations—
the feeling of the muscles in the mouth—when
producing the *ee* sound, as it will be of great
advantage later, when developing another vocal

point. When the pattern has been imitated successfully, I stop. The above explanations and exercises will have taken from twenty to thirty minutes—much too long as a regular thing, but when a new topic is introduced, and you feel that you have the interested choir with you, extra time may be taken once in a way. This remark applies to any subject relating to the work of the choir. At the next rehearsal we get a step further—taking, say, fifteen minutes—in developing unity of tone on all the vowels. This I do in the following manner:—I pattern Ex. 1 in key B♭ to the vowel *oo*, which the choir imitate. Then the vowels *oh, aw, ah, ai, ee*, are taken in succession. The choir then sing the vowels without pattern in keys C and D, patterning being resorted to when any glaring faults need correction. By the third week we get into what is the normal method of carrying on voice-building exercises, which should not take up more than five minutes, because choralists resent the time of rehearsal being taken up by things outside the music set down for rehearsal.

The procedure is as follows:—The accompanist strikes the chord of B♭ or C, and the choir immediately sing Ex. 1 to *oo*, very softly. Immediately this is done the chord of B is struck, and at once the exercise is sung to *oh*. Rising by semitones for twelve semitones the exercise is sung to each vowel in turn, until each vowel has been taken twice. At the second higher repetition of the vowels the contraltos and basses sing an octave lower than the sopranos and tenors. Although this unifying exercise is short (five minutes) its effect is great, because it influences the tone-production all through the rehearsal, and further, it is largely used in private rehearsal by those who are keen about improving their voices.

A few cautions may with advantage be given here. When oneness of tone has been secured, it must not be supposed that each voice is of the same quality (timbre). This would in many cases be an undesirable thing. What is wanted in choral singing is a rich compound tone, made up of voices of various timbres, which has the disagreeable excesses of individuality so modified that the characteristic qualities of one set of voices form the complement of another set or other sets, the combination making an agreeable whole.

Those who have seen great artists mix incongruous colours to get a certain tint will understand how it is possible to get, say, a glorified soprano tone from a mixture of ordinary voices. Therefore when a conductor hears, in solo, Miss A's rather shrill voice, he must not be worried, but think how beautifully it will add brightness to Miss B's heavy, full voice; and instead of being despondent at Miss C's dull, characterless voice, he must rejoice that it acts as a foil to Miss D's rather strident vocal organ.

Beyond certain limits, to which reference will be made later, it is a mistake to labour for too much similarity of tone. It is better to get good blending voices of varied qualities. I know of a choir which consists of the present and past pupils of a professor of singing. He has trained them well, but although they sing with taste and feeling and the voices are good individually, through their having been formed or trained on one model, and that on the rather hard, bright side, the effect is unsatisfactory, there being a disagreeable suggestion of acidity in the tone.

Another necessary caution is :—In all choral-voice exercises avoid too much use of the vowel *oo*. The forward tone is so easily obtained by this vowel that some conductors and many church choirmasters, taking the line of least resistance, use *oo* to such an extent that everything the choir sings is dominated with *oo*; consequently the dull, cavernous sound spoils the effect of all their efforts, just as the " ooey "—often hooty—wordless voices of many choirboys are an infliction.

Each vowel must be taken in turn, and if in the earlier stages any vowels are favoured, let them be *ai* and *ee*, as these favour "nasal resonance," which will be referred to later. It should be said however, that at the first few lessons it is sometimes necessary to use *oo* as a starting point for the other vowels, in order to coax the air current into its proper place, as *oo-oh* = woe, *oo-aw* = waw, *oo-ah* = wah, *oo-ai* = way, *oo-ee* = we.

EXTENDING THE COMPASS OF THE VOICE.

The next essential of a choir is adequate compass. In many choruses the sopranos and tenors " shy " at the high notes, or negotiate them badly. This is really not necessary, as both sopranos and tenors can be " nursed " into taking high G's, A's, and B's easily.

Ex. 1 is a splendid vehicle by which to extend the compass of the voices, and if in the exercises for unifying the voices it has been used with judgment, the compass of the voices will have extended to some extent unconsciously, and prepared the way for the time when more definite instructions as to the extension of the compass of the voice are demanded.

The following plan I have found to be very successful:—I strike the chord of F and ask the choir to sing Ex. 1 to the vowel *oo* very softly, to fix the air current. (The basses and contraltos sing an octave below the sopranos and tenors.) The same exercise is sung to *ai*, this time *mezzo-forte*, and again to the vowel *ee, forte*. F sharp is then struck, and the same process repeated. Rising by semitones, we proceed to key B♭, B or C. The singers soon realise that by proper placing of the voice they can reach the high notes with comparative ease, and in a short time there is little difficulty with respect to the high notes in any voice part.

The results of this compass-extending exercise are so satisfactory that the sopranos and tenors of all my choirs can easily sing the high B flat and B natural in Elgar's " Go, song of mine," leaping at the notes and hitting them in the middle with true "shock of the glottis."

DEVELOPING POWER OF VOICE.

The third requisite of a choir is power, or at least ring and intensity of voice. The unifying and extension of the compass of the voice, mentioned above, are very important elements, but if power and ring of voice be absent, you can at best only get smooth, sweet, decorous singing, such as is heard at genteel conventional suburban societies. But with tone of this sort it is impossible to get grand climaxes; consequently there are no thrills, no uplift of the heart, no stirring of the emotions—nothing, in fact, to send a glow of delight through the audience. Hence the power to produce the six degrees of *fortissimo*, which Mr. Kalisch referred to as being present in the Sheffield Chorus, must be cultivated and secured.

I am happy to be able to say that this power of voice can be obtained by a choir of good average voices, as I have demonstrated hundreds of times.

When a professional musical critic I was often struck with the effect produced upon the hearer by a few notes, or a phrase, drawn white-hot, as it were, from a violin by a brilliant player. The mental disturbance was quite disproportionate to the quantity or volume of sound produced, for the sum total of the sound could be drowned by a single strong-lunged chorister. On analysing the cause of the " thrill," I found that it was due to the *intensity* of the sound produced by the player's firm attack and nervous energy. This taught me a lesson, and gave me a principle which I applied to choral music in order to get thrills at a crisis or climax.

When a conductor has made up his mind that the time and conditions are ripe for cultivating power of voice, he must be alert to seize the favourable opportunity to introduce the subject. Let it be at a point where six *fortes* would not be too much—say the end of a massive chorus, or a phrase like " Overwhelmed," in Elgar's *King Olaf*, where the singers themselves realise that more power is wanted. With this as a cue to yourself, and as a splendid peg to hang your instructions upon, break in upon the rehearsal by giving them a dose of " Specializing," the subject being

" How to strengthen the voice so as to produce a
thrilling climax." Being a new, interesting, and
desirable topic, the choir will cheerfully tolerate
a twenty to twenty-five minutes' break—fifteen
minutes for explanation and ten for exercises.

The following is an outline of my explanatory
matter and the method I adopt when introducing
and working up this important feature of choralism.

I begin by saying that "At every concert the
audience should experience at least six thrills.
A concert without thrills is like a cloud without
water at drought time, or bread without salt—
unsatisfactory and unsatisfying. Thrills can be
produced by charming *pianissimos* and well-graded
crescendos and *diminuendos*, but most of all by
stirring *fortissimo* climaxes. It is evident to you all
that to get a rousing climax we shall have to sing
louder and with more brilliance. Seeing that you
seem to be singing with all your power, you may
think it impossible to sing louder. In that you are
mistaken. Though you had the impression it was
your loudest, you can sing twice as loudly and,
what is of greater importance, with greater *intensity*.
The question arises, 'How is it to be done?'
This I will show you after I have explained why
my instructions should be followed.

" The science of acoustics teaches us that
differences in the loudness of sounds depend
upon the amplitude of vibration of the sounding
medium—that is, say in a violin, upon the
difference in the size of the swing of the
sounding string. Further, the science teaches us
that the loudness varies according to the square
of the amplitude; that is, if a certain swing—say
the vibration of a violin string—produces one unit

of sound, a swing twice as great will produce not
merely twice as much sound—two units—but four
units ; and if the player causes the string to have
three times as much motion it will produce nine
units, and four times will produce sixteen, and
so on.

" Now compressed air agitating the vocal cords
produces the same results. Therefore, if you
compress the air in your lungs twice as much as
usual when you are producing a given note or
phrase, you will get four times the sound, and, what
is still more important, you give an impression of
intensity of feeling which heightens the thrill of
the *fortissimo*.

" It will be seen from the above that comparative
loudness resolves itself into a question of breathing
and control of breath. The correct manner of
breathing for vocal purposes, especially for strenuous
singing, is by the side-rib (Lateral Costal) method,
of which the following is an example." Here I
pattern the method by placing my left hand on
the pit of the stomach and the thumb of my
right hand on the side-rib, making the tips of
the fingers of the right hand touch the tips of the
left hand, as shown in Fig. 1.

I then take a deep breath, with the result that
there is an expansion all round the base of the
lungs. The expansion affects not only the muscles
at the pit of the stomach, which are on a level with
the floating ribs, but these ribs also. In the
following (Fig. 2) the side-rib expansion is
shown by the space between the finger-tips,
but the pronounced frontal expansion of the
muscles of the pit of the stomach is scarcely
discernible.

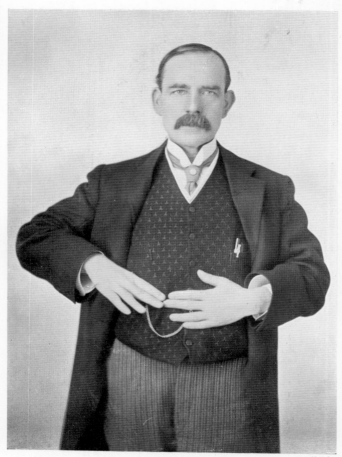

By permission of W. T. Furness, Sheffield.

FIG. I.

By permission of W. T. Furness, Sheffield.

FIG. 2.

It should be remarked that many professors of singing regard these particular muscles as the pivot upon which rests all breath control. While acknowledging that they play an important part, I recognise that the ribs are an effective factor in the regulation of the breath, hence my advocacy of the Lateral Costal method.

This outward expansion of the upper muscles of the abdomen seems to assimilate it with the abdominal method; but though incidental to the costal method it differs from the abdominal method, which causes all the abdomen—the lower as well as the upper muscles—to protrude.

If there be room for the choir to stand and go through the exercise I may ask them to do it, but if not they do it as well as they can as they sit; but they are urged to practise it at home. The next step is to show how, after taking breath, the abdomen is drawn in, and the diaphragm forced up to support the expanded ribs and thus compress the air. This done, I ask the choir to take a good breath, following my example, and to convey to them how to do it I ask the singers to breathe as though they were going to lift a heavy weight or to expand themselves as though they were trying to touch the sides of the room with their ribs! A scale or a particular phrase which requires the *fortissimo* effect is sung under this increased breath pressure, and the result is generally surprising to the choir. The success proves an incentive to further effort, and after a time astonishing *fortissimos* are realised by choirs who did not think they had such reserve of power. This practice gives to singers the power of " holding the breath at the waist," which is of great importance.

D

It should be remarked that these special *fortissimos* should not be used too often—say not more than thrice in an evening—and they should not be attempted until the words and the music are thoroughly mastered by the choir, in fact learned by heart, so that undivided attention can be given to the management of the breath and to the proper placing of the voices so as to avoid putting strain upon the vocal organs.

ATTACK.

The importance of attack—the striking of the notes firmly and cleanly—may be gauged by the fact that however well the piece may be sung in all other respects, if the notes are not struck firmly, especially high notes and points of imitation, the whole performance falls flat. Poor attack renders all performances unconvincing, while to hear each and every part triumphantly hit the bull's-eye is exhilarating to a degree.

There are two kinds of attack, which I name the Mechanical and the Artistic. The mechanical is that firm singing which arises from such a thorough knowledge of the music that the singer, confident of his powers, can " go for " the note or notes even in difficult passages. Though each note may not be struck in the most perfect way, the general effect is good and stirring. The artistic attack super-adds to the mechanical attack—which it includes—clean striking of each note, hitting it in the middle, without the trimmings or incubus of a scoop, drawl, or glide, the last-named occurring when the note is struck a shade sharp or flat. This artistic attack is the goal to be striven for, but it

must be clearly understood that it cannot be
utilised until the mechanical attack is attained.
When the artistic attack is mastered it means the
attainment of that consummation desired by all
singers—the true " shock of the glottis "—the *coup
de la glotte* of Garcia. This term, open as it is to
misinterpretation, is not a happy description of the
vocal action it describes, as there is not or need
not be a shock as we understand the term. It
merely means that at the moment of the air
passing through the larynx to make a sound
by means of the vocal cords, these cords are
firmly stretched at the right tension, and the
note struck is exactly the pitch required without
any adjustment being necessary, as there would
be if the note were struck half or quarter of a tone
sharp or flat.

This synchronization of the two factors—breath
and vocal cords—seems such a formidable thing,
and the term " shock of the glottis " appears so
fearsome, that it strikes a kind of terror into many
minds. But there is no need to feel alarmed.
The " shock of the glottis " comes naturally and
subconsciously to most people. Like the man who
was astonished to learn that he had been talking
prose all his life, many singers will be equally
surprised to know that every note which they have
sung, which was struck perfectly in tune, was sung
with true shock of the glottis. Some persons
possess this accomplishment naturally. Some
through carelessness have let it slip from them,
while a small percentage have great difficulty in
striking notes accurately.

Coming back to attack in choral singing, most
notes and phrases can be and are sung with

satisfactory clearness. But there are passages which present difficulties to every singer.

The chief of these are :—(*a*) detached *staccato* notes, (*b*) quickly reiterated notes, (*c*) high reiterated notes, whether sung quickly or slowly, and (*d*) high or low notes approached by leap.

To overcome these difficulties two things are necessary : (1) Exercises to train the required muscles to respond at will to make the proper adjustment of the vocal cords, (2) mental preparation on the part of the singer before the difficult notes are sung.

The following exercise is the one I use for developing " attack."

Sing to *ah, ai, ee, oo, oh, aw*—in keys B♭, E♭ :—

Ex. 2.

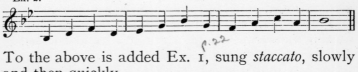

To the above is added Ex. 1, sung *staccato*, slowly and then quickly.

The best time to introduce the subject is when a good " peg " offers full justification—say the failure of the sopranos to sing a passage like the opening of " And He shall purify," or the leaps in the bass solo passage " Et iterum " in Bach's B *minor Mass.* When the opening has presented itself, explain why some exercises are necessary, and then take Ex. 2 *legato* and *staccato.*

During the course of the study period the conductor should pattern the exercise, explain about the shock of the glottis, and convince the choralists that good attack is easy of attainment with forward tone. Three or five minutes' exercise puts them on the right track, and with right principles in mind

the singers soon develop satisfactory "attack."
It should be pointed out to the choir that although
the vocal cords are in the larynx, they must never
associate the production of sound with the throat,
but always with the front part of the mouth, from
which all good tone seems to emanate. It used to
be said of Sims Reeves that you could always feel
and even see where his tones came from, and the
charm of the sounds was that they never varied in
the quality though they were wonderfully varied
in shading.

This is what singers must strive for, if they wish
to have every note cleanly struck. It is through
associating the voice with the throat that many
have gone wrong, and have been unable to strike
notes firmly, because they have tried to control by
will what should be done subconsciously; they
have tried to experience a "shock" where there is
no shock, but merely an automatic response to the
will by unconscious cerebration. If singers will
keep their minds fixed on the forward-in-the-mouth-
point of the breath impact, and ignore entirely all
thought of the vocal cords, difficulties of attack
and shock of the glottis will vanish.

When a series of high notes has to be struck—
for instance, the phrase in "And He shall purify,"
or the high A's in the *Choral Symphony*, or
the fugal subject in "Et vitam venturi" in
Beethoven's *Mass in* D — if there be bad
attack it is probably due to the giving way of the
muscles of the throat, rather than to any defect of
the voice. The partial collapse or shrinkage of the
muscles causes a disturbance and diversion of the air
current, and the muscles not having time to recover
before the next note is struck, we get that uncertain

scooping effect due to the gliding up to the note from a semitone or even two tones below pitch.

Bad attack due to this cause is easily remedied. Tell the singers to *will* that the muscles of the mouth remain in one position while they sing these high reiterated notes, in order that the air current shall not be deflected from striking the front of the mouth (just where the teeth join the palate) and they, knowing precisely what to do, will accomplish their desire with brilliant effect. This at least has been the experience of my choruses.

To get clean, firm attack on high or difficult notes, where dramatic intensity is required, it is necessary for the singer to prepare for the attack by mentalizing the note and controlling his voice-production. If there be no inertia in the singers, this can always be done and success achieved.

PIANISSIMO, MAINTENANCE OF NASAL RESONANCE, AND "ARTIST" TONE-QUALITY.

There are several things pertaining to the management of the voice, such as obtaining tone colour—white, dark, bright, sombre—and characterization of tone—the laugh, the jeer, the snarl, &c. —as well as particular features in the management of the voice,—such as the *staccato*, the swell, *sforzando*, and other points of the dynamics of sound,—which might be considered in this chapter, but which will be better dealt with under the head of "Expression."

PIANISSIMO AND PERFECT PITCH.

There is however one exception to this, and that is "How to obtain *pianissimo* in choral singing."

This point touches so many vital considerations in connection with the voice that it must be considered under the head of "Voice," rather than in the chapter on "Expression," although it is an important factor in that topic.

To sing *pianissimo* with firmness and at the same time to maintain the pitch postulates a vocal technique which comparatively few people possess; and yet with proper instruction a choir can be trained to meet the severe demands imposed by the dual task. Of course an indifferent choir can sing *pianissimo*, and, at times, come through the ordeal of keeping the pitch successfully—more by good luck or elation of spirit than by mastery of voice; but what I wish to show is that choristers can be trained so that normally they will be able to sing *pianissimo* and maintain the pitch without being surprised,—the surprise being when they fail to do so. As already said, soft, firm singing demands great skill, and as every artistic attainment necessarily involves a long preparation, I will go to the root of the matter and note the evolution of the necessary equipment and control of breath.

When a new or inexperienced choir have been rehearsing a modern work for some weeks—say six—the time will have come for them to endeavour to sing certain passages with really soft tone. In all probability they will fail to satisfy the conductor, even after two or three attempts. These repeated failures should be welcome, as they give the conductor his opportunity to introduce the questions of soft singing and artistic voice control.

The first step should be to fix a standard of *pianissimo*, and make the choir realise what the

standard is. To do this the conductor should
pattern Ex. 1 to the vowel *oo* very softly, asking
the choir to listen for the ticking of the clock
above his voice. The choir then imitate that
pattern, and, after a few attempts, with sundry
admonitions from the conductor to keep the tone
at the very lips, they will be gratified by hearing
the "tick, tock" of the clock over all their voices.
Some people may think this impossible, but I hear
this many times every week. A short time ago,
when Sir Frederic Cowen was conducting the final
rehearsal of his fine work *The Veil*, I told him
to listen for the ticking of the clock, as when we
heard this we knew we were singing sufficiently
pianissimo; and sure enough, under his beat, we
could hear distinctly, in every part of the room, the
ticking of the ordinary eight-day clock over the
four hundred voices, every one singing.

When the choir have grasped the standard of
pp or *ppp*, ask them to sing the exercise again, this
time noting the physical sensation—or lack of
sensation—of the muscles of the throat, mouth,
tongue, and lips, and to realise mentally how they
place the breath current, or "tube of air," near
the lips. Now ask for the phrase in the work which
is being rehearsed to be sung to the words. The
probabilities are that while there is a gain of
softness there will be a loss of pitch. Try again,
and the result will be nearly the same. The
choir by this time will probably be as interested and
as anxious to remedy the fault as is the conductor;
therefore their palpable shortcomings give the latter
his chance of making the welcome announcement
that at the next rehearsal he will give most
important and definite instructions how, in future,

to avoid flattening when singing *pp*, and, growing out of these instructions, how to secure " the artist " tone-production.

During the next rehearsal, at the first favourable opportunity—an effort should always be made to do the right thing at the right time—introduce the subject of " Flattening, and how to remedy it." Briefly state that flattening may be due to a number of causes, such as fatigue of body, indolence of mind—inertia, of which much will be said later—not knowing the music and words, vitiated air, atmospheric conditions, &c.; but more than all by faulty voice-production. This last cause may be said to be chiefly an ignorance or disregard of that modification of the voice known as nasal resonance.

Here let me insert a short disquisition on the important topic of Nasal Resonance, because so few of the conductors whom I have met are sufficiently acquainted with, or sufficiently understand, its import.

By " singing with nasal resonance," is meant the enriching of the voice by so adjusting the sounding air current that part of the " tube of air " which passes over the vocal cords, goes behind the uvula and passes into the nasal cavities, there producing sympathetic overtones which blend with and enrich the sound which proceeds, in the main, from the mouth.

There is no doubt that, generally speaking, the English choral singer favours a backward voice-production. This would appear to arise from the tradition that a choral singer must make as much noise as possible in *fortes*, and this develops a species of bellowing and a thick, heavy throat tone; and because singers can vividly feel the vibration of the sound at the back of the mouth, they are satisfied that they are doing effective work. Here, unfortunately, they misapply a physical sensation, just as did the man who said he knew his razor was sharp because he could see the edge !

It requires great persuasive power and tact on the part of the conductor to remove this idea, and to get singers to alter their method ; but if, in order to get unity of tone, attack, &c., the exercises and plans mentioned previously on pages 22 ff., 34 ff., have been followed, they will have been taught to realise and obtain forward tone, and the ground will have been prepared for the addition of this important superstructure ; and it will only need a little care, skill, judgment, and time to get them to follow the conductor's lead with respect to nasal resonance.

The question might fairly be asked, If nasal resonance be of such importance, why not introduce it to the choir at once, instead of so long delaying its introduction ? The answer is very simple. You cannot introduce with success any advanced artistic accomplishment connected with the voice until the mind has grasped the importance of the idea, and the muscles of the throat and mouth have been trained to respond to the demands of the higher achievement. In other words, preparatory technique is absolutely necessary. Many times have I tried to make a short cut and get to the desired quality at once, but every time I have failed to secure success, and have always had to proceed afresh from the beginning. Therefore I urge every conductor not to hurry in the matter of the voice, but to keep pegging away at the earlier stages, making the most of the voices he has, and to be satisfied with a little progress at each rehearsal, until the time comes when the majority of the singers have assimilated his ideas and instructions, and can do what he wants spontaneously. Only after this should the more difficult subject be introduced.

After this digression I will resume the hints on how to deal with the choir.

To get the choir to apprehend nasal resonance, first pattern Ex. 1 to the vowel $\bar{e}$ ("ee") or $\bar{a}$ ("ai") softly with pure non-nasal quality, and get the choir to imitate it. Then sing the exercise again rather loudly, very nasally—indeed with nasal twang. Tell the choir to imitate it, imparting a derisive, mocking character if possible. "He trusted in God" (*Messiah*) and the "Demons' Chorus" (*Gerontius*) are fine preparatory exercises if properly sung. This excess of nasality will help them to realise nasal tone, and predispose the muscles of the mouth for the next step.

Pattern once more Ex. 1, but this time with proper amount of resonance, and ask the choir to imitate. Of course success will be limited. This partial failure will enable you to introduce the device of humming on the letter *m*, which later on will be used frequently in the developing of *pp* and *ppp*.

The choir having got an idea—though perhaps a hazy one—of nasal resonance, ask them to sing to words the *pianissimo* phrase in the work under rehearsal. Afterwards ask them to hum the passage very softly, with the sound on the lips, at the same time calling their attention to the attenuated, nebulous, almost despicable sound, which should be such that one could hardly call it

singing. If this is done correctly they will have
realised one of the most spirit-reaching effects in
all music, the mysterious ethereal quality which
I call "floating tone," which seems to belong to
the seventh heaven.

While this entrancing effect is in their mind and
moving their hearts, ask them to sing the phrase to
the words, but producing the voice in the same
way and avoiding any increase of tone, and very
likely under the enthralling surroundings they will
produce that rare delight, a real *pianissimo*, with
true maintenance of pitch, because the effort to
produce tone in the proper way gives that mental
uplift, that psychological stimulus which, joined
to the freedom of the throat, makes singing in tune
almost an absolute necessity.

Here, in a few words, is the secret of the
pianissimo singing of my choirs. To sing a true
pianissimo get the tone quite to the lips of the
nearly closed mouth, and let the sound be a half
hum, so as to secure nasal resonance. The loose
throat, absence of muscular strain, and forward
breath induced by this production, together with
the accompanying mental alertness, tend to maintain
the pitch; the quality of the tone gives it clear
definition and carrying power; and the union of
the whispered fundamental sound of the mouth
with the nasal harmonics gives quality and character
to the tone, the whole satisfying the mind both as
to quality and quantity of sound and intonation
(pitch).

The classical quotation, "The price of Liberty is
eternal vigilance," is equally applicable to *pianissimo*
singing. The choir will always need pulling up
because some singers have not exercised enough

restraint. But notwithstanding this it is an incalculable gain to the conductor and the choir to have a definite system, which enables the singers to aim at the goal unerringly. Conductors under these conditions can work hopefully, and with more heart than when they are uncertain how to achieve the desired ideal of real *pianissimo* and true pitch. Other aspects of *pianissimo* will be dealt with under the head " Expression."

NASAL RESONANCE.

The conductor having inculcated the advantages of nasal resonance by its easiest mode of present-ment, namely, soft and very soft singing (humming), and the choir being by this time convinced of the practical value to the voice of this form of modifying the production, the way is now open for a decided effort towards making nasal resonance a vocal habit of the singers, in *mezzo* and loud singing as well as in *pianissimo*.

This will be a more difficult task than getting the tinge of nasality in soft singing, because in loud singing there being more strain on the muscles of the mouth, it is harder to overcome the regular " set " of these muscles, and determination on the part of the singer is required to deflect the precise amount of the air current to the back of the uvula, so as to produce the tone flavour required. Still, with care it can be done.

The conductor must set himself to nurse this quality of tone on every possible occasion. He should carefully note any phrases in which occur forward vowels, such as " Blessed are the men who fear Him, they ever walk in the ways of peace "

(*Elijah*), " Sing ye" (Bach), &c. He should in these phrases pattern the tone-quality, and as the vowels favour the sounds required, the choir will respond with fair success, until in time the tone becomes habitual.

The basses generally give the earliest and best signs of progress; therefore in solo phrases like—

But like an earthquake was the din when

where the climax note on the word "din" is particularly favourable to the right production, ask the men to repeat the passage as an object-lesson to the other parts.

Whenever a combined phrase is sung with fine, ringing tone of the right quality, as may happen to words like "Sing praises to the King of Heaven," or "Hail to the Chief," stop the choir to call attention to the beauty and quality of tone. The choir will welcome the stoppage, as they like nothing better than an interruption in order to be complimented. On high notes in the soprano part, frequent stoppages will be necessary to get the singers to place the tone forward, especially on words like "high glory," "for honour," &c., but even they will fall into line fairly quickly.

Of course one must always be careful to avoid excess of nasality, or more harm than good will result; but I must say that, except in two cases in the United States, where the people have an excess of nasality in speaking, I have never yet heard a choir go beyond the limits of good tone in the way of nasal resonance, whereas one often hears excess of throatiness in England.

Choral singers, by the law of sympathy and the influence of example, seem to improve up to a certain point with wonderful quickness. Here I would caution conductors not to be misled into ceasing their efforts because of this apparently exceptional progress. It is when the finer stage of artistic voice-production is reached that choirs dishearten conductors. Then they seem to make no progress, the same faults recurring again and again. But the conductor must persevere. Progress even under well-directed effort is slow, but this is always the way in the higher stages of every branch of artistic culture. To paraphrase the proverb, "Art is indeed a long time in coming, while time is decidedly fleeting."

PRESERVATION OF VOICE.

Before closing this chapter a word should be said as to preservation of the voice. Great musicians like Sir Hubert Parry, Sir Edward Elgar, Granville Bantock, and others. who have seen the apparently remorseless way I make my choirs sing, have frequently expressed the fear that I was putting too severe a strain upon the voices; but I have always been able to convince them by results that their fears were groundless.

This is because when a voice is properly produced it can stand a strain and be fresh after it, whereas an improperly produced and imperfectly trained voice would collapse. Therefore I endeavour to get perfect tone and ease of production, and proper placing of the voice, from the first rehearsal.

The first thing I insist upon is a loose throat. This I explain is produced by getting the tone as near the lips as possible, and never associating the production of tone with the throat. To secure this, the general instruction is to sing rather softly until the music and words are fairly well mastered. When this is done, we sing with expression ranging from *pp* to loud or louder or loudest according to what is required. But in this later stage the choristers are always told to rest the voice while they sing—that is, they are to regard each soft passage as an operation of massage on the vocal organs. They are urged to change the position of the mouth with each degree of force, and thus strengthen each part of the throat, instead of wearing out the voice with persistent use of one part only, *i.e.*, keeping the sound in one position all the time.

I illustrate this by the story of Dead Horse Road. This road, somewhere in Norfolk, is so called because it is the cause of the death of so many horses. This is due to its length and flatness, on which account only one set of muscles of the horses which traverse it are called into play, with the result that the beasts are soon worn out. Further, when brushing up well-known works, like *The Messiah* and *Elijah*, for the usual annual performances, at the first two rehearsals I disregard the expression marks, and ask the choir to sing a soft *mezzo* most of the evening with the avowed purpose of massaging the vocal muscles, toning the voices by getting rid of " clatter "—that is, the harsh harmonics which produce strident voices—getting a loose throat, developing nasal resonance, and securing general ease of production.

Some conductors may think that this continued soft and medium singing will have a weakening

effect on the voice, but it has not. Take the case
of the Huddersfield Chorus. I mention this choir
by name because, rightly or wrongly, it has the
reputation of having the strongest voices—singer
for singer—of any choir in the North of England,
which, as everybody knows, is the home of strong
voices.

This choir knows *The Messiah* so well that I
would risk a performance with one copy to every
twenty singers, or, if the necessity arose, with one
copy to a part. Notwithstanding this, we always
begin the rehearsals as though we did not know a
note, because it is by this assumption alone that
perfection of detail can be maintained. When we
begin, I instruct the singers to be prepared for
taking the choruses either as a voice exercise, or as
a finished display. As they know the music so
well they are asked to concentrate their attention
on voice alone, purity of tone being the Alpha
and Omega of the rehearsal. But to develop
mastery of certain phrases, and general alertness,
whenever I say " Sing " they must change from
mezzo voice to *forte* or *fortissimo* according to the
markings of the copy, but at the word " Voice,"
they must at once resume the soft voice-cultivation
manner.

This yearly toning of the voices, together with its
influence away from the rehearsals, is of inestimable
value, while the well-known vibrant resonant quality
of the Huddersfield Choir is strengthened.

If further testimony of the efficacy of the above
methods were needed, I would point to the wonderful
test of endurance of the World Tour Choir, where
the singers—except in rare isolated cases—never
lost their voices, and where a great proportion
E

attended every rehearsal and every one of the one hundred and thirty-four concerts without a trace of voice weariness or hardness; in fact, the only thing that seemed to affect the voices was the severely cold weather of which we had experience in East Canada and the United States.

Other aspects of treating the voice will be dealt with in the chapter on " Musical Expression."

BREATHING.

The importance of a correct method of breathing is such a commonplace that one is loath to lay stress upon it. But the lack of clear, definite knowledge of the various methods, and the inability of many to note the points of unity and harmony between the conflicting and apparently irreconcilable systems, make it necessary to repeat the trite saying that to attain the highest results in singing it is imperative that the art of breathing be thoroughly understood, and the respiratory organs strengthened and put under perfect control.

In the preceding chapter on " Voice," when dealing with the question of " How to obtain a *fortissimo* vocal climax," I foreshadowed the correct method of breathing ; but as only the fringe of the subject was touched upon, a more complete statement and a review of the question in all its bearings will now be given.

The dual object of respiration in relation to singing is to inhale sufficient breath to fill the lungs *entirely*, and to get such command of the respiratory muscles as to exhale the acquired breath to the best advantage. The question of breathing therefore narrows itself down to

1. What is the best way of taking breath ?
2. What is the best way of giving it out ?

HOW TO BREATHE.

Many books have been written on this subject of "How to Breathe,"—some very useful and informing, others harmful on account of the fanciful theories propounded, while others have been very good, but so obscure in statement as to darken counsel instead of giving illumination.

Having during the last thirty years studied every book of importance on the subject, with the object of learning the views of the best authorities, in order to apply the knowledge for the benefit of my societies, I have been able to put every theory to the test, and from the process I have evolved a fairly clear grasp of the practical application of the various theories, their points of agreement and difference, and their degrees of value.

I propose therefore to epitomise my interpretation of the different theories of "How to Breathe" in a popular and, I hope, so clear a manner that at any rate everybody who reads this résumé of the subject will know what I think and teach.

Now as this is not a physiological treatise, but a guide to the practical application of approved methods, I shall only deal with breathing as a medium for obtaining the best vocal results in the development of artistic phrasing, and incidentally as a source of health to the body, a brightener of the spirit, a foe to indigestion, a beautifier of the complexion, and a promoter of good carriage.

To those who desire fuller knowledge on the physiological side, as well as a series of well-considered breathing exercises, I strongly recommend

Dr. Hulbert's "Breathing for Voice-Production" (Novello, 3s.) as the safest, most logical, and on the anatomical basis the simplest book published on the subject.

I use the word "simplest" in referring to Dr. Hulbert's book. Some conductors may wonder at the use of the word in connection with a subject that has the reputation of being anything but simple. The popular notion is that the subject of breathing is involved, hard to understand, very controversial, conflicting, and irritating.

Notwithstanding this current notion, I repeat that the essential features and principles of correct breathing are simple.

As a matter of fact it is surprising, especially to those who have waded through innumerable books, in what a small compass the kernel of the subject lies. This kernel is merely the filling of the lungs in a natural way, and the emptying of them in an equally spontaneous manner. The method of doing both these things, and the scientific reasons for the processes, can be given in a couple of pages, so that it may well claim to be simple. The elaborate anatomical experiments, and the long series of deductions made from these involved researches, cannot be so briefly stated; but the results can, and these only are what concern vocalists.

The question may be asked, "If this be so, why have so many books with conflicting views and statements been published?" This I will try to explain.

There are two chief methods of breathing :—

    (1) The Clavicular, or collar-bone, so called because in this method the collar-bone is raised at each inspiration ; and,

(2) The Diaphragmatic, so called on account of the important part played by the diaphragm, or midriff, in controlling the style of breathing.

Diaphragmatic breathing may be used in two different ways:—

(a) The abdominal (stomach);
(b) The costal (rib), now generally spoken of as the Lateral Costal (side-rib).

It should be here stated that in some treatises the methods of breathing are set forth as follows:—

(1) Clavicular.

(2) Abdominal.

(3) Costal.

(4) Side costal (for medical purposes only).

It is from the opposing champions of the abdominal and costal theories that all the conflict and ensuing confusion have arisen.

In making a comparison and giving an estimate of the two methods, it may be said that both schools of thought rightly insist that the lungs should be completely filled at each inspiration, by inflating the lungs at their base—the broadest part—and not merely using the upper part as in clavicular breathing. It is when we ask "How is this filling to be done?" that the methods differ fundamentally.

To make these differences clear, it will be necessary to consider briefly the diaphragm, which has been compared to an inverted *muscular* basin. This dome-shaped muscular partition between the chest or thorax and the abdomen is capable of being altered somewhat in shape. The arched portion can be flattened, with the result that the floor of the thorax—that is, the base of the chest— is lowered, and the pressure of the diaphragm on the abdomen causes the latter to protrude. The diaphragm may also have its shape altered by being distended through pressure from below, resisting the pressure from above. These combined forces result in the dome becoming shallower, and, the enlargement of the circumference demanding more room, the muscles at the pit of the stomach are pushed forward and the ribs are thrust outwards and upwards. By these means the lungs are enabled to expand to their utmost capacity.

The Abdominalists—led by Mandl—claim that as more breath space is secured by this protrusion of the abdomen, therefore theirs is the best method, and the one to be followed.

The Costalites say that by the expansion all round the base of the lungs and uplifting of the side-ribs, they get an equal amount of breath space, while it is more natural, more healthy, and much better for breath control.

Sixty years ago the idea of treating the subject of breathing, as applied to singing, on a scientific basis was hardly considered. People said there was no need for it. Vocalists were able to sing brilliantly without knowing anything of the laws of inspiration and expiration, except in a vague way. They were taught, and followed, the traditional empirical methods of their singing-masters, and managed to do so well that they did not bother their heads about the theory of breathing so long as they could do it naturally. Their way of breathing, and the success that they achieved, are such inspiring traditions that it is now the aim of every teacher to get back to the old Italian methods. In 1855 Mandl caused the first flutter in the singing dovecotes by advancing the theory that as abdominal breathing gave the greatest amount of breath capacity, therefore not only was this method the correct one, but all other methods were wrong.

This theory was enthusiastically taken up in England by two well-known gentlemen, who collaborated, one for the breathing and the other for the voice. Being backed up by physiological reasons and seemingly irrefutable anatomical demonstrations, their advocacy of the new method was most successful. Being first in the field with their data, the abdominal system of breathing had a tremendous vogue,—for what chance had an empirical system against one which was based on scientific principles ?

But most people felt that something was lacking in the system. It was quite correct that it gave great breath capacity ; but did it ensure breath control, especially for great crises, and for getting power and ring of voice ? Still, notwithstanding these doubts as to its efficiency, the system kept the field for a long time, chiefly on account of its supposed scientific sanction. Then there came a reaction, and clever men thought that what was really true in practice must have a scientific basis; for it was hardly believable that the old natural way of breathing, as used by every great singer consciously or unconsciously, could be based on error. Therefore the anatomical and physiological aspects of the problem have been re-studied, with the result that the older traditional empirical usage has been found to rest on scientific sanction.

The results of this research have now been set forth in the system known as the " Lateral Costal Method," which can bring physiological fact to show that not only is it the best for inspiration, but also that *it gives perfect control in expiration*, which is the singer's chief asset, because it is the power to use a tool or implement which makes it effective.

Briefly, the new discoveries and the deductions which have restored the side-rib breathing to its now unchallenged place of supremacy are as follows :—In deep inspiration, by drawing in the abdomen, the liver and stomach, being firmly held in the basin-like dome or arch of the underside of the diaphragm, prevent any downward movement of this strong muscular partition below the level of the flying ribs. It is therefore forced to extend with an outward expansion. This expansion, coupled with the existence of the intercostal muscles, causes the ribs to widen in an outward and upward direction, thus giving the widest possible breath space, as well as aerifying the upper part of the lungs.

Further, this pressure of the abdomen against the thorax enables the singer to regulate the air current to the requirements of the sound he wishes to produce.

I showed on page 30 how to get supreme pressure and condensation of the air in a *fortissimo* climax. A corresponding control of breath is necessary to secure *pianissimos*, *staccatos*, and *swells*, and this method enables singers to acquire these accomplishments, as I shall show later.

As a result, this confirmation of the best traditional usage by modern physiological research proves to me, at least, that the correct way of breathing is by the Lateral Costal method.

Therefore, reverting to my previous statement that the kernel of correct breathing lies in a small compass, we find that as the outcome of all the patient, baffling, anatomical researches of both Abdominalists and Costalites we get practically the clear, simple directions of many an old singing-master, "Stick your chest out, keep your stomach in, hold your breath at the waist and sing."

To complete our consideration of the different methods of breathing, a passing notice of the clavicular method must be given. This method is so universally condemned by all authorities, that were it not that Jenny Lind is reputed to have used the system it would have been ruled out of court at once. Personally I am not quite sure that Jenny Lind used the clavicular method so exclusively as we are led to believe, for the following reasons.

During the last thirty years I have conducted very many concerts, oratorios, cantatas, &c., at which scores of the finest artists of the day have sung. Many of these singers have been trained by the finest and greatest teachers known, and on the most approved and up-to-date methods, and in the matter of breathing their style and method have been above suspicion. Yet I have many times seen these artists at important crises in their interpretation of a song, solo, or scena, lift their clavicles as though they were breathing by the forbidden clavicular method. This, however, they were not doing. As a matter of fact they were simply making an extra physical effort under the stress of temperamental excitement, and using

every available means to increase their stock of
breath for the great effort they were about to make.
Consequently they instinctively called into play the
whole of the respiratory muscles, and the additional
pressure of the abdomen on the diaphragm and the
greater condensation of the air in the lungs made it
quite natural to supplement all the other muscular
disturbance by lifting the clavicles. This action, then,
under conditions of temperamental and dramatic
excitement, instead of proclaiming clavicular
breathing, while it masks and obscures the ordinary
action proclaims the highest development of
breathing — Lateral Costal in excelsis. Hence,
when I see members of my choir raise their
shoulders when preparing for a grand outburst of
sound, I do not condemn them for breathing
wrongly, but rather commend them for the implied
instinctive effort to gain an extra amount of breath
and increased air-pressure.

These facts have often made me wonder whether
after all Jenny Lind did use the clavicular method
exclusively, or whether she merely used it as an
auxiliary to the costal method, but in such a way
as to hide or mask the action of the side-ribs.
Failing proof to the contrary, I believe that her
method was a combination of the two systems, as
this explanation falls more easily into what is now
known of the physiology of the art of breathing as
applied to singing, which in her day was not
seriously studied.

In relation to this mixing and masking of
methods, it is worth remark that when abdominal
breathing was the vogue, I have time and time
again seen singers, who had been trained by this
system, breathe by the costal method, and in

justification explain that because they breathed by means of the diaphragm therefore it was abdominal, only it was in another form. As the precise and definite theory of the Lateral Costal method was not then known or formulated, this reasonable explanation was allowed to pass; but the wrong method got the credit of the right usage.

HOW TO INHALE BREATH.

Having shown conclusively the best method of respiration, I will now deal with several secondary, but still important, matters connected with the subject.

With respect to the question of inhalation, should it be through the mouth or through the nostrils? For many reasons of health, and for special reasons of voice, breath should be inspired through the nose, as the air thereby taken in is warmed and filtered before it reaches the larynx and lungs, both of which temperings are necessary to the preservation of the voice and health. When the body is in repose there is no difficulty about breathing in this manner, but even when walking, exercising, running, and speaking, this breathing through the nose must as a general rule be followed.

Nevertheless this law must not be regarded as of the Medes and Persians, which altereth not, for in singing it cannot be carried out always with advantage.

In singing there is not time to breathe through the nostrils, especially without such effort injuring the smoothness of the musical effect—particularly in bravura singing—and impairing the beauty of the phrasing. The artist must not be worried or disturbed by mere physical actions or methods. Whatever is done should be carried through automatically, and absolutely without conscious effort.

The rendering of a piece being the chief concern, the merely mechanical means must be subservient to the ruling principle. Therefore the rule for taking breath may be stated as follows:—Whenever possible inhale through the nose, but in singing take breath subconsciously; or, in other words, *do not take breath, let breath take you.*

If the singer is unconscious, say, in a quick passage, of how his breath supply is replenished— whether through the mouth, or nose, or both—he will not be far wrong. The problem at issue with all singers is how to acquire automatic nasal inspiration. This subconscious habit can be acquired, as I shall show later.

BREATH CONTROL.

It is evident to everyone who knows anything about singing that however correctly one may breathe, it is necessary for professional singing purposes to have a super-ordinary chest development and highly-specialised breath control. This development and accomplishment can only be brought about by special exercises, (1) to enlarge the lung capacity and (2) to give quick and responsive action to the breathing apparatus.

Such a set of exercises are to be found in Dr. Hulbert's " Breathing for Vocal Purposes," which should be followed by all who wish to excel as vocalists. Personally I feel very strongly on this question of the cultivation of lung power and responsiveness. I regard command of breath as the touchstone of a young singer's success. Singers who cannot breathe well may take it that their fate is practically sealed. Many débutants have good voices and good style, but if they have not good breathing powers they always have a short singing life. They somehow recede from the public eye, and they wonder why this should be so with "people of their ability." The solution is to be found in the fact that in not developing breathing power by strenuous and sustained effort they cease to grow vocally. The same power of voice which is considered quite satisfactory in a new singer is quite inadequate and disappointing in a singer who has been before the public for some time. I have heard singers express surprise that they have been coldly received, instead of being rapturously applauded as formerly. The secret can often be traced to lack of development in power through defective breathing. The public have an unconscious way of weighing people in the balance; and those who are "work shies" —for breath development means real hard work —those who have followed the line of least resistance, *i.e.*, taking it easy, are found wanting, and are passed over for others who show progress in their art.

Whenever in performances that I conduct I find young principals failing to take the runs in the *Messiah*, *Judas*, *Creation*, or similar works, in one breath, I usually wipe them off the slate, as their lack of determination to excel in this direction is a sign to me of arrested development, connoting premature vocal decay.

When spoken to on this point these young singers invariably quote the example of some old, well-tried vocalist. They forget that these old singers are favourites for general all-round excellence, and though, through advancing years, or neglect, or indolence, they take breath in the middle of a run or interpolate words so as to hide their weakness, and use other devices to cover their deficiencies, these subterfuges cause a pang of regret to even their warmest admirers, who inwardly lament "How are the mighty fallen."

From the above remarks upon the importance of breathing, it will probably be thought that I favour a very rigid application of a systematic course of breathing exercises for choirs and choral societies. Though I may favour such a course theoretically, I am afraid I cannot recommend it with advantage to either conductor or choir. I wish that I could.

It would be easy to follow the example of some writers on this subject, and compile a list of things that should be done—*e.g.*, ten minutes' breathing exercises before each rehearsal; certain muscular evolutions, &c., to be performed; but I shall refrain. It is a mistake to insist upon an impracticable thing simply because it is desirable theoretically. I shall restrict my advice to a minimum of what is strictly practicable for choral singers. My reasons for this are :—

(1) Though elaborate breathing exercises are imperative for soloists, for choral singers a few definite, well-directed exercises suffice.

(2) Whenever I have tried to impose a systematic course of breathing exercises upon a choir, the members all with one consent began to make excuse, and arrived after the exercises were over.

((3) I have never known a case where the persistent use of breathing exercises in rehearsal time has not had the effect (*a*) of killing the interest in the rehearsal, (*b*) of doing more harm than good, and (*c*) of causing, if persisted in, the dissolution of the society.) Therefore, instead of drawing up an ideal scheme of what is theoretically desirable, I shall confine my remarks to what experience has shown me is practicable.

Now while my experience has proved to me the futility of the bad tactics of a frontal attack in the matter of imposing or attempting breathing exercises during rehearsal time, I never neglect the subject, but gain my object by a flank movement. (On all possible occasions—say, when long runs have to be negotiated, long notes sustained, staccato passages attacked, a climax realised, or a *pianissimo* phrase controlled—I always refer to breathing as the key of the situation, and by taking a short exercise that seems to grow out of the necessities of the music I get the choir to do it willingly.) The conductor must seize such opportunities, and keep his singers engaged on breathing exercises until interest begins to flag. This, however, does not often happen, because the object will have been achieved before that time arrives.

In my own societies I point out to the choir that though breathing exercises have to be somewhat crowded out at rehearsals owing to lack of room and time, yet there are daily opportunities of practising breathing in a most pleasant and agreeable manner, without any limitation to their duration or consideration as to space for exercise—the two drawbacks in the rehearsal room—and that without loss of time to anyone.

I emphasise the importance of these exercises by stating that they are what I have done daily for years, so they see it is a case not only of " Do as I say," but of "Do as I do."

An additional recommendation to the singers is their knowledge of the fact that I can sing the longest and most difficult " runs " or " divisions " in one breath, which is due to the use of a certain time-saving exercise. I also mention that, useful as the principal exercise is for singing purposes, I practise it chiefly for hygienic reasons, which will be mentioned later.

This wonderfully useful exercise is very simple. It consists in taking deep breaths as I walk along the streets—say for a distance of two hundred yards. Each respiration is taken rhythmically—that is, during each six strides, allowing three steps for each inspiration and three for each expiration. The time allowed can be varied according to the wishes of each singer, some only allowing four steps for each respiration, while others will allow eight steps—four for inhaling and four for exhaling.

The following is a sketch of how I deal with this subject in rehearsal. (It is all done, by the way, in about five minutes.) Having spoken of the evident necessity of developing the breathing powers of the choir as a whole, if we are to do full justice to the work in hand, I tell them that there is an exercise which will produce wonderful results, that it can be done in an easy and pleasurable manner, and that it will not take more than five minutes daily.

I then repeat an exercise which many will have seen before—that is, I place my hands on my lower ribs and breathe deeply, making the enlargement of

F

the chest at the base, by means of the expansion of
the side-ribs, very evident (*see* Fig. 2).

I ask them to imitate the pattern. This having
been done a few times, I explain how they may
perform the lung-strengthening, chest-expanding
exercise which I practise every day, and which—
for its inherent benefit—I strongly recommend to
them. I then place my hands on my ribs as
before, and, while I breathe, I either walk along the
platform or step as though I was walking, breathing
audibly in order to show how to inhale and exhale
rhythmically. To every intake and outlet of breath
four, six, or eight steps are taken.

I then tell them how, every time I go for a walk,
whether on business or pleasure, whenever I come
to a gentle incline I make it a rule to practise deep
breathing for, say, from two to three minutes to
give my lungs an air-bath, and thereby (*a*) improve
my breath power and control for singing. It,
however, does much more than this. From a
health point of view it is very important, as
(*b*) it oxygenises the blood ; (*c*) it improves the
circulation and strengthens the heart; (*d*) it gives
that peristaltic action to the stomach, which
promotes digestion and is a foe to dyspepsia ;
(*e*) it raises the spirit and often banishes headache ;
(*f*) it improves the carriage and the figure ; and
(*g*) it beautifies the complexion.

But of more importance than all is the correct
subconscious habit of breathing which this daily
exercise establishes. In my own case, whenever I
walk uphill I unconsciously begin the deep-
breathing exercise, and carry it on for about the
usual two minutes. One can see how important
and useful this habit must be to the vocalist, as

rhythmic inhaling gets the breath apparatus under proper discipline.

The charm of it all is the ease and pleasurable manner in which it can be acquired, without any loss of time. To the faithful following of these instructions by many of my singers we owe a great deal of our choral success.

To the above hints and instructions I add the recommendation that all singers should, when passing through doorways, inflate their lungs as though they were going to lift a heavy weight, and with arms extended push or thrust against each jamb of the door for about five seconds, as though they wished to push them down. This strengthens the breath pressure enormously.

WHEN AND WHERE TO BREATHE.

The "How" to breathe having been dealt with, attention must now be given to "When" and "Where" to breathe.

A great fault with choral singers is to leave inspiration until the very last moment, or quarter of a moment, with the result that they take snap breaths and catch breaths instead of full breaths.

Ample time should be given for full respiration whenever possible. To achieve this end a good rule is to take breath with the conductor's beat which precedes the singer's entry or beginning of a new phrase.

All these things can be done with a little trouble if only there be method. What I suggest is that every breathing place be marked by each singer; then this sign is the signal for taking breath in the right place.

The above remarks apply chiefly to each fresh beginning, when broad principles can be followed. Much more important is the management of breathing for artistic phrasing.

There is a general tendency amongst undisciplined singers to sing as long as they can in a breath, irrespective of the finer shades of phrasing. The only remedy for this is to pattern the phrase and get the choir to mark the breathing places carefully. The fault is often very noticeable at the beginning of a phrase, when, being full of breath, they object to stop and take another breath for what seems to them a trivial reason.

But these phrasing breaths must be observed, and the conductor must not feel discouraged if in such phrases as—

> *For* unto us a child is born,
>
> *Go*, song of mine,
>
> *Strike*, strike the lyre,

he has to go over the phrases a score of times to cultivate this habit of breath control for artistic purposes.

Conductors must read carefully the words of each piece, and in all places of difficulty, or where special care is necessary to get a particular emphasis and shade of meaning, the breathing places must be indicated. As a rule the divisions fall so naturally that in three-fourths of the piece there is little or no trouble. It is in the remaining fourth that care will have to be exercised.

When choice of a breathing place has to be made in a complicated phrase, the following considerations will give data sufficient to tread the mazy path with firmness:—Breath may always be taken after a full stop, colon, semicolon, and comma. Also before a preposition, an adverb, a relative pronoun, and, when necessary for emphasis, before an adjective which comes after the noun, as " Spirit Divine " (Cowen's *The Veil*). Latitude is also given in breathing before or after the verb " to be."

A burning question with some conductors is how to manage runs and long, sustained notes in one breath. Theoretically this is the correct thing to do, but as it cannot be done as successfully as they would like, such tests of breathing cause them much anxiety. In these and similar cases I always tell my singers to take two or three breaths so as to make sure of a bold and confident finish. But some may ask, Is this not incorrect? It would be if care were not taken to make it pass unnoticed by the auditors. People judge by results, not by processes ; therefore if the effect is all that it should be, the way in which a thing is accomplished does not matter much. This unity of effect I manage to get by the following method.

In all long runs, divisions, and long phrases of any sort—even in sustained notes—which cannot be well managed by one breath, I ask all the singers whose name initials commence from A to H to take breath on the first beat of any bar except the last bar, which must be sung with unbroken power and firmness. Those singers whose initials are between I and P to take breath on the second beat and those from Q to Z to take breath on the third or fourth beat, in any bar except the last (for the reason stated above). To make sure that this is done correctly, I ask every singer to mark his or her book.

The carrying out of this instruction usually results in a brilliant finish to runs and sustained phrases which would otherwise have the effect of an anticlimax.

Further consideration of the subject of breathing will be given in the chapter on " Expression," where *pianissimo*, staccato, breathing tone, breath afflux, &c., will be discussed.

WORDS :
ARTICULATION—DICTION.

Clear articulation is one of the points upon which both conductors and choirs deceive themselves. They imagine efficiency to exist in performances which, if tested by a clear, definite method and unbiassed judgment, would be found woefully deficient.

Through having adjudicated very often for over twenty years, I have naturally acquired the analytical, mark-giving bent of mind, and when I hear a choir sing, instinctively the appraising habit asserts itself, and comparisons are drawn between what is being done and the competition "bogey" of 100 per cent. When I hear, and in this way subconsciously adjudicate upon, a soloist or choir, in drawing a comparison I generally find that while for correctness of music the performers would get, say, 100 per cent., for voice 95, and for expression 90 to 98, the percentage for words would be 80 or much less. This lamentable imperfection would probably be due to the impurity of the vowels or neglect of vowel quantity, and the lack of sharp, clear, initial and well-defined final consonants.

These defects being so patent to every listener, how is it that in spite of all the severe things

written and said, choralists so universally fail to
overcome this vital shortcoming—I was almost
saying "vocal sin"?

As I have remarked above, it is largely due to
self-deception on the part of the conductor and the
choristers. The conductor deceives himself by
dwelling in the realms of fancy, instead of living in
the region of solid fact. He hears what he knows
he should hear, or, in other words, he mentally
hears words and phrases because he already has
them in his mind; hence he allows defective
articulation to pass, which he would never do were
he conscious of being a victim of his own obsession
and absent-mindedness.

The proper attitude of a conductor is to take his
standard of sense-conveying distinctness from
something outside himself. Personally I always
think of an old gentleman rather hard of hearing
seated in the far gallery, and if the words are not
very clear the choir are reminded of the imaginary
deaf gentleman in the gallery, the result being a
marked improvement in distinctness of utterance at
their next attempt.

Choristers deceive themselves by imagining that
in ordinary conversation they speak plainly, and
that if they sing as they speak they must be heard
and understood.

This is a complete fallacy, as not one in ten, or I
might say one in a hundred, sings words distinctly,
unless special pains be taken to make each word
carry. In the first place it is a great mistake to
fancy that conversational speech is clear and
distinct. As a rule it is quite the reverse. The
great majority of people are guilty of muttering
their words, clipping the consonants, corrupting the

vowels, and running words into each other. To make matters worse it has become a fad of many fashionable ladies to finish each sentence as though they wished their voices to proceed from the bottom of their throats. Fortunately the majority of these irrationals do not speak for long, or they would have to undergo treatment for laryngitis. As it is, not a few are troubled with vocal ailments which can be traced to this ventriloquial, speak-in-the-boots fad. We may here transcribe Madame Roland's famous words, and say, "O Fashion, how many crimes are committed in thy name."

As a matter of fact, people speak very indistinctly in ordinary conversation, but they are understood by means of the context. The listeners hear one or two words in a sentence, and as they know the subject of conversation, they instinctively supply the missing vowels and consonants.

For instance, if you hear " It's ver fi de to-day," you know the speaker means to say, "It is a very fine day to-day." A striking test of our usual indistinctness is furnished by introductions. How few ever catch the right name, and how many have to ask privately the name of the lady or gentleman to whom they have been introduced! This is chiefly because there is no context.

A fine example of the use of the context was furnished a short time ago by a party of navvies. One of the party came up to his friends, and said, rapidly, "an-ony-onye-ony-onyer?" They understood him at once, because as he spoke he pulled out his pipe, and they responded with the offers of tobacco. What the man asked was, "Have any of you any of it [tobacco] on you?"

Choristers further deceive themselves, even when they have been made conscious of their deficiencies by facts such as those just mentioned, by believing that the amount of effort required to speak distinctly will suffice to get satisfactory results in singing.

Alas, this is not so, because in singing the words have to battle against the vocal tone, and there is the further handicap of the muscular effort of the tongue, lips, and cheeks in the production of the quality of tone required, all of which effort the singers mistakenly think is given to the production of the words; hence the universal prevalence of deception number two. The remedies for these errors will be suggested later.

But a more potent reason for the prevalent indistinct articulation is the fact that few conductors, and still fewer choristers, know how to set to work to get the desired results; how to prevent that set of mouth which is responsible for the sound-position being usually one degree more backward than it ought to be; how to obtain the particular muscular action of the tongue, lips, and cheeks which will secure the desired crisp, sharp, incisive delivery of consonants.

The usual instructions *re* diction, " Get pure vowels and clear consonants," are fine examples of the " counsel of perfection "; but what good are they if the people advised do not know the precise point to aim at to attain these results?

When in South Africa I asked one of our party who had been through the Boer War, and had been engaged in sixteen fights, whether he had ever killed a Boer. He said he thought not, for though he had fired scores of rounds at the places where he knew the Boers to be located, he never knew the exact spot at which to shoot, and therefore he thought he had failed in his object.

This is the position of nearly every conductor I know. They have a good idea of what is wanted, and the direction in which successful delivery of words is to be found, but not the exact point to which they can unerringly aim. To those who desire this open sesame, I propose in the following pages to disclose the plans I have followed for years, which have made the clear articulation and convincing diction of my choirs noteworthy. These plans will enable everyone who will take the trouble involved in following the instructions to secure clear, understandable words in whatever class of vocal work they may undertake.

INERTIA.

Before proceeding with the exposition of the plans referred to above, it will be absolutely necessary to refer to a subject the consideration of which cannot be any longer deferred, because without complete mastery of the faults and drawbacks inherent to it, the effort to improve articulation would be futile. The subject is *Inertia*. Inertia is in evidence in every department of choral society work. It is shown in the irregular manner of going on and off the platform at a concert, the listless rising and sitting of a choir, the attack and release of notes, and the lack of responsiveness to the beat of the conductor. These things being very obvious to conductor and officials, efforts are made from time to time to remedy the defects, and a smartening-up period ensues, but alas! it is usually short-lived. However baneful inertia may be in the cases mentioned above, its subtle influence is much more pernicious in the region of words, because, its connection with articulation not being obvious, its presence is not suspected. Yet inertia seems to have every singer in its grip, and, like Sindbad's Old Man of the Sea, will not loose its hold until it is forcibly thrown off.

It is through taking no cognisance of inertia that conductors have failed in their efforts to improve the articulation of their choirs. It is therefore almost useless to give instructions how to remedy lack of clearness in speech until the head and front of the offence—" inertia "—is conquered.

On account of the importance of mastering this infirmity, and attaining its corollary, the perfecting of articulation, I take advantage of any special choral event, such as the World Tour, the visit to Germany, Paris, &c.,—in which every member is keenly anxious to attain perfection,—to give a résumé of the principles of perfect articulation and how to attain it. This little lecture is usually given at an extra meeting, when all the evening is devoted to the exposition. Its purpose is to initiate new members into the mysteries of lingual muscular equipment, as well as to revise, revive, and strengthen the knowledge of the older members of the society.

This recapitulation, even in the case of those who have heard the explanations before, is very useful, for choristers are very much like human clocks, and need to be occasionally re-wound.

Please imagine that such a special meeting has been called and I am addressing the full choir— each singer, as desired, provided with note-book and pencil—on the "Imperfections of Articulation: the causes and the remedy." The following is a rather full outline of what I would say.

" The subject that we have met to consider this evening is how to master words, how to secure clear, correct articulation, how to get perfect diction. This is most important, because words are, in my opinion, the most powerful things on earth. You might think that I, being a musician, attach more importance to the music than to the words, but I do not. In vocal music the words are paramount, and it is the function of the music, by sound, by rhythm, and by expression, to intensify and make more living the thought embodied in the words ; hence the importance of having the message clearly and understandingly enunciated.

" To go through a piece without letting the audience know what you are saying is, in my opinion, as you have often heard me say, a deep disgrace. It is like playing ' Hamlet' and leaving out the Prince.

" The lack of clearness and enunciation, joined to the often incorrect pronunciation, are two of the standing weaknesses of nearly all singers. This is certainly true of most choral societies, and you yourselves know that we usually fall short of our ideal, namely, the making of ourselves understood by our old friend the man in the gallery, whose hearing is dulled.

" Considering that you are all anxious to be heard, and most of you try to speak clearly, you think that the fault cannot be in you personally—that it is because your neighbour does not speak clearly. As a matter of fact, you both may speak clearly, as you think, but *you do not speak clearly enough*. The reasons for this are twofold. First, because you do not know exactly what to do, namely, how to use the muscles of the mouth to advantage, and secondly, because of the inertia which prevents the required freedom of muscular action.

" The question arises, What is the inertia of which we speak? It is the strong indisposition of the muscles to work, and their refusal to move, except under the impulse of a strong will, conscience, or necessity.

"Some people would call this idleness, but idleness is such only when the muscles refuse to work, though desire, conscience, or necessity demand that work should be done. In this obedience of the muscles of the mouth to the call of the mind, soul, and will lies the salvation of pure articulation and graphic diction.

"It may be taken as an axiom that every muscle in the body is afflicted with the infirmity of inertia, and none more than the muscles of the mouth, tongue, lips, and cheeks. St. James spoke of the tongue being an unruly member. This is true in another sense besides that meant by the Apostle.

"I have said that salvation from inertia lies in the fact that our muscles would respond to the *will*. While this is true, we must not think that it is an easy matter. When any of our muscles have acquired certain habits in the course of years, they rebel against the slightest disturbance of those habits. Let a man whose foot turns slightly inwards decide to turn it outwards. The struggle to achieve this will be so severe that in all probability he will abandon the contest, unless the impelling force be a sense of duty. But, you may fairly ask,

'If everybody is naturally idle, why have we so
many unidle men and women?' It is because the
sense of duty comes in to strengthen the will.
For duty, people deny themselves indolent ease,
selfishness gives way to self-denial, and 'taking it
easy' is replaced by strenuous effort. This is the
key to the situation. So long as singers' consciences
are content with 60 per cent. or less of efficiency,
they will make no effort; they will follow the line
of least resistance, namely, their old easy-going
habit. But let them get an ideal of perfection, and
feel that it is their duty to *art*, to the *society*, or the
city to which they belong, and a transformation
appears.

"This sense of duty to our society and to the
audiences who honour us by their presence I wish
you to feel, and you will then overcome the Giant
Despair against whom all conductors, including
myself, have to wage eternal war. Therefore I
beg you to be so determined to combat this
insidious weakness that, when the muscles of the
mouth say, 'Oh, leave us alone,' you must reply,
'No, I won't, you don't do your work efficiently,
consequently you must respond to my demands.'

"Here let me give some cautions, instructions,
and hints with regard to mastering inertia.
Remember that the slightest muscular effort beyond
what is habitual will seem to be greatly exaggerated;
therefore make up your mind to give twice or
thrice the effort you at first think necessary, and
then you will probably give half the amount which
you should.

"Persevere until the unaccustomed muscular
action becomes natural, as it will in a short
time, and later it will become a subconscious

attainment. Remember, though it be hard at first to get the tongue to move promptly and sufficiently, it is harder to control the lips, and hardest to dragoon the cheeks. In other words, in point of inertia the tongue is bad, the lips are worse, and the facial muscles the worst, as we shall see presently when we discuss how to use these muscles in developing pure, clear articulation.

"But be of good courage; you will triumph over all difficulties and come out conqueror, if in your struggle with about ten square inches of muscular fibre you decide to make your will the controlling power.

"Having seen that by mastering our natural inertia we shall be able to control the organs of articulation, we will now consider the principles of clear and correct articulation and its consummation, —diction, *i.e.*, the accomplishment of picturing out and giving living power to every word spoken or sung.

ARTICULATION.   DICTION.

"To get clear, distinct, intelligible articulation you will have to devote special attention to two things :—(1) Correct vowel quantity, and (2) distinct consonant delivery.

VOWELS.

" It is astonishing in how many cases the mere act of singing changes the vowel-sound. Ask even an educated person to sing the word ' man,' and the chances are that he will sing ' maun,' while the

word ' my ' is oftener than not sung 'moy.'
Similarly, the short vowel in ' the ' is changed to
' thuh ' ; ' ow ' often becomes ' o,' and most of the
other vowel-sounds are more or less perverted.
Probably you would do the same yourselves. This
would be so, not because you do not know better, but
from inertia, which, as I have said, compels you
to miscalculate the amount of muscular movement
necessary to produce any vowel when singing. This
strong indisposition to work causes the mouth to
make the minimum of effort, with the result that
the vowels are placed a degree further back in the
mouth than they ought to be. The remedy for this
is to sing with forward articulation, such as is
favoured by the use of nasal resonance. Those
who shoot for prizes at Bisley always ' make
allowance for the wind.' Similarly, you must
make allowance for the muscular disturbance
caused by placing your mouths in the position for
singing, and by will power project your voices and
words much more forward than you deem necessary
to attain the same position in your mouths that the
words would demand if you were speaking.

" The vowels *oo*, *oh*, *aw*, *ah*, *ai*, *ee*, and their
corresponding short vowels should be practised to
Ex. 1 (page 22), with special reference to *vowel
quantity* rather than to tone-quality, which has been
the object in the past.

" You must realise that some vowels and
diphthongs are more difficult to sing than others,
and that a vowel is often more difficult to sing on
a high note than on a low note.

"A very difficult vowel to get pure is *ah* and its
short form *a*. Unless great care is taken it
becomes perverted to *aw*. To give one example

G

only, you are familiar with 'Mighty in battle,' which, as you know, is frequently pronounced 'Moighty in bottle.' Alertness and determination are required when the vowels *ah, ai, ee,* and their short sounds are sung on high notes, otherwise every one will sound like *aw* or short *o,* as in the case of 'His mercy' (*Elijah*), which is nearly always sung as 'morcy,' on the high G.

" The reason why the much-abused *i* is perverted to *oi* is because *i* consists of forward *ah* and *ee,* the former dwelt on, and the latter just glanced at as the diphthong is left: if the *ah* is not forward then it becomes *aw,* the result being *aw-ee = oi.* Should the *ah* be quitted too soon, and the *ee* dwelt on too long, we get that quaint effect which we have heard so often —but of which few know the real cause—in the verse :—

> ' When I-ee can read myee tieetle clear
> To mansions in the skiees,
> I-ee'l bid farewell to every fear
> And wi-eep my-ee weeping eyees.'

The importance of the two things mentioned above —the forward *ah* and the rapid quitting of the second vowel of the diphthong—is shown in words containing *ow = ah-oo.* This is reversed in one diphthong, *u = e-oo,* as in dew, where the second sound must be dwelt upon and the first vowel quitted rapidly, or we shall get such a result as 'bee-ootiful.'

" Some of our great singers have so far transgressed in the matter of vowel quantity that they have sanctioned some of these errors, and have caused less gifted singers to copy such peculiarities, just as Spurgeon's students used to copy the pulpit mannerisms of the great preacher. But let it be said that these singers are great in spite of these faults, not on account of them. Even they are victims of inertia; hence their fall from perfection in articulation. But these blemishes are overlooked on account of other great qualities which throw them into the shade. The public unconsciously measure them as profit and loss is gauged; they count as gain all that is left of the profit when the loss has been subtracted. Thus if a singer shows a good balance of voice and artistic effect, we forgive in one the 'swoop' with which her name is associated, the wretched 'wobble' of another singer, the slight out-of-tuneness of another, the hanging-on-below-pitch of another, and the bad control of vowels of quite a number. Nevertheless these great singers would be better without such defects. The great choirs of the future *must be without them*, and their influence will cause artists to remedy their own defects. Signs of this are not wanting even now.

CONSONANTS.

"However important the vowels are, the consonants are still more important, for on these depend the precise sense and graphic power of what is sung, and in their delivery rest a great deal of the spirit and verve of a piece. Notwithstanding the reiterated injunctions in elocution books to make the final consonants clear, we still find the same old slipshod way of articulating consonants.

"Why are consonants so widely neglected? After making due allowances for the ever-present inertia,

I think that the non-success is due to the singers
not knowing precisely what to do, what to aim at.
They do not know what particular muscular action
of the lips, tongue, and palate will secure the
desired crisp, sharp, incisive delivery of consonants.
I will therefore endeavour to put in a new light,
and to state in a new way, what a consonant is,
promising that whenever a pupil or a class has
grasped this, all indistinctness will vanish.

"By a consonant we mean a letter which
represents a particular impression made upon the
mind when a sound is abruptly, forcibly, and
markedly stopped by the lips, teeth, palate or
throat. These sounds may be stopped entirely or
only partially.

" As illustrations of what is meant, let us take the
explodents, which are classified as under :—

> Labials, *p* and *b.*
> Dentals, *t* and *d.*
> Palatals, *ch* and *j.*
> Gutturals, *k* and *g* (hard).

" If we wish to say ' rope ' we first say ' ro,' and
then make a stoppage of the sound at our lips, and
this particular kind of stoppage we associate with
p, and we then hear the word ' rope.' If we say
ro, and make a heavier stoppage at our lips, we
get ' robe '; if we stop the sound at our teeth we
get the impression of *t* or *d*, as in the words ' get,'
' rote,' or ' road '; if at our palate we get *ch* or *j*,
as in ' church ' or ' judge,' while if the stoppage
is made in our throat we get ' roke ' or ' rogue.'
Though this is not quite the same with all
consonants, it is quite near enough for our purpose
to make the general and important statement that

to get clear consonants what we have to do is to *make the stoppage of our sounds complete, and in such a manner as to give the hearer no doubt as to where it is made.*

"From what you have heard you will realise that to get keen, incisive articulation you have to know the exact spot in the mouth or nasal cavities where each stoppage of the sound is made, so that each click, hum, buzz, and aspirate can be located. This can be done by the rapid, crisp, smart, well-controlled movement of the articulatory muscles, as opposed to the conventional sluggish manner in which many of you now sing.

"Just imagine what this knowledge should mean to you. Instead of floundering about in the bog of uncertainty, you can act with decision. Whereas in your will-o'-the-wisp-like search you had metaphorically to sing, 'Thou art so near and yet so far,' you should now be able to sing, 'Thou art my guiding star.' Summarizing the whole, here is the talismanic key to unlock the gates of indistinctness of speech:—Hold the vowel-sounds as long as the notes sung will allow, then by an instantaneous movement of the muscles of the mouth effect the stoppage of sound in the place required, and the result will be the production of perfect consonants.

"On account of the inertia already referred to, the most anxious student cannot perform these actions as cleanly and as swiftly as they should be done, without preliminary exercises, which should be designed to give a maximum of benefit with a minimum of trouble. Such a set of exercises is provided for initial consonants in the following alliterative sentences, which, as many of you know, have proved to be very advantageous to those who have used them conscientiously :—

P.   Pearls please pretty Penelope.
B.   Big Ben broke Bertha's bouncing ball.
T.   Try teaching to tax temper.
D.   Dear Dora danced delightfully.
Th. Thin things think thick thoughts.
Th. Thee, *thou* them that *thou* thee (*thou* used as a verb).
Ch. Church chaps chirp chants cheerfully.
J.   John Jones jumps jauntily.
K.   Clever cricketers keep catches.
G.   Guy gives good gifts gracefully.
F.   Fair flirts fancy French fashions.
V.   Vain Vernon vowed vengeance.
M.   Mild-mannered men make money.
N.   Nellie never noticed Norah.
R.   Round rough rocks ragged rascals ran.
L.   Lion lilies like light.
W.   Wise women won't whine.

" Exercise for final consonants is provided in phrases like the following :—

Tip-top trip.   Search church porch.
Bob rub tub.   Madge lodge Hodge.
Bright white light.   Mike woke Luke.
Fred led Ned.   Snug swag-bag.

" In practising these phrases, bear in mind that it is not the mere saying of them, but *how* you

say them, that counts. For instance, in words
containing *p*, *b*, *f*, *v*, *m*, or *w*, which involve
the use of the lips, see that they close with
rapid action, because the lips are very reluctant
to close.

" The *th* groups require great care, for you
know we have often to stop to get ' the ' clearly
pronounced. In fact, any choir which can sing
' the ' perfectly is in the highest class. When
singing a final consonant, avoid the common error
of ceasing to make the sound before you actually
reach the end of the word, with the result that
' sheep ' sounds like ' shee,' ' Help, Lord ' like
' Hel, Lor.' To remedy this serious shortcoming,
introduce the faint-sounding *uh* at the end of
each consonant. This acts as a sound-carrying
' glide,' or, in other words, enables the sound to
glide to the click, hum, or buzz necessary to
make the consonant distinct. To secure this
carrying ' glide ' some singers add *er* or a
short *ah* to their words: thus ' sheep ' becomes
' sheep(er) ' or ' sheep(a) ' ; ' Help, Lord ' becomes
' Help(a) Lord(a).' This is exaggerating the
glide unnecessarily and disagreeably, but if the
glide *uh* is given delicately, it imparts definition
to the consonant, without being in the least
objectionable.

" Up to the present I have spoken of not
giving enough prominence to the finals, but in
the case of the sibilants *s*, *z*, *sh* and *ce*, please
curtail them as much as possible, and never
introduce them till the last eighth of the beat.
Usually there is a disagreeable hissing sound at the
close of such words as ' peace,' ' hush,' ' pass,'
because many singers pass to the sibilant too soon,

and nearly everybody keeps the tongue to the roof of the mouth instead of withdrawing it quickly, say to the lower teeth, or letting the lower jaw fall slightly. Attention to this will remedy a grave defect.

" In conclusion I would remark that the practical application of clear articulation to the laws that govern diction will be treated when we study ' Expression.' "

It is strictly on the lines enunciated in the foregoing little lecture, supplemented by passing remarks at rehearsals, that such success as we have had in diction has been achieved; and I feel sure that others may be equally successful, or more so, even to the obtaining 100 per cent., if they will follow the hints given.

It has been assumed in the foregoing that the singers were perfectly familiar with the correct pronunciation of every word, and that every deviation from correctness was due to imperfect control of the vocal muscles. But there are districts in which even educated people have certain peculiarities of pronunciation which call for a word of caution. For instance, a city in the south had some of its peculiarities well revealed by a verger who was showing a party of Yorkshire people round a well-known cathedral during a recent Handel Festival week, immediately after he had ciceroned a party of Americans. He said, " Oi can understand what you Yorkshire people sye (say), but the wye (way) those Americans murder the King's English is enough to give anybody the ' amp ' (hump)." He was blissfully unconscious that he was not using perfect King's English himself. The same can be said of those who turn every g into k, as in the word " nothink," while in the north

there are those who say " deeficult waird " for
" difficult word." The importance, in an artistic
sense, of being absolutely correct was shown to
me by a famous Scotch baritone singer. I asked
him how a common friend, who had a really
good voice, was getting on in the profession. He
answered, " Oh, he is not getting on at all, and
won't, because he sings English songs like a
Scotchman "—*i.e.*, with a Scotch accent.

In every case the conductor must be sure of
King's English, and, if necessary, pattern every
doubtful word.

MUSICAL EXPRESSION.

Of the many factors which go to make a pleasing and successful musical performance, the most important is that combination of colouring, intensifying, and shading which we term Expression in music. A composition may be ever so cleverly written, but its vitality often depends upon the way it is presented,—whether the spirit of the work is revealed, the proper atmosphere caught, the crises well arranged. There is no doubt that scores of compositions have been killed by first performances which have lacked the requisite artistic tone of expression, while other works which have happily and properly survived ran great risk of being consigned to oblivion through the same cause.

The now historical example of the first performance of *The Dream of Gerontius* is a case in point. When this classic was first put into rehearsal the new idiom was incomprehensible to the choralists, while every one failed to grasp the then strange combination of mystical, diabolical, and ecstatical elements which run through the whole oratorio. The result was that at the initial performance the musical expression which should have illuminated the work and made the whole intelligible was almost entirely absent, and the performance was a complete fiasco. Those

of us who were convinced of the supreme merits
of the work—which in my opinion marked an
epoch in choral composition—were very sad and
depressed.

This incident shows how imperative it is for
conductors to grasp the principles of artistic
expression, to cultivate critical acumen and to
enlarge the faculty of taste, not only to do justice
to works which they may have to conduct, but also
because the ultimate status of a choir or conductor
depends upon artistic renderings as embodied in
musical expression.

This pre-eminence of musical expression is so
universally felt that singers and instrumentalists
take their rank more from possessing the power to
sing or play with expression than from possessing a
good voice or digital dexterity. It is true that a
singer with a good voice alone, or a player with
special technique, may win a temporary reputation,
but it is only temperamental artists who achieve and
maintain positions in the front rank.

The difference between the two is : one is merely
a singer with a voice, and the other is a singer
who can sing ; in instrumentalists one is a mere
technician, while the other is an artist.

To emphasise the importance of expression it
will only be necessary to recall to mind the present-
day vocalists who occupy leading or front-rank
positions, whose voices are of very mediocre
quality, but who, by virtue of their emotional,
temperamental, and expressive interpretations, carry
conviction to their hearers, and thus make their
artistic position secure.

There are two great impediments connected with
the acquisition of the power to impart expression

to music, which prevent hosts of otherwise good musicians from advancing further than the fringe of the subject. The first drawback is its subtle elusiveness, and the second is the length of time required by even artistic temperaments to inhale so fully its principles that they can exhale its fragrant essence.

As I have remarked, expression is one of the most elusive things with which a conductor has to grapple. Its difficulty lies in its indefiniteness. I do not mean that it is a difficult task to realise and get the observance of the different marks of expression *piano*, *forte*, &c.—although many conductors do not get even these—but to acquire that subtle perception, a kind of " sixth sense," which dictates what is suited to every note and phrase, how to develop the æsthetic and dramatic idea of the composition, is by no means easy. But when one has become infected with the " microbe of expression " and means business, this instinctive feeling for expression will develop rapidly.

That a conductor or performer may lose sight of the expression of a piece and be unconscious that he is so doing, is a commonplace. This may arise not so much from lack of artistic perception as from his giving undue attention to some particular aspect or aspects of the work in hand—correctness of music, rigid regard to tempo, literal performance of the *p*'s and *f*'s of the copy—so that it or they crowd out the poetic element of expression, and instead of his being an emotional artist he is merely a human metronome.

The relation of a personal experience may illustrate this point. Some thirty years ago, when

the Sheffield Musical Union was in its infancy,
I, as an enthusiastic amateur, was very keen on
the members becoming good sight - readers of
music, and we got to be so expert that I was very
proud of our attainments in this direction. In my
pride I invited a critical and musically cultured
friend (Mr. Sam Johnson) to come and hear us, as
I wished to surprise him. He came ; we sang,
and then I asked for his verdict, expecting
that he would be enthusiastic and say that he had
not heard anything like it. I was terribly
disappointed. He said, " Your sight-singing is, in
its way, very clever, but you can't sing. Where
are the quality of tone, the shading of expression,
the phrasing, the smoothness of delivery, in fact,
all the points that go to make artistic singing ?
Though you may get through the music in a
wonderful manner, you can't sing."

This cold douche set me thinking, and showed
me that if a conductor lacks ideality, the
potentialities of taste and expression will remain
undeveloped, and dull and heavy singing will
result. It altered my whole course. While not
neglecting sight-singing, I determined to wipe out
the reproach and make the choir "sing." Here it
will be well to repeat a story, which, in my then
disturbed and receptive state of mind, greatly
influenced me. A poor French artist invited a
number of his friends to a fish supper, which
proved to be so enjoyable that they were all in
raptures. Not one, however, of the guests could
tell what kind of fish they had eaten. After great
pressure the artist told them that the fish was
merely herring, at which his guests marvelled, and
inquired how it was possible for herring to be so

extremely enjoyable. He replied, "It was the sauce that did it."

Here was my cue. It was the way pieces were served up which made them palatable or otherwise It should be my quest to find out the underlying principles of expression, so that music served up by myself should, in future, have the advantage of enriching, appetizing musical sauce.

In this search I became conscious that mere *pianos* and *fortes* were not the sum total of expression, even when given with bandmaster-like fidelity, but that something more was required to differentiate between the common expression in a piece and an artistic rendering. The question arose, "What is this subtle essence, this ether-like quality which must be present, but which, like the overtones of a Stradivarius violin or nasal resonance, must not be in evidence except as it enriches and glorifies the sounds produced?" Two or three remarks by Ruskin *à propos* the sister art of painting put me on the right track, and from these arose that scheme of expression which I now follow, and which for the guidance of others I have attempted to codify.

The first point was: The curve is the basis of beauty in design. The second was: Beauty in design is something almost symmetrical. The third was: Every speck of paint should have its climax, or should tend to, and be part of, a climax.

These hints were extremely useful; but I felt that something was still lacking, and for a long time I was searching for this missing link, when I came across two illuminating statements of the same thought by two great painters—Haydon and

Watts—which made me cry out, like Archimedes of old, " Eureka ! Eureka ! I have found it !" This fourth suggestive thought was : The line of beauty in design is such that no two parts of it contain the same arc of a circle. Haydon illustrated this by a spiral, which showed his contention convincingly. From the above fundamental principles of art I deduced the scheme of musical expression which I have ever since followed, with, I hope, decided success. This scheme may be formulated as follows:—

(1) Regard the swell as the basis of the beautiful in music, and the chief source of all effective expression.

(2) Take care that the patterns of design do not occur with mathematical regularity, or the effect will be mechanical.

(3) Always go from somewhere to somewhere, rising directly or indirectly to some rousing climax, or toning down to some equally effective point of repose. Have an Ideal to aim at.

(4) Conform to the demands of the " line of beauty " by getting, when needed, variety of force and design in each note, phrase, or movement.

(5) Never treat a note, phrase, or movement in an isolated manner, but let it be considered in relation to the whole movement, cantata, or oratorio—learn to think in musical continents, or, as Rodin says, in " mass."

From the above guiding principles comes the grand deduction that musical expression resolves itself into the "art of phrasing." By phrasing is understood the art of securing proper expression to every note, bar, and phrase, and so arranging them that each phrase has some point of variety and contrast with every other phrase, and so bears a proper relation to the context, the whole merging into an artistic unity and producing a sense of harmonious design in expression.

Expression will be dealt with separately, but the dominant fact of the relationship and subserviency of all its separate limbs to artistic phrasing will ever be present, although the word "phrasing" may not be often mentioned.

Let us now consider the subject in detail.

Musical expression may conveniently be said to consist of three main divisions :—

(1) The regulation of rhythm.
(2) The application, variation, and control of dynamic (tonal) and emotional force.
(3) The portrayal of various mental states, extreme moods, and fancies, such as laughter, hatred, derision, ribaldry, anger, despair, &c.

To the above must be added, in vocal music :—

(4) Management of words, diction, verbal shadings by emphasis, tone-colour, &c.

Rhythm. What is rhythm ? We all know that music moves in beats or pulses, and at regular intervals—say, at every two, three, or four beats—some of these beats are stressed or accented. It is these accents which produce rhythm ; therefore rhythm may be defined as a pattern of accents, or a phrase of pulses made characteristic by the effect of its contrasted strong and weak accents. Rhythms may be observed even in statuary and architecture. Rhythms may be regular, as when they follow the time-signatures ; and irregular, as when many syncopations are introduced.

Of all the branches of music, I think that the study of rhythm is the most neglected, and its possibilities least understood. We learn as a matter of course the tune, time, and perhaps expression of a piece, but rhythm often escapes us. And yet the grasping of this somewhat elusive element is of the utmost importance.

It is the absence of well-defined rhythm which makes so many pianoforte recitals become wearisome, and causes so many otherwise fine players to be concert failures. I say advisedly that of our leading pianists Paderewski owes his pre-eminence more to his mastery of rhythm—his delicious control of accents—than to any other single factor. I personally know and have heard other pianists who have as great or greater technique, but the peculiar charm of the Polish master pianist is absent from their playing, consequently they are comparative failures—the cause, according to my analysis, being their defective rhythm. It is this same element, a delightful sense of rhythm, that makes M. Pachmann's renderings of Chopin supreme.

In the organ world, Mr. Edwin H. Lemare has a more wonderful faculty of imparting the sense of rhythm than any other organist I know, and this rhythmic swing, coupled to his brilliant technique, produces that exhilarating effect which draws crowded audiences to all his organ recitals.

H

The lesson of these pregnant facts has been burnt into my mind, and fully utilised by me in the training of my choirs.

In view of the importance of this observance of accent, two questions arise :—(1) Why is so much choral singing lacking in rhythm, and consequently in interest ? and (2) Why is rhythmless music favoured in some circles ?

The first result is due in many cases to the fact that so many choral conductors are organists. They have grown so accustomed to the lack of spring in the music they most frequently hear, that the absence of rhythmic pulsation does not strike them as it does the general public, who, though critical and conscious of a lack of something, are not analytical enough to hit upon the true explanation.

The result, in the second case, arises from the hyper-sensitive taste of a limited class of musicians who prefer the nebulous, dreamy, and inconclusive, rather than the clear and well defined. Whether this is an indication of superior judgment or merely depraved taste is a debatable point which need not now be discussed.

My own view is that whether it denotes growth or decay, a conductor's outlook should be wide enough to embrace and treat sympathetically even rhythmless music.

But as this class does not appeal to the ordinary cultured ideal, and as rhythm is the vitalizing element in music, conductors should cultivate rhythm—not the bald, rigid thing, but poetical pulsations, *i.e.*, with the corners rounded off, accents with an atmosphere; and if this is done successfully the works performed will come upon the critic with the freshness of a stream of water in a thirsty land.

Quite recently I heard a mild-mannered lady asked how it was that she got her very determined husband to do just what she wanted. She said that it was simply that she "managed" him without letting him know that she did it. This is precisely what conductors and performers generally must do with regard to obtaining rhythm. They must "manage" it without making the means employed or the accents themselves too obvious— in fact, the successful achievement of artistic rhythm may be set down as a good example of "art concealing art."

I will now explain the principles by which this management may be accomplished :—

1. Always preserve the sense of the rhythm of the time-signature.

2. Add the element of variety by making on all possible occasions two-, three-, four-, six-bar, &c., rhythms.

3. Secure modifications of the accents by means of delicate pressures and swells, and thus obtain contrasts between dynamic (masculine) and emotional (feminine) accents.

4. Remember that it is possible to maintain the idea of signature rhythm without the crest of the accent being on the first beat.

5. Emphasise the accents—sometimes every note—in working up to a *fortissimo* climax.

6. Strike firmly all syncopated notes and other salient parts of irregular rhythms.

7. In cross-rhythms let each individual rhythm be well-defined, while preserving the swing of the whole.

8. Sustained notes and reiterated notes should be sung with *crescendo* when they terminate at a strong accent, or are followed by a higher note on a strong beat.

9. Frequently a note, by reason of its being a discord—prepared or unprepared—or a resisting harmony note, requires special emphasis.

10. The first notes of triplets should be well defined.

It may be thought a very easy matter to secure the sense of the rhythm of the time-signature. But sometimes the swing of the rhythm is obscured by the form or shape of the melody, by the introduction of syncopation, or by the grouping of the notes. Take, for instance, the well-known phrase :—

and all flesh . . shall see it to - ge - ther,

This is usually sung incorrectly, the high notes being sung too loudly, thus perverting the rhythm. Take again the subject :—

And with His stripes we are heal - ed,

the usual loud singing of the high notes destroys

not only the rhythm, but the poetry and the effect. By taking care to get it sung as follows :—

And with His stripes we are heal - ed,

the passionate grief and artistic beauty of it are preserved. Scores of similar examples might be given, but these must suffice, with the remark that constant watchfulness is required to keep the rhythm well defined.

Rule 2 is an effective corrective to the popular notion that rhythm is merely the giving of a strong accent at the beginning of every bar. This is perfectly true in theory; but if the accents are struck remorselessly with metronomic regularity they become an irritation, and produce an effect similar to that caused by the recurring jolt of a tram, or the whirr of machinery.

Of course there are certain pieces and declamatory choruses, such as " He gave them hailstones " (*Israel*) and " O! never, never, bow we down " (*Judas*) in which this persistent accentuation is necessary. But even these strenuous choruses must be regarded as merely passing contrasts to other movements, to which they act as agreeable foils.

Generally the rule of securing variety in accent must be followed, and care must be taken not to get a monotonous rhythm :—

Here we have quite a variety of forms of accent in the eight bars, which may be said to consist of two one-bar rhythms, a single two-bar rhythm, and a final four-bar rhythm.

The next two examples are taken from *Elijah:*—

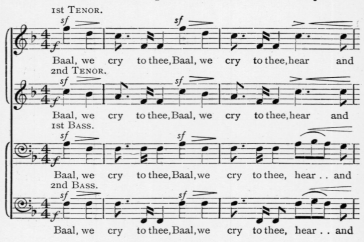

The markings will show how varied are the rhythmic phrases.

It is surprising how long the regular current of accents can be interrupted—say, at a prolonged *crescendo,*—if only a well-defined accent restores the rhythmic swing.

Innumerable other examples could be quoted of the fine artistic effect of this element of variety, but I will only mention the opening phrase of *Blest Pair of Sirens* (where we have two two-bar rhythms followed by a four-bar rhythm), the opening of Elgar's "Lullaby," and "The Marksman" (*Bavarian Highlands*), where the same thing occurs. In the last-named stirring piece, delightful changes of variation, from one-bar to eight-bar rhythms, occur all through.

With the above suggestions the alert conductor will not have much difficulty in devising a scheme of varied rhythms for each composition. In addition to the variety secured by Rule 2, a great deal of monotony can be avoided by the application of Rule 3.

Except in a few choruses like "He gave them hailstones," and "Have lightnings and thunders in clouds disappeared" (Bach), the dynamic accent can be modified by the swell, which converts the hard pulsation to an emotional throb. Further, so long as the feeling of signature rhythm is preserved, the crest of the accent need not come on the first part of the first beat. As an illustration of Rules 3 and 4, take the well-known air "Kathleen Mavourneen," as sung by a well-known great artist :—

Kath - leen Ma - vour - neen, a - wake from thy slumbers,

Here, instead of a mere accent on the first beat there is a gentle pressure on the first quaver and a swell to the second, then a shading off. In bar 2 variety is secured and the emotion heightened by the swell being continued to the end of the third quaver. In bar 3 the climax is reached by continuing the swell for four quavers before shading to a soft finish.

It will be observed that the phrase consists of a four-bar rhythm made up of two incidental one-bar rhythms and a two-bar rhythm. The next quotation is a fine illustration of varied accent pattern:—

It may be regarded as a compound nine-bar rhythm phrase—as no two accents are alike.

In working to a climax of a phrase or of a movement (Rule 5), life, power, and vigour are imparted by seeming to exaggerate the accents at the very end. As examples take the runs in "For unto us" and "Why do the nations," and an excerpt from *The Veil* (Cowen):—

thing? Why do the na - tions rage . . . .

. . . .

Allegro vivace.
COWEN, *The Veil.*

O Spi - rit di - vine, ... Come . . . and

bless, come and bless . . . . The flower . . .

of the world. . . . .

Many soloists fail in bravura passages like the above by not attending to these final stimulating, action-quickening accents.

Many conductors of choirs also neglect this important point, and the choruses fall flat, whereas if the runs be ended with marked accent a thrill invariably follows. Another example is the following passage from "For unto us":—

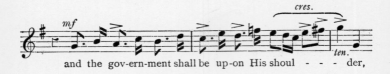

and the gov-ern-ment shall be up-on His shoul - - - der,

It should be borne in mind that when at the *fff* end of a massive chorus you seem to have reached the limit of force, and still more power is wanted, the emphatic accent, by its nerve-rousing stimulus, produces the desired effect.

With respect to Rule 6, it should be said that all departures from the regular and conventional, whether in accent, tempo, voice, or treatment, should be carried out boldly whenever musical or dramatic reasons call for such special treatment. Hence syncopated passages like the following :—

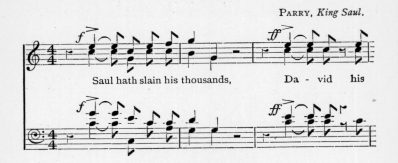

PARRY, *King Saul.*

Saul hath slain his thousands,   Da - vid his

ten   thou-sands,   etc.

require incisive attack.

In carrying out Rule 7, to make every part clear it will be necessary to emphasise each important accent, whether regular or syncopated, and to soften the voice immediately, so as to allow the accent of the next voice to be heard. To get my choirs to realise and accomplish this difficult feat, I compare it with expert football, where, as soon as a player has had his short passing-kick, he gets out of the way to allow his colleague to make his kick effective. The following marked examples will illustrate this point clearly:—

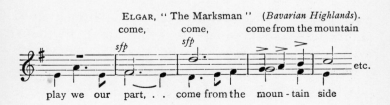

The stimulating effect of a *crescendo* on a sustained note or reiterated notes is ample apology for the temporary disturbance of the regular flow of accents—strong, weak, medium, &c.—while the *crescendo* is often wonderfully effective, as is shown by the following examples :—

This fine composition contains a great many effective examples of this point.

Rule 10 calls for special attention on account of the frequent—nay, excessive—introduction of tripletted notes in the scores of modern composers.

Generally when they are introduced against duplets they should be given supremacy, because when they lack this distinction obscurity often results. This is why the vocal *cadenza* near the end of the *Choral Symphony* (Beethoven) is so unsatisfactory even when sung by singers of the first rank.

The two examples which follow illustrate how similar passages should be sung :—

BRAHMS, *Requiem* (Novello's edition).

THE DYNAMICS OF EXPRESSION.

Having dealt with this important adjunct of musical expression—rhythm—we can now consider what is generally associated with and regarded as the chief factor in musical expression, namely, the artistic application, regulation, and modification of the amount of tonal and emotional force required to secure a desired interpretation of a musical composition. The colour palette from which the conductor may draw his varied shadings may be said to comprise the swell; the *crescendo;* the *diminuendo;* stress pressures; *sforzandos*—in fact all degrees of force from *pianissimo* to *fortissimo;* marked entries; imitative passages; antiphonal effects; the dovetailing of parts and phrases; attack and release; variation of tempo, such as *accelerando, rallentando, tempo rubato,* and the pause; shortening and lengthening individual notes as in *staccato* and *tenuto;* management of sustained notes; working to a climax whether of *fortissimo* or *pianissimo;* characterization by means of variation of tone-quality and facial expression, as in the laugh, the sob, the jeer, the shriek; onomatopoetic effects, such as the howling of the storm, the soughing of the wind, bringing out the meaning of special words, the booming or tinkling of bells; diction and rhetorical accents of words; sudden contrasts of force and mood; and the strengthening or weakening of parts, so as to secure due prominence to the principal theme, or to avoid undue obtrusion of subordinate parts. As most of the above attributes of expression are governed by the line of beauty, and as this is referable to the curve of the sound, it will be seen that the *swell* is the basis of most of the dynamic and emotional aspects of light and shade embodied in the above catalogue of possible constituents of the tonal colour-box.

THE SWELL.

From an emotional aspect the swell is paramount.
The unbroken swell may be short, as when confined
to a single note or phrase, or may extend for
quite a long period. It may begin and stop
at any point. The *crescendo* may be regarded
as the first part of a swell, the *decrescendo* as the
latter part. The connection of most points of
expression with the swell will be shown as the
subject unfolds. It may therefore be laid down
that the management of the swell is the basis of
musical expression. With this axiom in mind, let
me say that the emotional effect is nearly always in
proportion to the breadth of the design. The span
of a large railway viaduct is more impressive than
the arch of a small bridge. The span of St. Pancras
Station excels in effect the curve of the top of a
railway carriage, while the rainbow transcends both.
In like manner the long, majestic swell, *crescendo*,
which leads up to a grand climax is more overpowering than the short *crescendo*, and the prolonged
swell on a sustained sound is more thrilling than
the gentle increase of power which should be used
to give interest to every note. With these
preliminary remarks, we will now consider
expression in detail, and show the application of the
theory as the subject unfolds. Although the swell
is the basis of expression, it cannot be used
indiscriminately. Great care must be exercised to
use it aright. At the final chord of a piece a
perfect curve of sound may be used with good
taste, as in Brahms's *Requiem* (pp. 55, 93
and 96, Novello), because there the swell
is not subject to comparison; but in other

cases the curve of sound must be usually
slightly irregular to meet the artistic dictum that
beauty of form is something *nearly* symmetrical
—except it be as a point of comparison with an
adjacent curve. I recently heard a conductor
rehearsing an amorous part-song, and the following
is an exact reproduction of the expression used :—

every phrase an exaggerated swell, each *exactly like*
the other.

Well might Sir Arthur Sullivan stop the choir
at a Leeds Festival rehearsal when a specimen of
this kind of expression cropped up, and say:
" Please, let us have no more of that accordion
expression." I know some singers who ever since
that time have contemptuously referred to a swell
as " accordion expression," thereby showing their
limited outlook. It was not that Sir Arthur
condemned the swell ; it was the recurrence of the
same pattern over and over again to which he
objected. In his own compositions some of the
finest effects possible are due to the well-regulated
swell, as I shall show later.

As examples of perfect curves of sounds
contrasted with other perfect curves, thereby
realising diversity in unity, we may take :—

Gerontius, last bar, page 116.
The Kingdom, "Let his habitation be deso-
late," &c.
Atalanta in Calydon, page 30.
Brahms's *Requiem*.

Though short swells may be symmetrical curves of sound, long swells are usually parabolic. Two fine illustrations of this are afforded in " Since by man," and " As in Adam " (*Messiah*) (see page 126), and " Open the heavens," and " Then hear from heaven " (*Elijah*) (see pages 126, 127), which emphasise the dual points of securing something nearly symmetrical and the avoidance of repetition of mathematical regularity.

THE LINE OF BEAUTY.   ARRANGING CRISES.

The fourth and fifth rules laid down in the preceding pages say that we must always go from somewhere to somewhere else. That is, we must have as an objective a climax of some sort, and we must proceed to this by the " line of beauty."

One of the mistakes of some conductors and composers is to be always itching for a grand climax every two or three bars. They ignore the fact that the larger the design the nobler the effect. Restraint is what is often needed. The conductor should fix his mind on what is to be the grand climax, and work steadily up to that, though not in a hurried manner. But the question arises, How is the interest in a piece to be sustained until the climax is reached? The answer is, Follow the " line of beauty." This may be defined as giving an ebb and flow of sound to each note or series of notes, and, while passing through a series of cumulative crises, so varying the curve of sound as never to repeat the same design, and always keeping in view the consummation of the whole in the final bars.

This working for and achieving well-planned crises is of immense importance to a conductor. It is part of that " thinking in continents " spoken of in a previous chapter. Handel owes a great part of his popularity to this feature. He proceeds from the simple to the complex in regular sequence in most of his choruses. The crises follow each other in ascending ratio until the final effort carries the conviction that the end has really been reached. Sir Charles Santley, of all the singers I know, is the one who owes most to this great gift of arranging crises. If the thousands who have heard him will look back and analyse the impression of his singing, they will find that he seemed all the time to be rising to something,—that figuratively he was always coming towards you with increasing power, and that his arrangement of the crises of his song or aria was always artistically correct.

This arranging of crises must be carefully planned by the conductor, and he might, for private use, do this graphically by means of curves, to see that he gets variety as well as interest in each phrase. For instance, he may wish to arrive at a climax at the end of, say, one hundred bars. He will have to study the words and the form of the music, discover which points can be emphasised in the unfolding of the scheme of expression, and then sketch it out as follows :—

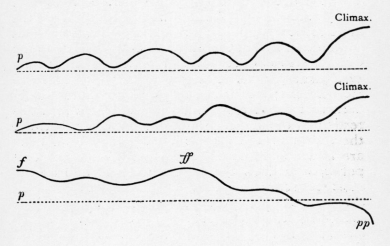

The conductor must bear in mind that there are *many right ways* of performing a piece, and though, as a rule, the place of the climax is usually clearly defined, the sectional crises are not obvious; therefore great latitude is allowed in fixing these, always provided the "line of beauty" is followed.

For instance, in a given piece each of the following plans would be correct :—

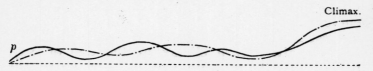

It will be seen that they both reach the same point, but with variation between the start and the finish. This explains why Joachim seldom played a solo twice in the same manner. There was always the same ebb and flow of sound, always the same sense of appropriate variety of treatment, but never a cast-iron interpretation. Similarly, Madame Clara Butt says she never professes to sing a song twice exactly alike. She is swayed by the feeling of the moment; but if she sings rather more loudly here, and softer there, than she did at a previous rendering, the audience are quite satisfied, because the charm of the artistic variety and good taste are evident. Most singers, as well as the general public, who knew Sims Reeves, place him as the most consummate artist in phrasing ever before the public; and yet he varied his renderings according to his mood. This opens another question, namely, the correctness of one artist singing a phrase loudly, and another artist singing the same phrase softly. Both the artists may be correct, because many phrases are open to two interpretations. For example, take the words :—

(a) " Why art thou cast down, O my soul."

(b) " Yea! Though I walk through the valley of the shadow of death."

The first example may be treated in a reflective manner, in which case it would be sung *piano;* or it may be sung in a confident, defiant way, when it would be declaimed *fortissimo;* and (*b*) could be sung as full of awe, or as an expression of joyful assurance. " O ! horror ! " might be whispered as embodying chilling terror, or shrieked as the outcome of ungoverned frenzy. A striking example of this contrasted treatment of the same words and music was afforded at two performances of *Gerontius*, both conducted by the composer, at which I was present. The phrase—

Thee, in Thine own . . ag - o - ny . . .

was sung by an eminent artist *fortissimo*, as marked, while at the second performance a still greater artist sang it *pianissimo*.

With this fact in mind it will be seen that there is little need to have two phrases sung alike. A phrase which might have been sung softly may, through being preceded by a soft phrase, be sung loudly without injuring the sense. This apparent contradiction is explained by the fact that it is viewed from a different standpoint by different artists. Again, in many phrases it does not matter whether they begin softly and end loudly, or *vice versa*, as long as they dovetail artistically.

This power of varying the form of expression, while keeping strictly within the line of artistic propriety, is in my judgment one of the attributes of an artist. Therefore conductors should not be afraid of following what they consider to be the true interpretation of a piece, although it may not always follow conventional lines; but let each change be well thought out, not adopted from mere caprice. If the interpretation is prompted by brain, and carried through with mastery, whatever else the conductor may make he will not make a failure.

Nevertheless, with all the latitude of choice which a conductor has, it must not be taken for granted that it is hardly possible to go wrong. If he thinks that, he is sure to make a mistake. And it is conductors endowed with temperament, and those who have a feeling for expression, who are most likely to go wrong unless their natural impulse is trained and kept under control by a course of severe discipline.

These temperamental people feel that monotony is unendurable, and they try to introduce variety without knowing the true principles of artistry. Hence they often put an accent or *crescendo* or *staccato* in the wrong place; and when this happens we get an effect like that of a dab of red on an actor's nose instead of on his cheeks.

Of many instances of this kind I will mention only two. When adjudicating at a National Eisteddfod in Wales, a choir came forward to render Mendelssohn's "Come, let us sing." The occasion being an important one, the conductor thought the choir must do something out of the ordinary. And it did. The chorus commences with the rhythm:—

The choir sang :—

Come, let *us* sing, Come, let *us* sing.

This had such a disturbing effect that all the judges looked up in amazement, and for a moment could not understand what was being done. Then we realised that to give emphasis to the word " us," they had changed the rhythm entirely, making it duple time, as though written—

Come, let us sing, . .   Come, let us sing. . .

which, it will be seen, produces quite a lopsided effect.

The next example was at a concert which I attended, to oblige a friend, on purpose to hear a singer full of musical feeling. He sang " Maid of Athens, ere we part " in rhapsodic fashion, as became the sentiment of the song, but unfortunately, in his fervour, he made a travesty of the expression by putting swells, staccatos, &c., in wrong places, something like this :—

Maid of Athens, ere we part,   Give, Oh give me back my heart.

A newspaper reporter seeing me present came and inquired whether it was a comic song. I said that originally it was not, but I would ascertain the singer's idea. When a friend remarked that he had never heard such a rendering before, the singer, taking it as a compliment, said, with conscious pride, that he tried to put his soul into it ; and he still recalls that effort as a triumph, quoting his friend's words as testimony. The moral of all this is, Study well the principles of expression before attempting any new departures.

THE CLIMAX.

Stress has been laid upon reaching the climax by well-ordered and consistent steps; but as the climax itself is the great thing, we must give adequate importance to it when it is reached.

As a rule it should be treated with breadth, dignity, and power. Care must be taken to approach its culmination soon enough to enable it to be held sufficiently long to be impressive, and when it has been reached it must not degenerate into an anti-climax by weakness of voice, insufficiency of breath, or failure to bear the strain.

Here comes in the value of (*a*) arranging the breathing places so as to have plenty of breath for the last bar, (*b*) breath pressure sufficient to enable the choir to put on extra power for the supreme effort, and (*c*) emphasising the words as a final stimulus to the feelings of the audience. Remember that a fine peroration will cover a multitude of weak places in the preceding parts.

It should be noted that the effects of climax depend very largely upon their surroundings. If, by the antecedent phrases being too loudly played or sung, the sense of cumulative effort has been destroyed, the climax *fortissimo* distresses the rather jaded nerves instead of rousing them.

Table Mountain is not very high, but on account of its surroundings it is very impressive. Thus conductors must be mindful of the context, and take care not to fire off all their ammunition too soon. In preparing for a climax I always remember Wolfe's direction at Quebec—"Don't fire until you see the whites of your enemies' eyes."

The wisdom of reserving your force till you can strike with effect is seen in :—

"O we cannot" (*Golden Legend*, page 3)—

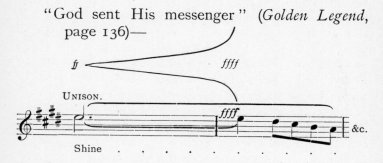

Here a rapid spasmodic *crescendo* on the fifth and sixth beats is required to depict despairing rage.

"God sent His messenger" (*Golden Legend*, page 136)—

Here a pronounced *crescendo* with breath pressure is needed on the third beat to lead to the real *fortissimo* on the first beat of the second bar. It is this which gives the *thrill*.

A further illustration may be found in :—

"His yoke is easy" (*Messiah*, page 154).

COLOURS ON THE CONDUCTOR'S PALETTE—

PIANO AND *PIANISSIMO*.

Having given a general view of the approach to and consummation of the climax, we will now study in detail the separate elements of the colours on the conductor's tonal palette.

Under the heading of "Voice" we rather exhaustively considered the question of "How to obtain soft singing with maintenance of pitch"; but there are several disturbing elements not touched upon, which demand serious attention.

At many final rehearsals for concerts I have been delighted with the singers' splendid realisation of soul-moving *pianissimos;* but at the concerts I have been bitterly disappointed at their failing to do what they had done time and again at rehearsals.

I do not say the audiences were dissatisfied. They were usually charmed at the measure of success attained, on the principle of "What the eye never sees the heart never grieves about"; but to me, who had heard them reach the ideal, it was heart-rending to note the fall from an ethereal seventh-heaven *pianissimo* to one of an ordinary type.

Considering that most of the choir are as anxious to achieve success as the conductor, the question arises, How is it that these lapses occur?

In my opinion the causes are three :—

(1) The ever-present inertia which has been previously mentioned ;

(2) The solicitude to be heard, coupled with the nervous fear that unfelt voice-production will not carry ;

(3) The law of sympathy.

With respect to inertia, there are always some singers who yield to its influence, and who do not exercise will-power enough to force themselves to put forth the necessary effort. To these lazy ones constant attention must be given, for, like the poor, they are ever with us.

To sing *pianissimo* the voices must be poised so forward, with nasal resonance, that the singers are often unconscious of singing at all. I ask them to sing by faith, and be content with a sound which is so nebulous as to be almost, if not altogether, too contemptible to be called singing. Under my personal influence in rehearsals this is done, but at concerts in a large hall their lack of physical sensation in the throat gives them the idea that the sound will not carry a yard ; therefore to do their duty they imagine they must sing louder. The lesson of all this to a conductor is to train choristers, by constant reiteration, to differentiate between the very slight physical sensations they feel in rehearsal, and the sensations they fancy they ought to feel at a concert. Urge them to sing by faith, assuring them that if the sound is only a kind of hum produced somewhere near the nasal cavities it will be heard, although they may feel doubtful about its carrying power.

Respecting the third drawback, the " law of sympathy," I would observe that in many cases it is of immense use in choral singing, because by its almost unconscious influence choirs move by common impulse to a rousing *fortissimo*, or catch the infection of the dramatic spirit, or realise the subtle atmosphere which pervades a piece. But it is often a serious handicap in *pianissimos*, and in cases where a single part has an independent phrase or swell which requires to be brought out very prominently.

In a choir no one lives or sings to himself. Therefore, when a person sings a shade too loudly, his neighbour—not hearing himself as well as he thinks he ought to do, sings rather louder also, and this singing a shade too loudly spreads throughout the choir. The worst of this is that the singers having unconsciously fixed a standard, it is impossible to get them to the bewitching softness they have often attained in rehearsal.

The remedy for this is to specialize for *pianissimo* at the last rehearsal, asking everyone to be responsible for himself or herself at the performance, even to cease singing—as some self-denying members of my choir do—when they hear other people singing too loudly.

ARTISTIC DISCRIMINATION.

There are certain phrases in pieces where it is practically impossible for a full choir to sing so softly as the ideal demands. In these cases I usually ask half the choir to sing, and balance matters by asking the other half to sing a similar phrase later.

For instance, I have the quartets "Since by man," and "For as in Adam" (*Messiah*), sung as unaccompanied choruses, commencing very softly, and, after a gradual *crescendo* to *forte*, finishing equally softly. To achieve an ideal rendering I ask the first voices of each part to commence the first bar alone, the seconds come in at the second bar, and the whole choir sing till the first note of the last bar, when the second voices finish very *pianissimo* :—

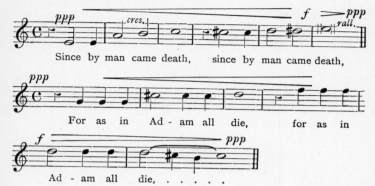

Since by man came death,   since by man came death,

For as in Ad - am all die,   for as in

Ad - am all die, ...

Take another example, "Open the heavens," and "Then hear from heaven" (*Elijah*), which I usually have sung as follows :—

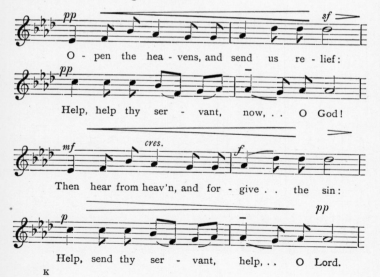

O - pen the hea - vens, and send us re - lief:

Help, help thy ser - vant, now, . . O God!

Then hear from heav'n, and for - give . . the sin:

Help, send thy ser - vant, help, . . O Lord.

K

The delicate close of " On Himalay " (Bantock) requires clear tone and true pitch, or its poetic flavour is destroyed. I therefore ask those whose voices are not of the light soprano type to deny themselves the pleasure of singing for two bars.

This selecting of legitimate means to an end I call artistic discrimination. Note that the doing of this always gives the conductor more trouble than the usual plan of letting all sing ; but the result justifies the task of finding out the phrases to be treated exceptionally, and the worry of soothing the ruffled feelings of singers who are asked not to sing for a few bars.

NEBULOUS *PIANOS:* EFFECT OF CLOSING BARS.

The last point in connection with *pianissimo* is also related to artistic discrimination. To sing an unadulterated *mezzo*, *piano*, or *pianissimo* would produce a weak, unsatisfactory effect. There may be a few cases where a dull, lifeless sort of expression is required, but they are very few. As an example :—

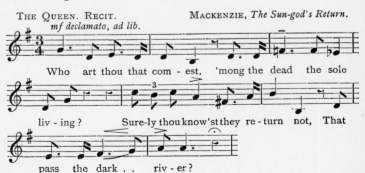

As a rule Weber's dictum that "a *piano* phrase should contain a *forte*," is true.

It may seem strange to introduce a *mezzo-p*, or even louder, into a passage marked *piano*, but singing it softly throughout—if it be of any length —would induce that monotony which must be avoided at all costs. Again, by the *decrescendo* from the louder tone the hearers have a standard of comparison, and as the voices get softer and softer the sense of real *pianissimo* is grasped by the mind of the listeners as the passage reaches its close, because the effect of the whole is almost entirely governed by the impression of the last few bars.

FORTE AND FORTISSIMO.

There is a general notion which may be expressed in the phrase "Take care of the *pianos* and the poundings will take care of themselves." There is an element of truth in this, but, as I have shown in the chapter on "Breath pressure," due attention must be given to the ways of producing *fortissimo*, or full sonority cannot be attained. In addition to what has been said, the attention of the choir must be directed to getting anti-throaty, vibrant tone, which bears the same relation to a shouting backward tone as a well-trained athlete does to a lumbering navvy.

The occasions when a real *fortissimo* can be used with proper artistic effect are comparatively few ; therefore when they do occur urge the singers to "knock sixes."

CONTRASTS OF EFFECT.   IRREGULARITY OF LINE.

From the foregoing it might be inferred that progress to a climax by the line of beauty is fairly regular—just a series of curves and sounds arranged so as to secure variety. In the main this is so, but very frequently an episodical phrase is interpolated which quite breaks the formal continuity of the ebb and flow to the climax. Sudden transitions from *ff* to *pp* or *vice versa*, abrupt changes of tempi, and unexpected changes in sentiment are cases in point. These erratic contrasts are welcome changes, as they take us from the commonplace and introduce the romantic element. Music is not always a series of well-ordered lawns set out with Dutch precision. Then, at times, the climax seems to be so far away that there appears to be no connection between what you are doing and the end in view. Another disturbing element is the obscure, nondescript, neutral passages which are parenthetically introduced without apparent reason. These things may be perplexing and annoying to those who want things to move on in symmetrical sequence, but they are the elements which give life and vigour to expression. The mind revels in contrasts. The mountain peaks and deep gorges of sound tend to picturesque effects. If expression were always in unbroken curves, however varied, we should get tired of the monotony, however beautiful. The obscurity of the other places just satisfies that speculative bias which many people have, and which finds expression in their depreciating things that are understandable.

These little "affairs of outposts" must be dealt with sectionally, each being made as interesting as possible, and treated as a relief to the grand forward movement to the brilliant finish which will come by-and-by.

With respect to the execution of the sudden contrasts a word of caution is necessary. The tendency is to keep in the last mood too long through lack of mental alertness. As a means to stimulate this I always ask the singers to mark these places with large *ff* and *pp* in blue pencil, which they can see long before they reach the place. These signs serve as helpful mnemonics, and usually produce the desired result. Examples of these sudden changes are to be found in Brahms's *Requiem* (pages 56, 139, 197, 207), Verdi's *Requiem* (pages 22, 27, 35, 87), *The Wedding of Shon Maclean* (page 50). It is worthy of remark that in the *Requiem* the same words are sung both *ff* and *pp*.

THE *CRESCENDO* AND *DIMINUENDO*.

The *crescendo* is used to express rising sentiment, to uplift the spirit, and give general vitality to the music. It may be regarded as the first—the rising —part of an incomplete swell. The *crescendo* may proceed in ever-growing force and intensity in defiance of the law of strong beats and weak beats, until at some point the swing of the rhythm of the piece be restored. Very frequently in emotional pieces the *crescendo* is made up of a series of smaller upward flights, as :—

The *diminuendo* may be regarded as the reverse of the *crescendo* in respect to expression of feeling,

and as being the latter—falling—part of the swell.
It may be a continuous decline, or it may, cascade-
like, be a series of descending phrases, as :—

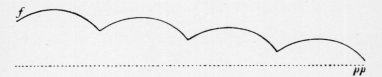

Here we get the feminine expression well
illustrated. When singing a *diminuendo* passage to
moving notes, the accent should be delicately given,
to prevent the feeling of nebulous uncertainty. It
is by these two elements—*crescendo* and *diminuendo*
—that ebb and flow of sound is secured, which,
when skilfully managed, is comparable to a well-
planned garden whose mounds and banks seem to
melt into delightful, undulating lawns. The highest
compliment which was paid to my Yorkshire
choir when we visited Germany was made at
Frankfort, where a musician of great influence said
that the greatest wonder to him in the choir's
performance was not the rich *fortissimos* or the
delicate *pianissimos*, but the way in which the
three hundred voices seemed to swing from *piano*
to *forte* and back again *on a single hair*. This
treatment of the *cres.* and *dim.* is the model I
always try to follow.

ATTACK.

I have previously spoken of one aspect of attack
in the chapter on "Voice"; but in addition to
striking difficult notes firmly, there is the firm, bold,
reliant singing of whole phrases—or through an

entire work—the absence of which gives the
impression of lack of attack. A choir may sing
with courage and good attack generally, but
sometimes abnormal places are encountered which
seem to paralyse their efforts. The difficulties
which, for a time, appal the singers are those of
pitch, as in Beethoven's *Choral Symphony* and
Mass in D; abstruse harmonies and difficult
intervals, as in *Sea-Drift, Omar Khayyám;* catchy,
involved rhythms, as in *The Mastersingers;* great
speed of performance, where the words cannot
be articulated, as in *The Flying Dutchman;* and
constant transitions to remote keys, as in most
ultra-modern works.

Sometimes the difficulties are so real that there
is justification for lack of confidence and some
excuse for bad attack, but at other times the reasons
for taking fright are quite absurd. However,
these gusts of unaccountable panicky fear *do* arise,
and they must be met with coolness and tact, and
with as little loss of time as possible. When the
uncertainty arises from real difficulties in the music,
the best way is to arrange for sectional rehearsals
for the " nervy " part—usually soprano—and to
go over the difficulties for, say, twenty minutes
until the singers can *feel* the music. If the difficulty
be one of pitch, as in Beethoven's works or—for a
few bars—in *Go, song of mine* (Elgar), I always
rehearse these parts a third lower in pitch until the
music is grasped, then gradually get up to full
pitch, by which time the dread of the strain will
have disappeared. But even this is not sufficient
to exorcise the demon of doubt from a part;
therefore other plans are sometimes necessary,
two of which devices I will mention. In special

pieces where the chromatic element is very pronounced, and where the leads are very difficult to negotiate, I ask for, say, six volunteers from each part who will undertake to be like Horatius and his two friends, and defend the bridge until the danger is past, or, like the "thin red line" at Inkermann, hold disaster at bay.

A notable instance of the need of inspiration in the singers occurred when the Sheffield Musical Festival Chorus first undertook to sing the *Choral Symphony* (Beethoven). At rehearsal after rehearsal the sopranos sang with an apologetic tone which lacked vim and power. When they got to the very high parts the singers looked at each other, and the infection of fear seemed to run through their ranks. At last I privately called eight singers on whom I thought I could depend, and asked them to learn the whole of the music thoroughly and be prepared to sing it, when called upon, with courage, boldness, and determination as a pattern to the whole choir. The next week I invited these eight ladies to come on to the platform and sing the soprano part, asking that while the remaining seventy sopranos were silent, the whole force of the contraltos, tenors, and basses—roughly about two hundred—would sing with all their power, the object being to demonstrate that eight confident sopranos could be heard over the whole two hundred lower parts.

Right nobly did these eight sopranos uphold my contention. They realised that they were on their mettle, and they sang with decision and enthusiasm. Their voices pealed above those of their two hundred opponents, who were singing for dear life. Everyone was excited, while the silent sopranos were carried away with surprise and admiration. At the close the ladies received an ovation for the victory they had won, and there was jubilation all round. But they had done more than win an individual victory; they had broken the thrall of fear which had held the sopranos in bondage. Henceforth these sang with courage and splendid attack, and with such ease that an enthusiastic lover of music, who had often heard the work at Festivals, in congratulating me on the result said that it was the first performance she had heard in which her throat had not ached by reason of the apparent strain on the voices of the singers.

As a final word on " Attack " get your singers to " leap out " to meet your beat in all cases of (*a*) high notes, (*b*) staccato notes, (*c*) marked entries, (*d*) fugal entries, (*e*) difficult and involved combinations of words and music.

STACCATO AND RELEASE.

Montesquieu says that the true test of a horse's quality and training is not in the way he starts, but the smartness with which he stops. A similar remark might be applied to singers, for as a rule the exact timing of the release of a note is often defective, and *staccato* effects are usually blurred by choralists. (I have more frequently to stop the choir to correct ragged release than for poor attack. *Staccato* is closely related to release rather than attack, but the sensation produced causes it to be regarded generally under the head of attack. I find that choirs may sing one or two notes *staccato*, but that they fail when they get to the third note. This is due in part to the physical effort required, but chiefly to the singers' fear of being too jerky. Conductors should therefore rehearse the *staccato* passage frequently to educate the singers' mental and physical sensations as to the kind of effort required to produce a good, recurring *staccato.* Note should be made of the fact that the law of sympathy operates very largely and beneficently in " attack." In " release " some singers stop too soon through indolence, while inertia causes another section to prolong the sounds unduly.

Most people do not know or realise that there are two kinds of *staccato ;* the short, detached, dramatic, forceful or delicately-crisp, and the emotional, which appears under the semi-*staccato* signs, but from which it is distinct.

Each variety has its own difficulties, and must be treated in a different manner.

Dealing first with release at the end of phrases, in all places where there is a disposition, through inertia, either to curtail or to prolong the final note, I always ask the singers to mark the end of the note with a downward stroke in blue pencil. Especially should this be done in cases like the following, where the parts do not finish simultaneously :—

King Olaf, page 17.

Spectre's Bride, page 140.

Brahms's *Requiem*, pages 4 and 8 (Novello).

In these ordinary cases of stoppage there is not much difficulty, only a little care being necessary.

But in the clean-cut stoppages of crisp *staccatos* and the quick shading off required in emotional *staccatos*, great skill is needed to accomplish them artistically. The difficulty of the really short *staccato* lies in getting the true shock of the glottis and cutting off the note smartly. These may be managed well on two or even three notes, but when it comes to a succession of *staccato* notes, as in "Haste thee, nymph" (Handel), or alternate *staccato* and sustained notes, as "I am the god Thor" (Elgar), the effect is generally blurred. This is due in the first case to the rapid tiring of the muscles brought into play in an unusual task. In the second case it is through lack of alertness—tiredness, or really indolence—after the thing has been done twice.

Elgar, *King Olaf.*

In the most advanced choirs these things have to be seriously dealt with, and more time has to be spent over these points than one would imagine. How to get the true shock of the glottis so as to get clear attack I have dealt with previously, pages 32-36, so nothing further need be said, except that in studying how to sing *staccato* the principles there enforced must be recapitulated. With respect to releasing the notes crisply, this can be done by the same means whereby "striking the notes in the middle" is effected, namely, dissociating the sounds from the throat and locating them close to the lips.

But the singers must have a reminder, or they will not do it at the critical moment; therefore all *staccato* marks should be emphasised with blue pencil, such re-marking to be used as a mnemonic to stimulate the will, which is the controlling force in all cases of muscular action—and inaction.

EMOTIONAL *STACCATO*.

The emotional *staccato* consists of striking the note softly but firmly and quitting it quickly; but instead of leaving it with the same amount of force or sound with which it was struck—as in dynamic *staccato*—there is a *molto diminuendo* on each note, merging into silence, this silence seeming to be part of the note, just as in Phil May's sketches in *Punch* an incomplete line suggests its continuance. By this treatment of the *staccato* we get a series of incipient sobs or delicate breath-pressures which have an immense emotional effect.

The importance of *staccato* singing somehow seems to escape the attention of conductors. It may be that the infrequency of *staccato* phrases has prevented the amount of labour involved in performing this particular accomplishment from becoming crystallized; therefore conductors do not give the necessary trouble to the technical side of the attainment, with the result that as a rule *staccato* passages are comparative failures. But really, it is worth while to develop their possibilities to the utmost, not only because of their intrinsic value as a musical effect, but because they are so seldom done well that when they *are* accomplished they stand out as something quite exceptional and memorable.

To attain perfection in these effects, to secure crispness and delicate shading, the conductor must explain his wishes and pattern the ideal model frequently. In doing this he must demonstrate that only by forward tone and tongue-tip utterance, joined to the singers' self-denying discipline, can these things be accomplished.

If a conductor wishes to make a sensation let him perform Handel's " Haste thee, Nymph " or " What have we to do with Kaikobád " (*Omar Khayyám*). Though of different types of *staccato* they both present arresting features when ideally performed.

THE DYNAMIC AND EMOTIONAL *SFORZANDOS.*

STRESSES AND PRESSURES.

Though the constituents of expression which we have considered are each of importance, I question whether any one is quite as effective as well-executed pressure-notes, be they heavy, light, or emotional. Perhaps a great measure of their striking effect is due to the rarity of their being done tastefully. There is a distinct tendency to interpret these marks too clumsily ; to give a kind of thud at each pressure, every one lacking the shading-off necessary to obtain a good effect.

Again, most conductors seem oblivious of the fact that there is the emotional *sforzando* and pressure-note, as well as the forceful, explodent variety ; further, that there is a wide field of use for the emotional pressure in cases which are not indicated in the music, because they cannot be well defined by mere notation. These must be felt by the conductor, and through him reproduced by the choir. The emotional variety consists of the usual

pressure-note ＞ preceded by a short *crescendo* ＜ ＞,
thereby destroying all impression of abruptness,
and at the same time imparting an atmosphere of
tenderness which has a peculiar charm.

To illustrate these pressures and stresses, take
the following examples :—

A. DVOŘÁK, *The Spectre's Bride.*

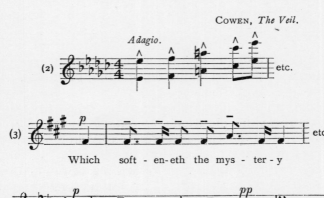

COWEN, *The Veil.*

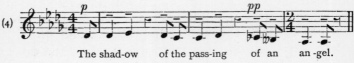

(5)

Unless the choir be warned they will put pressure on the soprano notes of Ex. 1, and by not diminishing the sound to *mezzo* they convert the whole phrase into *ff*, with the effect of crowding out the moving contraltos and basses, which are the important feature. In Ex. 2, the same thing happens with the instruments; we get a succession of stodgy sounds *fff* with no point, whereas if a marked *decrescendo* is made on each note, a series of impressive sobs—which contrasts finely with the other instrumental parts—emphasises the poignant effect required by the scene depicted. In Exx. 3

and 4 the pressure-notes, if not carefully treated, convert each phrase into a bold *mezzo* without any tenderness, but if each note is shaded off into the region of silence the effect is quite moving. On page 140, Exx. 1 and 2 are good illustrations of the dynamic pressure-note, Exx. 3 and 4 demonstrate the emotional pressure, while Ex. 5, page 141, is a striking example of contrasted *staccato* effects.

The essential fact which should be grasped by conductors and performers is, that pressure-marks should not alter the general character, be it *forte*, *piano*, or *pianissimo*. They should balance the pressure at the commencement of the note with a proportionate shading-off at the finish, so that the mean quantity of the tone is not disturbed :—

$$\text{Line of mean force} \Big\} \quad \mathit{ff} \overset{\overset{\mathit{fff}}{\mathit{sf}}}{\underset{\mathit{mf}}{\rule[-1ex]{0.5pt}{3ex}}} \mathit{ff}$$

The *sf*, *fff* followed by a *mf*, preserves the balance of *ff*.

$$\text{Line of mean force} \Big\} \quad \mathit{mf} \overset{\overset{\mathit{mf}}{>}}{\underset{\mathit{p}}{\rule[-1ex]{0.5pt}{3ex}}} \mathit{mf} \qquad \mathit{pp} \overset{\overset{\mathit{pp}}{}}{\underset{\mathit{ppp}}{\rule[-1ex]{0.5pt}{3ex}}} \mathit{pp}$$

The *mf* with pronounced pressure followed by *p* gives a mean of *mf*. The *pp* with gentle pressure followed by a whispered *ppp* secures a true *pp*. Exx. 3 and 4, page 140, should be regarded as *p* or *pp* phrases with the trimmings of a well-defined emotional pressure followed by a delicate *diminuendo;* and they must not degrade these and similar phrases by neglecting the shading-off, thus converting them into colourless *mezzos* without a tinge of emotion.

Some emotional pressure-notes are more telling than others. When these occur they should be rehearsed until the right effect is secured. For instance, the following examples can be made very impressive :—

In " Moonlight," while a rather full stress is required, it is the rapid *dim.* to *ppp* which shows the virtuosity and produces the striking effects.

L

Modern works such as *Omar Khayyám*, *Atalanta in Calydon*, &c., abound in effects of this kind. Sometimes the emotional pressure seems too assertive through the short initial *crescendo* being carried a shade too far, thus causing it to approximate to a swell <>, instead of <⊃>, a pressure-note with softened approach, or a *sforzando* preceded, as it were, by a buffer.

When such cases occur, I remind my singers of a boy who was trespassing, who, when asked by the farmer where he was going, replied " Back again." If they feel that they are overdoing the initial swell, and they " get back again " rather quickly, no harm will be done.

With respect to the signs > and ∧, I use the latter when a sudden *decrescendo* or *fp* is required. The pressure-notes which are often needed to call attention to the entry of a part, and to reveal obscure parts of imitation, will be dealt with later.

MANAGEMENT OF SUSTAINED SOUNDS.

It is atonishing how telling sustained sounds may be made, especially if they end on an accented beat. Figuratively they illumine with a flood of light the whole phrase in which they appear, if there be a steady *crescendo* to the last accent.

As examples it is only necessary to refer to the sustained notes in Brahms's *Requiem*, pp. 20, 47, 48, 50, 51, and 76 (Novello's edition), and to the splendid examples in " Blest Pair of Sirens."

These being chiefly in the soprano part, their proper treatment is fairly obvious, but when the sustained notes appear in the inner and lowest part, instead of allowing them to be inert, full advantage should be taken of their possibilities—as, for instance :—

Striking examples are shown in *The Messiah* analysis, pages 203-248.

Very frequently a swell may be made on a sustained sound even to the extent of drowning for a moment the other voices, but this obtrusion is redeemed by the charming effect produced when the *diminuendo* sets in, and the part which had undue prominence melts into obscurity, by the singers "getting back again."

A series of short vocal swells on a sustained note may be made wonderfully effective in cases like the following :—

moan - - - - - ing,

Other characteristic phrases will be shown later.

The chief caution which needs emphasising is to take great care that the choristers finish a swell as softly as they commence. It is an easy thing to commence a swell, but an extremely difficult thing to secure the proper symmetrical treatment of its latter half. Usually the singers commence the *dim.* too late and finish it too soon, producing an effect like this, pp———|⁓p, instead of pp———|———pp. Therefore always be alert to correct this defect of technique and taste.

EXALTATION AND SUBORDINATION OF VOICE PARTS.

For convenience we have hitherto studied expression from the point of view of one voice or the whole choir moving simultaneously, when one mark of expression applied to the whole. Though this rule obtains in a large proportion of cases, modern music and latter-day requirements demand more individualistic treatment of every section of the choir. From the time when the ravishing strains of Rossini, Donizetti, Bellini, Verdi, Gounod, and other "tuney" operatic writers flourished, up till very recent days, the chief desideratum in a choral piece was a melodious soprano part, with nicely flowing but subordinate lower parts; hence the popularity of the part-song, which, though often charming, was in fact little more than an elongated hymn tune. This "chief air" influence was so marked that everything was treated more or less in the same manner—"the tune" was everything. Even in fugues the contralto, tenor, and bass parts were secondary to the sopranos, who were never taught to modify their voices in the counter-subject—or even when their part was mere padding—so as to afford the other voices a chance of giving the subject, answer, or *stretto* due prominence.

This explains in a great measure why madrigals fell into disfavour and were seldom sung, notwithstanding the warm commendation given to them by all great musicians. As the interest of madrigals does not lie so much in their "tune" as in the byplay of the parts, the great mass of people saw no beauty in them. Hence their sad neglect.

When, in the 'nineties, I began to treat part-songs, madrigals, glees, and choruses with more freedom, by giving occasional prominence to the contraltos, tenors, and basses, I was bitterly assailed and charged with presumption, lack of taste, exaggeration, and other dreadful faults; but as I had been at the trouble of analysing the music, and felt that the chief feature, whatever it was, should be prominent, and that the accompanying parts, however interesting, were merely packing and must be subservient to the principal theme in whatever voice it appeared, I kept on my own way, and time has justified my action.

A change has now come over the scene. The very things which were condemned are now the things praised, and the eternal preponderance of the soprano, though at times delightful, is resented by all critics. This attitude accounts for the decline in popularity of many really good part-songs. For the same reason Spohr's violin quartets have gone out of fashion. There is too much first violin in them, and too little prominence of the other instruments. A general sharing of the interest by every part employed is what is now looked for. Audiences and singers alike want relief from the sopranos. They demand that the contraltos shall become prominent occasionally in charming melodic phrases. Then interest is evoked by the tenors springing into life and shining like bright particular stars, and the pleasure is enhanced when the rich voices of the basses loom large on the musical horizon, the other parts meanwhile making obeisance to them, although they are the lowest part.

INTERCHANGE OF PARTS.

This exaltation of a part, with its corollary—the subordination of the other parts—is now so firmly fixed as an artistic principle that its successful realisation has to be seriously considered by all conductors. The question arises : How can it be best accomplished ? After repeated trials with madrigals, imitative choruses and other works, I have found that the part which requires bringing out cannot *always* give sufficient power and emphasis to be heard as clearly as it should. This

may arise from the "lay" of the notes to be sung
or from the power of the opposing voices.
Therefore the best way of overcoming the difficulty
is to have a well-considered plan of *borrowing and
lending* of voices—an interchange of parts, which
can be effected at any moment.   In my own choirs
I always regard the second sopranos and first
contraltos as interchangeable.   They are the
"handy men" of the choir.   Whenever a contralto
phrase needs to be prominent, I ask the second
sopranos to mark their copies and sing the phrase,
and then go to their own parts.   Similarly the first
contraltos assist the sopranos.   This has the double
effect of strengthening the thematic voice while at
the same time weakening an opposing voice.   One
can see how effective such a plan is.   Thus in a
choir of a hundred sopranos and ninety contraltos
I get, at strategical points, one hundred and forty
contraltos to peal forth a theme like the
following :—

BRAHMS, *Requiem*.

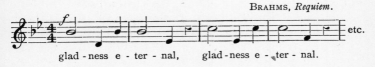

glad - ness e - ter - nal,   glad - ness e - ter - nal.

This subject is more fully dealt with in the
analysis of *The Messiah*, and the examples given
of the chorus " And the glory of the Lord" (*see*
pages 205, 207).   In "Worthy is the Lamb" (*see* page
240) this is reversed, the contraltos there assisting the
sopranos, the theme thus being given out by the
equivalent of 145 sopranos.   This principle I carry
still further by getting the tenors, when necessary,
to assist the contraltos, and the contraltos to join
the tenors and even the basses.   In fact, whenever

a part needs strengthening I use any available voices for that purpose. On page 239 a detailed account is given of how this is done in "Worthy is the Lamb."

Assistance to a voice part is sometimes confined to one note; for instance, a few tenors sing the first low G of the contralto lead in "In going to my lonely bed," or in "Laudo Deum Verum," and "God sent His messenger" (*Golden Legend*). In both these cases the tenors and basses, by means of great breath-pressure, work up to a glorious climax, but by reinforcing their high notes with the telling, nasally forward notes of the contraltos a brilliant effect is produced, which explains in part the six degrees of *fortissimo* already mentioned. Incidentally it may be said that the audiences are delighted with the wonderful reserve of force shown in the voices of the men (it is never suspected that any of the women join in), who are equally pleased that their efforts win commendation all round. Here let me urge once more that doing this is not in any sense questionable or illegitimate, but merely artistic discrimination. As an example of the application of this principle in an extended form I would refer to Granville Bantock's "Cruiskeen Lawn." It may be added that when I submitted this scheme to Mr. Bantock, he thoroughly approved of it, and the great success of its performance by the choir on the world tour fully justified the treatment :—

Bar 17. Contraltos reinforced by second sopranos :

BANTOCK, "Cruiskeen Lawn."

When the year's grown old and grey, When the hours slip

Bars 20, 21. Tenors joined by second contraltos:

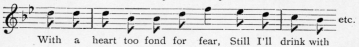

With a heart too fond for fear, Still I'll drink with

At bars 24 and 25 the second sopranos again join the
contraltos, and there are several other interchanges
of parts which are set forth in the detailed analysis of
the part-song given in Appendix I. (*see* page 291).

Cases like the following do not need any interchange of parts, but great care is required to keep
the accompanying voices a degree softer than
marked, while the solo voices can be a shade louder
than indicated :—

ELGAR, "Go, song of mine."

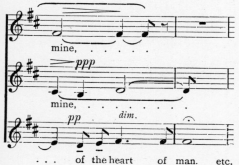

PART-SONG. (pp)   EATON FANING, "Moonlight."

Having dealt with the means at disposal for giving prominence to certain parts when required, let us consider how to treat fugal and other imitative passages, meanwhile giving the caution that the injunction to use special treatment, as in the cases

given above, is *exceptional, and only occasionally occurs.*
For instance, in the whole of *The Messiah* I only
adopt this interchange or borrowing of voices in
three choruses—in " And the Glory " for ten bars, in
"O Thou that tellest " for one bar, and in " Worthy
is the Lamb " for four bars. In *Elijah* there is not
a single case of adding of voices, but twice there are
cases of subtraction of voices for a few bars. The
two examples quoted from *The Golden Legend*
are the only cases that occur in that work. Therefore people must not think that wholesale choppings
and changings are indulged in or are necessary.
But it is a grand thing to know that upon occasion,
when necessity arises, it is possible to strike like a
thunderbolt, even if it be only for one or two notes.
A case in point is Parry's " Blest Pair of Sirens,"
where I put all available force on the high A of the
tenors to bring out a telling response to the
sopranos' A in the preceding bar, as well as to
crown the climax with a thrilling effect :—

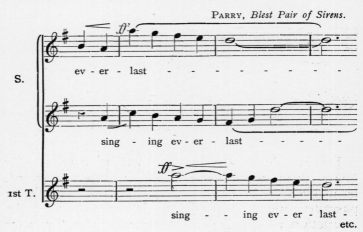

PARRY, *Blest Pair of Sirens.*

FUGUES, FUGAL ENTRIES, IMITATIVE PHRASES—

OBVIOUS AND OBSCURE.

In all fugal-writing the well-known rule is to commence with marked entry and sing every note of the subject firmly. But it is not so well known, or at least followed, that as soon as the subject has been enunciated the voice should at once become much softer and subordinate to the next entry of the theme, subject, or answer. A case in which the answer is often ruined by the non-observance of this rule is afforded in the Kyrie of the *B Minor Mass* (Bach) :—

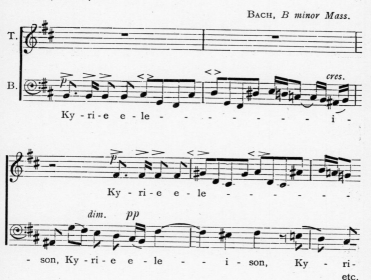

BACH, *B minor Mass.*

Here the basses should sing *pianissimo* to allow the low-placed tenor reply to be heard, and then the full meaning of the music is revealed.

The following example illustrates the general way of treating a fugal exposition :—

MENDELSSOHN, *Elijah.*

It will be noticed that the bass and contralto entries are differently marked from the printed copy. This is because of the " lay " of the parts. When sung according to the above markings, this exposition has an added charm because the last entry is heard supported by the rich harmony of the other parts. Each case however has to be analysed separately by the conductor, the marking given which is thought correct, and then the result tested in rehearsal and performance. This plan I follow absolutely. In cases where the dramatic import of the music will not allow any diminution of sound in the opposing voices, the entering voice must have a *hard, cutting tone* for the first bar or even longer, as in the following excerpts :—

MENDELSSOHN, *Elijah.*

His

His curse hath fall - en down up -

His curse hath

curse hath fall - en down up - on us,

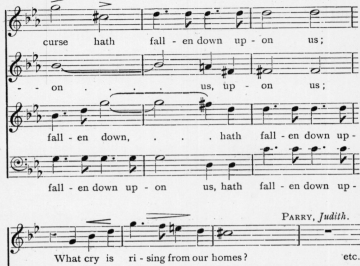

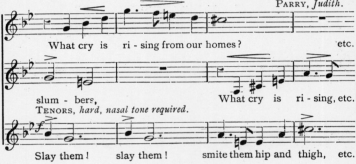

POINTS OF IMITATION.

A great deal of the convincing power of a piece containing points of imitation lies in each entry being made manifest to the ear, for in addition to carrying on the thematic scheme there is a kind of elation in listening to this throwing about of the theme, and wondering where it will next appear— a kind of musical " Hunt the slipper." Therefore each entering voice must be emphasised sufficiently to call attention to its entry into the musical scheme. This emphasis serves the same purpose as having the incomer's name called out at official receptions. The momentary prominence having been secured, the voice can, and generally must, gracefully subside.

OBSCURE IMITATIVE PASSAGES.

When a part has a rest and then takes up the theme, the singer can see at once that a marked entry is necessary; but when a part is continuous the "point of imitation" is most frequently missed, and the music is generally sung as though it was an ordinary part of the general harmonization of the "air," which, as mentioned above, is usually allowed to dominate the whole.

For instance, how many, or rather how few, have noticed that in the fifth bar of "He that shall endure" (*Elijah*) the interest is not in the soprano part but in the tenor?:—

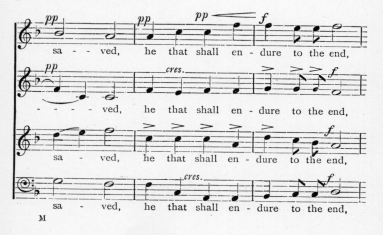

M

Similarly at bar 11 the contraltos should be prominent for five notes, at bar 14 the basses ditto, the contraltos again for three notes, then the tenors for three notes; while bars 20 to 26 should be treated thus :—

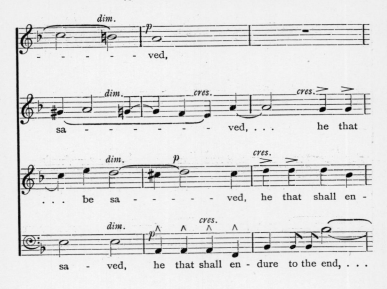

A particularly pleasing effect is made by observing the following obscure imitations :—

(1) 2nd Alto.   ELGAR, *Gerontius.*

Go   on thy course and   may, etc.

1st Tenor.

Go . .   on thy course,   go ;

(2) 1st Soprano.

peace, . .   thy place to - day   be found in   peace.

2nd Soprano.

thy place to - day be   found   in   peace.

There are many cases where the music, on paper, does not appear to call for special emphasis, but in performance a slight pressure adds point and meaning—as in *Atalanta*, page 4, *The Kingdom*, pages, 31, 167, 180, 183, *The Veil*, page 109. These may be often regarded as pulsation imitations.

WHEEL WITHIN A WHEEL.

Closely connected with this exaltation and subordination is the management of two or more independent melodies, and the bringing into notice the subsidiary designs, secondary motives, or intertwining melodies, so that they may be heard without shrouding the principal theme.

To do these things successfully involves quick changes in tonal force and skilful manipulation of the voices. As an illustration we will take the opening of Bach's " Sing ye " (*see* pages 197-199).

It will be seen that a single mark, *f* or *p*, would not be adequate, as each part proceeds on independent lines ; therefore each line must have its own markings.

In the past composers seldom indicated how a piece was to be performed, except by an occasional *forte* or *piano*, as they expected that those who performed the works, being experienced musicians, would know how to interpret them properly. Herein lies the danger of overlooking these subtleties of expression. Modern musicians are so used to having every nuance indicated that they often regard the marking of works—even old works—as final. To act on this assumption would be fatal to either an emotional or intellectual interpretation of the old masters. I have a copy of Bach's *Mass in B minor* which does not contain a single mark of expression. Is there any wonder that Bach was in the past unpopular ?

When a composition is manifestly inadequately marked the conductor must analyse it to ascertain its possibilities, and then have courage to carry out his ideas. But in addition to the trouble of searching out the salient points, there will be the additional labour of training the choir to overcome the " law of sympathy " sufficiently to act independently. Two illustrations of this " wheel within a wheel " are :—

ELGAR, *King Olaf.*

And flee, flee a - way . . . from each

Hoist up your sails of silk And flee a - way from each

o - ther.

o - ther. . . etc.

Intimately connected with these cross-currents of expression is the management of contrasted swells, as in this excerpt :—

H. COWARD, *Story of Bethany.*

O . . . Lord, how . . great etc.

O Lord,

CHARACTERIZATION.

One of the distinguishing features of modern choral technique is what I term " characterization," or realism, of the sentiment expressed in the music. Formerly this kind of singing was tabooed to such an extent that when in rehearsals and at concerts I induced the Sheffield Musical Union to sing with graphic power, musicians of the old school voted me a mad enthusiast, extravagant, theatrical, ultra, and many other things of the same sort. These people wondered why I wanted variety of tone-colour—who had ever heard of such a demand from a choir ?—and many of my friends even thought I was demanding too much when, in rehearsing Berlioz's *Faust*, I asked for something harder in tone than the usual fluty, mellifluous sound in order to depict the hearty laugh of the peasants in the first chorus. They were almost scandalised when I asked for a somewhat raucous, devil-may-care carousal-tone in the " Auerbach's wine-cellar " scene, and when a fiendish, snarling utterance was called for in the " Pandemonium " scene they thought I was mad. However, the performance settled all these objections. It was seen by contrast how ridiculous it was for a choir to laugh like Lord Dundreary with a sort of throaty gurgle ; how inane it was to depict wine-cellar revelry with voices suggesting the sentimental drawing-room tenor, and how insipid it was to portray fiendish glee within hell's portals with the staid decorum of a body of local preachers of irreproachable character.

Of course the battle in the rehearsal-room had to be fought sternly inch by inch, but frequent trials, approval of the progress shown, and brilliant success at the concert won the day. It was so convincing that many said they could taste wine and smell brimstone.

This vindication of characterization prepared the way for other experiments.

The derisive and despairing laughter in the "Demons' Chorus" (*Gerontius*); the contrast of sentiment in "The wraith of Odin" (*King Olaf*) between the boisterous mirth of Olaf's company at the opening of the feast, and their mysterious awe when they become aware that Odin's wraith had been present; the graphic touch of "Jarred against nature's chime, and with harsh din" (*Blest Pair of Sirens*); the strident cry of the conquerors, "Slay them, pursue them" (*Judith*); the re-echo of the song of the desert (*Omar Khayyám*); the forceful, rising *apportamento* to depict the rushing current (*Armada*), and many other examples, all assert the legitimate growth of characterization as an attribute of choral singing. Composers have noticed all these things both at recent triennial and competitive festivals, and as a result we have now compositions which open a new world of vocal effects. Contrasts of tone-colour, contrasts of differently placed choirs, contrasts of sentiment—love, hate, hope, despair, joy, sorrow, brightness, gloom, pity, scorn, prayer, praise, exaltation, depression, laughter, tears—in fact all the emotions and passions are now expected to be delineated by the voice alone. It may be said, in passing, that in fulfilling these expectations choral singing has entered on a new lease of life. Instead of the cry being raised that the choral societies are doomed, we shall find that by absorbing the elixir of characterization they have renewed their youth; and when the shallow pleasures of the picture theatre and the empty elements of the variety show have been discovered to be unsatisfying to the normal aspirations of intellectual, moral beings, the social, healthful, stimulating, intellectual, moral and spiritual uplift of the choral society will be appreciated more than ever.

THE TECHNIQUE OF CHARACTERIZATION.

"Tender-handed stroke a nettle,
And it stings you for your pains,
Grasp it like a man of mettle,
And it soft as silk remains."

Before stating how to produce the laugh, the sob, the sigh, the snarl, the moan, bell effects, ejaculations and "trick-singing," all of which come under the head of characterization, I would say that if an ultra thing is undertaken it must be done boldly. The spirit of the old rhyme quoted above must be acted upon, or fear will paralyse the efforts put forth, and failure will be the result. In choral singing, as in other things, the masculinity of the doing, the boldness, the daring, the very audacity with which an extreme effect is produced carries success with it. Therefore do not attempt a daring thing feebly or by halves.

THE LAUGH.

There are few more effective and legitimate effects than the laugh, when properly and graphically produced; but this is seldom accomplished. The frequent failures arise from the singers not using the right kind of tone. To get the "ring" of the joyful laugh the tone must be of bright, hard quality with an edge on it. Otherwise it sounds flabby and non-infectious, which is the reverse of what is wanted. Further, it must be *staccato* even in such phrases as the following :—

WAGNER, *The Flying Dutchman.*

Knows the worth of hunters bold! Ha ha ha ha ha ha ha!

Knows the worth of hunters bold! Ha ha ha ha ha ha ha!

THE GIBE.

Contemptuous gibe and derisive scorn are, as regards voice - production, closely allied to the ironic and sardonic laugh. The chief ingredients in all these effects is nasality reinforced by tonal flavour infused by the feeling of the singer. Thus in *Gerontius*, at the scornful words, "What's a Saint?" the singers should approximate the upper lip and nose and thus assist the nasal twang. In "He trusted in God" (*Messiah*) the same thing should be done, but without such a pronounced nasal twang. As the passages in which this treatment occurs are very infrequent, the charge of repetition of effect is not likely to be brought, especially as the singer can infuse variation of flavour in depicting hate, scorn or disparagement.

To the question, "Can you get a large choir to sing such passages quickly," the answer is "Yes," if you regard this and similar instances as "trick-singing," which we will now consider.

TRICK-SINGING.

There are certain phrases in most modern works which present such difficulties in one form or another that they can only be sung when they are so well known that the voice sings them as it were involuntarily, without any conscious effort. The above excerpt is an example; the chorus commencing "Surely she'll refuse him," from the *Mastersingers*, "What have we to do with Kaikobád?" (*Omar Khayyám*), the subject in "His yoke is easy," and many other quick phrases such as the following are further cases in point :—

BACH, *B minor Mass.*

Et i - te - rum ven - tu - rus est cum

glo - ri - a, ven - tu - rus est cum glo - - - - -

- - ri - a, cum glo - ri - a ju - di - ca - -

- - - - - - - re vi - vos . . et mor -

- - - - - tu - os, ju - di - ca - - re

vi - vos   et mor - tu - os, vi - vos et mor -tu - os;

Some passages may not present very great difficulties, but when taken at great speed the difficulties are magnified, for in technique speed is the test of proficiency.   Now it is impossible to get the rank and file of an ordinary choir to learn a work with such a keen edge of perfection.   Life is too short. But if they can be persuaded that certain phrases are out of the common, and to master the difficulties of such phrases these must be treated as a conjurer or juggler does a trick—that is, practised assiduously until they can be sung without mental effort—the singers will tolerate reiterations without number till the required fluency is attained.   It resolves itself into the glorifying of the words " trick-singing " until they become a motive for special effort.

Therefore all tricky phrases must be specially dealt with by being classed as trick-singing, and the music reiterated for a short time every night, first slowly, then gradually quicker and quicker till the desired effect is realised.   By this means I have obtained perfect rippling laughter in the passage quoted from *The Flying Dutchman.*

The sardonic and the derisive laugh, to be effective, requires a very marked nasality and a hard, cutting tone.   In *The Dream of Gerontius* the hitherto unexplained effectiveness of the derisive laugh of the Demons is produced by making a very marked *crescendo* on the last note, as :—

This reverses the marking given, but Sir Edward Elgar said when he heard the effect, "That is splendid." It is the lack of knowledge of this that has caused this chorus to be often described as being performed by dress-coated demons.

As a final word on the laugh I would say that to get the proper effect the notes must generally be sung *staccato*, except in cases where contrast is purposely introduced, as in *Gerontius*. This can be done if full advantage is taken of the nasal forward tone required for this medium of mirth or derision.

THE CUMULATIVE EFFECT OF REITERATED PHRASES.

The power and cumulative effect of reiterated passages, burdens, and refrains, as well as the diversity of treatment demanded by such phrases, are most frequently overlooked by conductors, with the result that dulness is often associated with what should be full of delightful kaleidoscopic variety. Two such phrases occur in *King Olaf*—

"Dead rides Sir Morten of Fogelsang," and "Hoist up your sails of silk." Each of the eight entries of "Dead rides," and the five reiterations of "Hoist up," should be treated differently, but with such a cumulative effect that the audience looks out for each reappearance with excited expectancy.

An example, short but expressive, of how to sing reiterations occurs in the following excerpt:—

SOPRANO.   ELGAR, *Gerontius.*

As if   aught,   aught,   aught   could stand

The first "aught" is said smartly, the second with the final "t" snapped out, while the third is pronounced almost like aught-*a*, the carrying glide (*uh* or *a*) being accompanied by a quick emission of breath like a miniature explosion from a steam engine, to express demoniac vehemence. The cumulative effect in "A Franklyn's Dogge" and the "Kaw" in *Hiawatha* have already been referred to; therefore as a final example I will return to the word "fou" (full), which is reiterated five times under similar conditions in *The Wedding of Shon Maclean.* The way I treated it was as follows: The first time short, and very softly; the second time for one beat, loudly; the third time it was held for two beats, with a swell on the vowel; at the fourth recurrence, to surprise the audience, who by this time had doubtless surmised that each time the word would be prolonged, it was sung *staccato* very loudly; and at the fifth and final utterance the word was held for three beats with an exaggerated emphasis and a swell on the vowel to enforce the fact that the pipers *were* drunk.

SPECIAL ONOMATOPOETIC EFFECTS.

There are certain imitative vocal effects, such as bell sounds, violin tone, and banjo accompaniment which call for special explanation. Years ago I heard the "Bells of St. Michael's Tower," as arranged by Sir R. P. Stewart. The result was so disappointing that I never gave it a further thought till some three years ago, when I asked a musical critic of great experience in choral work whether he had ever heard an effective performance of the old glee. He said that twenty years ago he had heard a really convincing performance, but never since. This was sufficient for me. If it were possible then, it would be possible now, and by reviving the ancient glory I should fill a long-felt want. I studied its possibilities, and as a result, during our World Tour, we had requests to sing it at every concert, some even desiring it to be interpolated during the performance of *The Messiah* or *Elijah*.

This success was doubtless the result of the striking imitation of the bell-tone, which was due to the following method of singing. The opening, "Ding, ding, dong, bell" is sung nasally, in such a manner that by singing through the final "ng" with closed mouth, the octave harmonic is heard in the latter half of the sound. This gives a decided metallic tinge to the tone. The ebb and flow of the *pianos* and *fortes* add charm to the ensemble :—

It is however at bars 12 to 15 that the most striking results are produced :—

STEWART," The Bells of St. Michael's Tower."

N

Here the words " boime " and " chang " are struck
with a relentless *sforzando*. The clashing of the
explodents " b " and " ch " and the conflicting
vowels produce a kind of sound-confusion associated
with the clang of a bell. The singers immediately
get to the nasal consonants " m " and " ng," which
they sing in the nasal cavities. Meanwhile another
quick change in the dynamics has been effected, to
represent the booming of the bell immediately after
it has been struck by the hammer, namely, the ultra
quick *decrescendo* followed by the rapid *molto swell*,
as shown by the expression marks *ff* > <> in

the foregoing example. These three chords are all slightly varied in length. " Bell-oom " is varied from the other words by having an unbroken swell ⟨=⟩ ; the last three words are treated with pronounced swell on " ng."

Thus there is variety in every separate sound, each presenting a bell-tone in various aspects. The good impression produced by the " bell " section was strengthened by the graphic way the words were spoken and every point of imitation brought out, special attention being given to " a *crabstick* would take," in which Richard's muscular Christianity was made evident. As a climax to the whole, the bell effects of bars 12, 13, 14, 15 were repeated, the interpolated closing word "bell" being struck *fff* and gradually shaded off with the nasal bell-like sound to *pppp*. It should be said that in bars 12, 13 and 14 the effect of the overtones of the bells is made more convincing if the contralto G and the baritone D are made slightly prominent.

It is well known that the tone-quality—timbre— of instruments depends upon the order and strength of their harmonics or overtones ; thus an oboe differs from the clarinet by reason of the double oboe reed producing a different set of harmonics from those produced by the single reed of the clarinet. Having grasped the importance of harmonics, singers will realise why it is that nearly all characteristic tone is produced by the nasal cavities, as it is in these that nearly all the modifying harmonics connected with the voice are produced. Therefore in imitating violin tone by humming, or the "pang, pang" of banjo accompaniments, all that is required is to experiment in nasal tone-qualities and practise till the desired effect is obtained. With respect to the banjo trick, care must be taken to get the thin, wiry upper octave harmonic well defined, and success will be assured.

DICTION.

Not the least of the elements which go to give point to graphic characterization is that way of saying or singing words which is best described by the word " Diction."

This implies not only clear articulation, but also investing words with those subtle inflections and shadings which reveal the essence of the thought and make them glow with life, as for example :—

PARRY, *Pied Piper.*

ver - min,   was   a   pi - ty,

ver - min,   was   a   pi - ty,

ver - min,   was   a   pi - ty,

ver - min,   was   a   pi - ty,

RHETORICAL ACCENT.

The first thing to add to clear articulation is correct rhetorical accent. A common fault is to sing every syllable with one force of voice, without reference to how the words would be accented and inflected if they were spoken. In singing, the inflection of a word, if not prevented, is to a large extent, though not entirely, governed by the notes sung; but the proper balance of the word-accent need not be interfered with. Unfortunately this fact is not grasped. Thus in the words "Surely," " Hallelujah " (*Messiah*), " He is gracious, compassionate " (*Elijah*), the final syllable is nearly always sung too loudly, as " Grâcioûs," " Sûrelŷ," " Hallelûjâh," instead of being sung as " Sûrely," " Hallelûjah," " Grâcious," " Compâssionate." A well-known example of this misplacing of the rhetorical accent is :—

The en - e - my shout - eth,

One authority says that never yet has he heard the word " Hallelûjah " correctly sung. This fault is more markedly displayed when the second syllable is carried forward to the beginning of a fresh bar, as :—

kind - ness,   mer - cy,   peace - ful,

moan - - ing, . .

In these cases the singers follow the musical accent, whereas the rhetorical accent, in which the second syllable is sung delicately, should always be followed if the characteristic feature of the word is to be imparted to the listener. Special care should be taken with phrases which have feminine endings.

KEY-WORDS.

The next thing which claims attention is the dramatic or descriptive import of the words. But it must be borne in mind that it is only one word in a sentence or several sentences which demands graphic picturing. This word I call the key-word, as it decides the import of the sentence. There are certain words which seem to epitomise the leading idea of the sentences in which they occur in such a way that if these words be missing the other words have no meaning. This key-word or words needs emphasising sometimes graphically, sometimes quietly, according to the sentiment. If more than this be done, over-emphasis results, which in many cases is worse than under-emphasis. The words " Take all the Prophets of Baal, let not one of them escape us, bring all and slay them," are regarded as a very dramatic series of short sentences, and yet the only words which are specially emphasised with strenuous utterance and dramatic colouring are " Take " and " Slay them."

Even in the lurid "Demons' Chorus" in *Gerontius* the only words which call for special emphasis and tone-colour are " What's a saint " and " Psalm droners." The fact is that the mind is satisfied with the graphic key-word or words in a sentence. Care must be taken, therefore, to secure the proper presentment of these key-words, especially when, as sometimes happens, these words are unfamiliar.

The following are a few examples of words and how to sing them. Words like "flashed" want singing with emphatic "fl" and quickly uttered sibilant, and the final "t" sound must be well defined. To get a proper "f" the lips must be made almost to close so as to get a real buzz. The rush of air at "sh" must be rapid, and the carrying glide *uh* must come at the end of "t" to give it clear definition.

"He shall die" (*Elijah*) demands excess of aspirate, a hard tone, and a fiercely-set mouth. In the phrase "Of those that hate him" (*The Veil*) the word "hate" wants a hard, steam-whistle tone, almost a shriek. How to sing the words "slay them" (*Judith*) I have referred to on page 157. In "able to pierce" (*Blest Pair of Sirens*) the explodent "p" must be well-defined, and the final must be a *staccato*-making sibilant. "Woe" (*King Saul*) should show the spirit of hopeless gloom by means of cloudy tone with a sob-like swell in the word. A particularly fine example of the effect of characteristic diction is found in the following :—

WALFORD DAVIES, *Everyman.*

I lie here in cor - ners   Trussed and piled so   high,

And in chests I'm locked so   fast.

When this was sung real *staccato*, with nasal tone and coloured by the mocking spirit of the singers, Dr. Davies was so pleased that he stopped the choir and said, "Oh, you horrors! how can you be so cynical?"

The function of diction is to invest words with fragrant charm and brightness, as well as to fill them with terror. Therefore delicate phrases like "and the gossips" and "Hoist up your sails of silk" (*Olaf*), "Blessed are the men" (*Elijah*), "Sleep" (*King Saul*), "O, pure in heart" (*Golden Legend*) should be made a delightful memory by means of gentle pressures, the perfect closing of the lips at the explodents "b" and "p," and the graceful use of the carrying glide *uh*.

BREATHY-TONE AND BREATH-AFFLUX.

One aspect of characterization in diction which has been overlooked in the past is the important part which breathy-tone and breath-afflux may be made to play in choral singing. It is astonishing how few solo-vocalists and still fewer choralists take advantage of using breath with the tone or after the sound, as in breath-afflux. The surprise is greater when we remember the great models Reeves and Santley, who made much use of this adjunct of artistic singing. With respect to choral-singing, the natural objection that one has to breathy-tone, and the fear that the occasional use of this special production may develop into habitual use, may in part account for the non-use of this accomplishment. But I believe the neglect is due to conductors not knowing how to get a large body of singers to manage it successfully. The way I set about getting the choir to sing in this manner is as follows :—

(1) I decide upon the special kind of tone—what degree of breathiness—is wanted.

(2) I practise privately until I can personally produce the desired effect.

(3) This model is then patterned to the choir.

(4) I make full allowance for the spirit of distrust and fear of new effects which afflicts all amateur singers, and do not give up in disgust when I find that singers do not respond or are openly sceptical of and unsympathetic to what I am trying to teach them. As it is the *unknown* that is the terrible, I know that their suspicion of the strange demand will grow less and less as the effect is studied more and more.

(5) When, after many attempts, the effect is perfected, I compliment the choir on their achievement, and everybody, including the conductor, is happy. Then the many bad quarters of an hour are forgotten, and another asset is permanently added to the armoury of expression.

By means of breathy-tone many shades of characterization can be expressed in a way that other means cannot touch. It must be borne in mind that whenever breathy-tone is introduced for dramatic or picturesque effect it must be done in an unmistakable manner, or the cloudiness of tone arising from only partially doing it will be put down to bad tone and properly condemned, whereas if the tone be almost a negligible quantity and the words are spoken in a kind of stage whisper, then the intention is made manifest and appreciated accordingly.

The following are a few cases where breathy-tone should or must be used to get the proper spirit of the situation :—

" Will then the Lord be no more God in Zion " (*Elijah*) (expressive of fretful despair).

" Let Him be God " (*Elijah*) (solemn awe).

" Upon your faces fall " (reverential submission).

" Then for a moment the Veil was lifted and the Face was there " (*The Veil*) (overpowering solemnity).

" And none had seen the stranger pass " (*Olaf*) (mysterious surprise).

"Who hath you these tidings brought" (*Everyman*) (fearsome inquiry).

" There is a spectre somewhere near " (*Spectre's Bride*) (hushed affright).

BREATH-AFFLUX.

Closely allied to breathy-tone is breath-afflux, that is, the substitution of breath for what would otherwise be sound in the singing of a word, such breath giving a kind of upward inflection to the breath sound produced. The difficulty of getting this done by a large choir is due to their amateur fear of overdoing it. When it is first attempted, the affluxion of breath is practically a minus quantity, through the sound being continued too long. To inspire singers with courage and to give them the proper lead, pattern the model as frequently as you would to a professional pupil, emphasising the fact that the sound must be merged into a swift current (afflux) of breath as soon as it is struck. By this means choristers are able to give convincing characterization to rapturous delight, as in "Ah! my heart upbounds" (*Bavarian Highlands*); longing desire, as in "O! may we soon again renew that song" (*Blest Pair of Sirens*); overwhelming grief, as in "Mors" (Verdi's *Requiem*); dramatic affright, as in "Ah" (last word of *Samson and Delilah*); wild jubilation, as in "Hooch" (*Wedding of Shon Maclean*).

Although the opportunity of using breath-afflux may only occur *once* in a work, its successful accomplishment reveals a mastery of technique which captivates an audience and gives distinction to a performance. Therefore conductors should not let opportunities for its introduction pass, as has been so often done.

WHEN NOT TO SAY WORDS.

In the saying of words it sometimes happens that artistic discrimination has to be exercised. It is a well-known fact that the eye can only definitely see one thing at a time—the object which is on the point of sight. Similarly the ear can only hear closely one sound or series of sounds. Therefore in cases where, through several phrases being spoken together, the words come into conflict with each other, tending towards a jumble of sounds, it is necessary to discriminate between the principal words and those of less importance. Having decided this point, act boldly. Ask the subsidiary parts merely to mutter their words, so as to enable the principal phrase to dominate the whole for awhile, as in *The Spectre's Bride* :—

Dvořák, *The Spectre's Bride.*

† Her tender feet were tired and sore, Her mouth betrayed the pain she bore, Her

The reason why some phrases sound confused and indistinct is because conductors have not realised sufficiently that everything written is not of the same importance. They therefore treat every word or note with the same respect, whereas they should discriminate between the wheat and the chaff, and relegate the mere filling-up parts to a secondary position.

WHEN NOT TO SING WORDS.

There are frequent occasions when, for descriptive effect, it is advisable to *speak* the words instead of singing them, although the words are set to notes. This is best done when a word or phrase is repeated several times. Then, to give variety, and as a climax,

---

* These words should be hummed rather than sung.

† The words in the bass part must be very clearly and distinctly articulated.

the word is spoken. For instance, in the reiterated
word " Kaw " (*Hiawatha's Departure*) the first
is sung, the second harshly semi-sung, and the
last (page 130) *spoken* with incredulous disdain.
In *Gerontius* the last sardonic laughs (page 90) are
uttered with a contemptuous, despairing cackle, with
the sound in the throat.   This cuts through the
instrumentation and produces the desired effect.
A delightfully humorous effect is produced in
A Franklyn's Dogge, by saying the seventh repetition
of " Little Bingo " in a shrill, piping voice.   In the
second verse, at the words " good stingo " (bar 68),
" good " is prolonged with a sort of sepulchral tone,
and "stingo" snapped out; while in the third verse
(bars 30 and 31) the audience is usually convulsed
by the words "by Jingo " being all breath, with
emphasis on the explodents " b " and " j." In
cases where words are directed to be spoken,
great care and many trials are necessary to get
the choir to sing with convincing utterance and
unanimity.

It seems almost an insult to caution well-
conducted, experienced singers against making a
travesty of or turning to ridicule any special effects
of characterization.   Still, it is necessary to do so.
When anything out of the common is done for the
first time, or while a new effect is being developed,
the strangeness of the idea and the imperfection of
the first attempts often sound so ludicrous that a
certain number begin to snigger at the result.
This may be overlooked for a few times, but the
spirit of levity must be suppressed, and self-restraint
substituted, or a performance will in whole or in
part be spoiled in six seconds.   This has happened
to my knowledge in phrases like "He leapt"

(*Spectre's Bride*), the "Demons' Chorus" (*Gerontius*), "Little Bingo," the quaint Turkomani melody (*Omar Khayyám*) (page 198), and other places too numerous to mention.

FACIAL EXPRESSION.

A most important adjunct to characterization in singing is an animated, mobile facial expression. It is important in two directions. It not only promotes good articulation, but the reflection in the face of the sentiment, be it laughter, ardour, hate, or disdain, carries conviction to the hearer. Unfortunately British singers are afraid of showing emotion, and are especially so anxious not to show it in their faces that it is almost an impossibility to get anything like expressive facial movements. This perhaps did not matter much fifty years ago, when we were more insular than we are to-day; but now that we have to come into competition with the more volatile or dramatic singers of the Continent, it is imperative that we acquire the power of facial expression as a living commentary on the words spoken. This can only be done by the encouragement, stimulus, and magnetic power of the conductor. To change stolidity of face to versatility of feature he must brace himself up for a formidable task. In showing the precise form of muscular action he desires, he must throw convention aside and illustrate it in a somewhat exaggerated manner. If in response to this pattern some venturesome soul breaks through the hard crust of stolidity and does what is wanted, he should call out the singer's name and commend him warmly. He should do this to others at every favourable opportunity, and make all the members feel a desire to win commendation. The singers must be shown that immobility of face prevents that free muscular action of the articulatory organs which all graphic singing demands. By good-natured banter the conductor must ridicule singing a joyful chorus like the opening of *Faust* (Berlioz) with an immovable, bored countenance, or the words " He shall perish ; let him die," with a Sunday-go-to-meeting expression of face. These " flank attacks " will have to be continued until a sort of standard has been fixed, and the fear of looking ridiculous has been driven from the minds of the singers. In attempting this task let the conductor, as an incentive to perseverance, keep in mind the old saw about dropping water and the stone, because when a British choir *does* wake up to its possibilities it can and does unmistakably excel in this unfrequented domain of expression.

HOW TO SING DIFFERENT STYLES OF COMPOSITION.

Some time ago I heard a conductor who was reading a criticism of his concert ask the question, " What does the fellow " (the critic, of course) " mean by saying the chorus was performed very well, but it would have been better had it not been rendered in the style of a part-song?" This point, which is very obscure to many conductors, I will try to make clear. To differentiate between the style of singing a madrigal, glee, part-song, and chorus is a task which few conductors can undertake. They may have a notion that there are differences of treatment, but their views on these are very hazy. Yet there are well-defined characteristics which clearly mark one class of composition from the other, and which call for a somewhat different kind of treatment.

We will take the simplest form—the *part-song*—first. In this class all that is necessary is to have a well-defined melody supported by well-balanced under parts. The expression is governed by the top line, be it soprano or first tenor, and owing to the general simplicity of the music, great expression can be infused into the rendering. In the more recent part-songs this does not absolutely apply, as much more independence of parts is introduced, —in fact they often incorporate the characteristics of the glee and madrigal, and have to be treated in similar styles.

The *madrigal* suffers most from being sung in part-song fashion. The strength of madrigals lies in their "points of imitation." The cleverness and learning displayed in these, as well as the possible musical effect, are their chief recommendation from an artistic point of view. It follows therefore that the clear presentment and unfolding of these imitations should be the main object of attainment in singing madrigals. Yet I have heard dozens of performances in which this feature was ignored, through each voice going on regardless of the other, or of the claims of "the points of imitation." The result of such performances is disappointing to general listeners, the impression being that the madrigals are unmelodious and therefore dull. At the close of this work (*see* Appendix I.), a tabulated scheme of how to sing madrigals is given, but to enable these tables to be interpreted

more readily, the following example of how I mark
" In going to my lonely bed " is given :—

EDWARDS, " In going to my lonely bed."

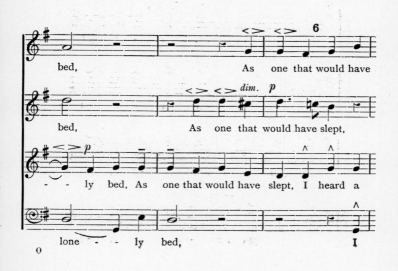

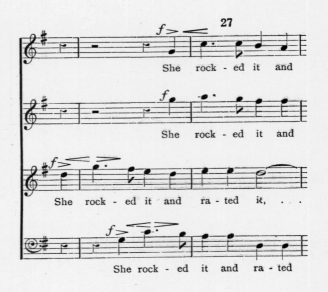

It will be noticed that marked entries are the centre of interest. In the homogeneous plain chordings the soprano takes the premier place, as in a part-song. This affords a welcome period of repose. Careful analysis is often required to ferret out the imitations, and still more skill to get the imitating voice heard; but by bold anti-part-song singing, and, may be, borrowing and lending voices, this can always be accomplished.

The *glee* differs from the part-song and madrigal in that it is usually laid out to give, at sundry times, solo phrases and prolonged passages to each voice in turn, and when these melodious tit-bits or even long sentences occur, this favoured part must be allowed to dominate the other voices, although they may not be "imitative" as in the madrigal. When these special melodic phrases are absent from the lower parts, the soprano takes the lead, as in a part-song. When a glee includes points of imitation, as it frequently does, these must be treated in madrigal fashion.

The following excerpts show how the dominating parts of a glee are treated :—

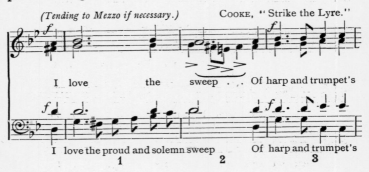

(Tending to Mezzo if necessary.)   COOKE, "Strike the Lyre."

I   love   the   sweep . . . Of harp and trumpet's

I love the proud and solemn sweep   Of harp and trumpet's

1   2   3

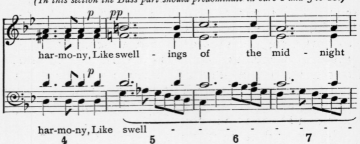

(In this section the Bass part should predominate in bars 1 and 5 to 10.)

har-mo-ny, Like swell - ings of   the mid - night

har-mo-ny, Like swell - - - - - - -

4   5   6   7

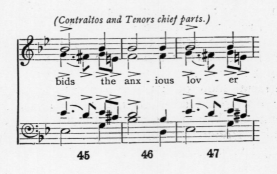

(Contraltos and Tenors chief parts.)

bids   the anx - ious lov - er

45   46   47

The *chorus* usually needs to be treated in a broader style than either the madrigal, glee, or part-song; and being very often framed on bigger lines, and not being bound by any convention, it generally includes all the attributes of the three classes already considered, to which is added fugal treatment. Therefore a chorus frequently requires great variety of treatment. The answer to the question of the conductor at the beginning of this chapter is that he had probably let the soprano dominate the whole instead of giving emphasis to the inner and lowest voices in points of imitation, had neglected to give prominence to the solo phrases in the lower voices, and had imposed too much restraint in working up to a climax—all of which points must be attended to when performing a chorus.

Sometimes a chorus is built upon one plan— fugal, madrigalian, or part-song—in which case the particular style dominates the rendering; for instance, " He that shall endure " (*see* page 159 ff., *supra*) should be sung in madrigal fashion in the working up of the principal and secondary subjects, which are repeated so frequently in imitative form.

The following Example shows how I mark for expression the first six bars of Bach's great motet:—

Chorus I.
Allegro moderato.   J. S. BACH, *Sing ye to the Lord.*

Bearing the foregoing points in mind, it will be an easy matter for conductors to get each style of composition sung in the manner appropriate to it.

A caution is needed here. Some people suppose that it is only part-songs which should be sung with ultra-refinement. This is a mistake. Every class of composition—even the choruses of Bach—may be and should be sung with ethereal delicacy if the sentiment demands it. No rendering, be it vigorous or emotional or sentimental, should be open to the charge of being " part-songy " if the characteristics of the class of the composition are preserved. Therefore do the correct generic thing, and if critics " say,"—well! " let them say."

THE CRUX OF ARTISTRY.—THE ELUSIVE " THREE PER CENT."

Conductors and choristers generally fail to realise how small a percentage in actual work done lies between a fairly good and an excellent performance, and that this excellence is the result of attention to seemingly insignificant details. But so it is. Take three performances of a given piece at a competition—one good, the second very good, and the third excellent. It will be found that in the notes sung and the words said, and the general scheme of expression—constituting, say, 97 per cent. of the actual work presented during the performance—there is little to choose between them, each choir being fairly correct. But the spirit, the verve, the subtle points of expression, both in tone and diction, of the one choir place it far above the other two. Their ebb and flow of force, their colouring of voice, their clear diction, due to quick action of tongue and lips combined, and their carrying glide *uh* and convincing facial expression, seem but small additions to the effort and skill put forth by the other choirs; but they make a convincing performance which cuts like a keen-edged razor, while the comparatively blunt-edged, ordinary rendering makes little impression.

Unfortunately this three or five per cent. spirit or flavouring takes almost as much trouble to obtain as the remaining 97 or 95 per cent. On this account both conductor and conducted frequently act on the thought, " Why should we have toil without end merely to get the turn of a phrase, the shading of a *piano*, the placing of a word, the colouring of the voice, and the changing of the countenance, when everything is satisfactory without these wearing efforts ? " They forget that it is this three or five per cent. which is the elixir of artistic life, and makes all the difference in the result. It is the difference between gingerbeer and champagne. The flavour which counts is absent, and its place is taken by something offensive.

I was taking supper with a physician, who was for the time on vegetarian diet. He said that his meal had been spoiled by the mushrooms having been burnt in the cooking—pleasure turned to nausea by the smallest of percentages.

When I spoke to Professor Arnold, the great authority on steel, on the importance of small percentages in securing artistic results in singing, he said he quite believed it, as the difference between common steel and high-grade steel was less than one per cent. To illustrate this he kindly provided me with photographs of two specimens of steel—one specimen perfect, the other ruined through containing one-hundredth part of one per cent. chromium less than the other.

The moral is that conductors must not despise, as beneath notice, the most insignificant details which tend to a perfect rendering of a piece. The amount of work required to get this distilled spirit of artistry may seem out of proportion to the result, but the necessity is laid upon them to reach the goal of excellence, otherwise they become fossilized.

A good solvent of the difficulty is to act on the principle which I have found necessary to adopt, namely: To achieve any artistic ideal, give *three times* the amount of work and attention to it that you consider *ought* to be necessary. When you have adopted this as your standard you will give, *con amore*, the additional labour required. *See* Appendix I. for illustrations how to mark for expression various types of compositions.

ANALYSIS OF *THE MESSIAH*.

THINKING IN CONTINENTS.

In a previous chapter I remarked that in the matter of artistic phrasing—the perfection of each note and phrase, and the linking them up so as to form a complete and satisfactory whole—we should think in continents rather than in a few isolated notes, or even a complete chorus. To make the performance of an oratorio meet the demands of an artistic interpretation, each chorus must be performed with some reference to what has gone before and what follows after, so as to secure proper contrasts, sufficient variety in treatment, and the correct musical centre of gravity.

I propose to show how to do this by giving a brief outline and analysis of my way of interpreting *The Messiah*, with sundry reasons why I adopt this particular rendering.

My reasons for illustrating "thinking in continents" by means of Handel's great epic are: 1. It is so well known that the explanations can be easily followed. 2. Its possibilities of variation of treatment seem to most conductors to be so remote, that if it can be shown that even in the hackneyed and non-dramatic *Messiah* there are possibilities of obtaining pleasing, effective, and artistic diversity, it should be certainly possible to secure telling contrasts of effect in more modern dramatic works.   3.   I have had so many applications from conductors to explain by letter and marked copies how to perform certain (or all) of the choruses, that this chapter may meet a real want.

I shall deal with each number seriatim, but I shall merely glance at the instrumental and solo portions, reserving for the choruses a more complete and comprehensive treatment.

No. 1.   The Overture.   The *Grave*, though marked M. 69 for each crotchet, should be taken much more slowly.   I take it M. 100, beating eight quavers in a bar.   In the repeat, the wind instruments *tacent* and the strings play real *piano* or *pianissimo*.   This stately movement prepares the way for the finely-contrasted *Allegro*, which I take at or about crotchet M. 132.   The oft-recurring subject should be given boldly in whatever part it appears.   At bar 26 there should be a *dim.* to bar 27, after which each successive bar to bar 32 should be played with marked accent and increasing power.   A *poco dim.* follows for three bars, when the subject is re-stated in the first violins.   At bar 48 there is another *dim.*, and at bar 50 a cumulative passage begins (as at bar 27) and progresses vigorously to bar 57, when the subject is again introduced, and is bandied about with vehemence till the pause.   The concluding *Adagio* should be very loud, broad, and impressive, reinforced by the organ, if this be a good blending instrument and in tune.

No. 2.   "Comfort ye."   This is usually sung a little slower than quaver 80, but this speed, with due regard to *tempo rubato*, is correct.

No. 3. "Every valley." The general tendency is to sing this rather quicker than crotchet M. 84, and it gains in effect by being taken about M. 96. In both the above solos, see that the instrumental interludes are firmly and cleanly given.

No. 4. "And the glory." Here we come to the real object of this analysis, which is to be a review of the potentialities of the choruses of the oratorio, and to suggest means of providing variety of treatment and contrasts in effect during the working up of each chorus, through various crises, to the ultimate glorious climax of the final "Grand Amen." Therefore the points to be kept before us are (*a*) the features of interest in each chorus, when considered as a unity complete in itself, and (*b*) the unfolding of those special characteristics in each chorus which, in the scheme of expression, allow of a different treatment so as to introduce variety and contrast between the various choruses, and thus prevent monotony of effect.

"And the glory." Being the opening chorus, great pains should be taken to make a good impression from the commencement. It is a confident, prophetic assertion of the coming victory of the Lord, and therefore of masculine expression. M. 100 is rather too slow. I take it about 112, with marked rhythm. The opening words "And the glory" should be most clearly articulated, with a swell on the first syllable of "glory."

The phrasing is as follows :—

And the   glo - ry, the   glo - ry of   the   Lord
(*not* Laud).

This pattern is followed in every part in which the subject appears. To secure this, the passage should, in rehearsal, be sung in unison by all the parts a dozen times over, to get clear words. I attach much importance to the clear saying of the final " d " and the initial " th," and the smooth glide to *uh* in glo(uh)ry. I tell the choir to hold the audience by their glittering speech, as the Ancient Mariner held the wedding-guest by his glittering eye.

Here we must make a digression to consider the question of the reinforcement of a part to strengthen the clear definition of an important musical subject or phrase. It will be observed that the contralto part is so very low that contraltos cannot sing it loudly. This sometimes gives the impression that the contraltos are weak, as at a recent festival in Yorkshire (not Sheffield) one of the London critics spoke of the "weak contraltos," citing this entry as proof, whereas the contraltos in question were a splendid body of singers, the very reverse of weak.

To obviate this false impression, I always ask the second sopranos (whom, as I have mentioned before, I regard as auxiliaries of the contraltos, to be called on at any time) to sing with the contraltos here, and also at bars 43-46 at the words "and all flesh shall see it together." By this means all sense of weakness is eliminated, and the hearers are satisfied, because, as I have remarked before, people judge by the results, not by the processes.

The other parts take up the strain jubilantly, but chief emphasis should be placed on the basses, because they, having the original theme, are the chief part. This same feature should be specially

brought out at the first *tutti* crisis at bars 33-38.
Here the second tenors might reinforce the basses.
A very impressive feature is the contralto phrase
(bar 29), when performed as follows :—

be re - veal - - - - - - - - - ed ; etc.

Following the advice and rule given on page 67, the
contraltos might take two breaths in this phrase.

Full advantage must always be taken of all
points of imitation, in order to keep up the interest ;
therefore at bar 97 the contraltos must be reinforced
by the second sopranos to make the following
phrases dominate the whole for three bars :—

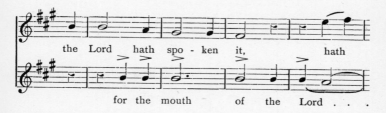

the Lord hath spo - ken it, hath

for the mouth of the Lord . . .

The climax utterance of the principal subject by
the sopranos at bar 107 must be given with great
brilliance, to which end it should be phrased as
follows :—

And the glo - ry, the glo - ry, the glo - ry of the Lord

In the peroration (bars 131 to end) the tempo might become a little more stately, but in any case the men must emphasise the words "mouth" and "Lord" by giving a firm swell on each word, and at the *Adagio* an impressive close must be secured by singing it with great breath-pressure.

No. 5, "Thus saith," and No. 6, "But who may abide," calling for no special remark, we will consider No. 7, "And He shall purify." The long runs, made up of two, three, and four divisions, being the distinguishing feature of this chorus, extra attention must be given to them until they are fluently performed: there is much difficulty in preventing the first two words running into each other and sounding like "an dee." I find it advisable and preferable to take breath after "and"; then the aspirate can be given clearly if the words "And He shall purify" are produced near the lips. To ensure clearness let the passage be sung by the whole choir in unison until perfect. There should be an accent at the beginning of each division, that is, on the odd beats, but not on the even beats, with a general *crescendo* to the end of the phrase. When singing the four reiterated notes, see that the attack is clean. The homophonic phrase "That they may offer unto the Lord," &c., must in each case be given *forte*, and at the end of the chorus *fortissimo*.

No. 8. "Behold a Virgin." No special remark.

No. 9. "O Thou that tellest." The compass of this solo lies in a rather awkward part of the voice for contralto singers, as they are seldom able to sing here with any power of voice. To counterbalance this weakness, conductors must instruct the orchestra to play more *piano* than they otherwise would. In the interludes get as much tone as possible, to prevent giving a colour of weakness to the whole. In the choral section several new features present themselves, the chief point of contrast being the *pianissimo* phrases. There is a shading off of the phrases instead of the usual *crescendo* effect heard in previous choruses :—

The sopranos, basses, and tenors each enter *forte* boldly—taking breath after " Thou "—and then in turn they each *dim.* after the first four notes. The contraltos enter *mezzo*, and the other parts follow suit until the word " arise," which is given *forte* with a rousing *ff*. " Say unto the cities " is *mezzo*, but " Behold your God " *fortissimo*. This is maintained till bar 16, which is sung as follows:—

It is observed that the sopranos, tenors, and basses sing *piano* after the first beat till the fifth beat. This is to allow the beautiful phrase of the contraltos—strengthened by the second sopranos—to stand out prominently. The *molto crescendo* which follows adds vigour to the whole section. Bar 19 is sung *mezzo* with *dim.* to the word "behold," which is given *ff.* At "The glory of the Lord" the force is reduced, and, as though filled with awe, the contraltos sing—

until the *molto cres.*, which anticipates the change of thought at the uplifting words, "is risen upon thee," which are sung *fortissimo*.

No. 10. "For behold, darkness." Should commence *pp*, as though the sound were emerging from void and darkness, then *cres.* to *forte* on the fifth quaver in bar 4, from which point *decres.* to the entry of the voice.

No. 11. "The people that walked." There is a disposition on the part of some conductors to take this about M. 90, but if the phrasing marks are well observed the interest will be maintained at M. 72.

Where the strings are in unison with the voice they must never dispute the supremacy of the singer, but form a sympathetic background. At bar 18, when the fascinating progressions of the wood-wind instruments appear, the strings must assume a subordinate place, in order to allow a fresh point of interest—the seldom-heard wood-wind tone—to have a full chance. The closing bars should be *forte* in all instruments.

No. 12. " For unto us a Child is born." This glorious chorus, the first great climax of the work, must be treated in a grand, majestic manner. A great deal depends on utilising the principle of the curves of sound, mentioned previously, by which great variety may be introduced. Some conductors, who have not grasped the secret of this ebb and flow of dynamic force, think it necessary to increase the speed to M. 100. This is a mistake, M. 72 to 80 being quite quick enough, with a slight *accelerando* in the peroration, which is counterbalanced by the short *rallentando* at the last ecstatic utterance of the words, " The everlasting Father, the Prince of peace."

It was the fashion some years ago to sing the opening very softly till the first grand outburst, " Wonderful." These sudden contrasts were the chief stock-in-trade of conductors thirty or forty years ago, but this is not the case now. My plan is as follows :—The words " For unto us a Child is born " are sung loudly and jubilantly, and not whispered as though the singers were ashamed of the announcement. At bar 8 "unto us " is sung *mezzo*, and each succeeding utterance is sung with rising emotion and power. The following is the way we practise the run of eight divisions in

unison until it can be sung without reference to
a copy :—

For un - to us a Child is born,

etc.

This unison singing is necessary, if only to correct
the tendency to sing semitones instead of full tones
in the under passing notes.

Another potent reason for this unison practice is
to familiarise the singers with their own particular
breathing places in these long runs. As mentioned
elsewhere, to secure a firm, triumphant finish
I tell the singers they can take several breaths in a
"run," provided that those whose initials range
from A to H take breath on the first beat, those
from I to O on the second beat, and those
from P to Z on the third or fourth beat. This
explains the brilliant effect produced by these
and similar runs, especially at the close of
"His yoke is easy."

At bar 49 a fine effect is produced by treating the contralto phrase as follows :—

The contraltos also have a chance of distinguishing themselves at the passage commencing at bar 53. The long run must be firmly sung *mezzo* until bar 57, when a *molto crescendo* must be made :—

This is immediately followed by the tenor phrase, which is repeated by the sopranos. If sung with firmness and growing enthusiasm, it always produces a thrill of excitement :—

The top G must be sung resolutely, with a fine swell produced by breath-pressure, as before explained.

The displays for the separate parts are very effective and telling, but the supreme moments are the glorious *tutti* outbursts, at the words "Wonderful! Counsellor!" &c. To get the full transcendent effect it is necessary to make each word glow with ardour, by means of the well-managed quick swell, as follows :—

There is all the difference in the world between striking the notes with a heavy *sfz* and this short *fff* swell. One gives a sort of shock to the word, while the other makes it glow with warmth, life, and artistic effect.

Having dealt in detail with the main features of this chorus, I will now give a general display of the whole scheme of expression.

" FOR UNTO US A CHILD IS BORN."

BAR.	BEAT.	VOICE.	
1-6	-	-	Firm instrumental introduction.
7	-	S	To be sung *forte* to "born."
8	4	S	*Mezzo*, then *crescendo* to bar 12.
12	3	T	Tenor lead, *forte*.
13	3	S	Third beat, soprano lead, *forte*. At the beginning of the run sing *mezzo*, increase in loudness every bar and finish *ff*.
18	-	C	Contralto lead, *forte*.
19	3	B	Bass lead, *forte*. Begin the run *mezzo-forte* and increase every bar to end of phrase.
26	2	T	Commence *mp*, *crescendo* to the word "shoulder," then *crescendo* to bar 28.
27-29	-	S	Imitative tenor phrase.
29-30	2	-	All voices enter *piano;* gradual *crescendo* to bar 32.
32-36	-	-	*Fortissimo* with swells on the accented beats; make the words very clear.
36-44	-	-	General *mezzo-forte* with rise and fall according to phrasing.
45-49	-	-	*Double forte*.
50	-	S	*Forte* entry, with slight shading off.
51	-	B	Firm entry, with slight shading off.
52	-	C	*Forte* entry, *mezzo-forte* at the beginning of the run, which must be sung very clearly, but with something held in reserve until bar 56, which should be sung with all power possible.
57-60	-	-	To be sung like Exx. on page 213, *supra*.
61	-	-	All voices begin *mezzo*, and *crescendo* to "Wonderful."

64   -   All. From this point go from strength to strength. The *tempo* may be increased slightly to give more animation and excitement. At bar 86 as light *rall.*, to give emphasis to the words, is effective. The *tempo* is resumed by the instruments, and at the last two bars the full organ should increase the power of the *fortissimo* close.

No. 13. The "Pastoral Symphony." At the opening the wood-wind should be allowed to dominate over the strings, as a slight contrast to the string tone which is in evidence so much throughout the oratorio. In the repeat the strings play alone *ppp*. If they play above a whisper ask them to play with a single hair of the bow. This is to suggest the serene calmness of the hills of Bethlehem, with the sounds in the dim distance, carrying the thoughts heavenward. It should be remarked that the interest is increased by giving a little prominence to the theme which in bar 28 appears in the second violins, in bar 29 in the first violins, and at bar 30 in the 'cellos. At the close, before there is time for the audience to break the spell by applause, let the organist give the chord for the heavenly message, contained in the succeeding recitative.

No. 14. "There were shepherds." Beat eight quavers in a bar, and cease beating at the fifth quaver of the penultimate bar, to allow the soloist to finish *ad lib.* The concluding two chords are struck after the singer has finished.

No. 15. "And the angel." With organ only.

No. 16. "And suddenly." This commences as loudly as possible, and very quickly (M. 144), eight in a bar. Begin *decrescendo* at the third beat of bar 2 until *piano* is reached at bar 4. Cease playing the accompaniment at the seventh beat of the penultimate bar, and after the soloist has ended strike the last two chords immediately.

No. 17. " Glory to God." This chorus opens boldly, the tenor part being allowed special prominence in bars 1, 2, 3, 10, 11, 12, 13. Bars 5, 6, 7 should be sung very softly. Some authorities say that as the words " Peace on earth " are part of the announcement of the angels, it should be sung *forte ;* but as there is as much reason in singing softly as loudly, for the sake of artistic variety it is better to have the contrasted effect at bars 5, 6, 7, also at 14, 15, 16, 29, 30 and 31. Note that at the third recurrence of the words, " and peace on earth," the theme is in the bass part, therefore the other parts should be *pianissimo.*

No. 18. " Rejoice greatly." Though marked M. 104, most singers take this at about 112, and it gains in effect by this slight increase of speed. The middle section, " He is the righteous Saviour," is taken more slowly, but at the *réprise* the original *tempo* is resumed.

No. 19. " Then shall the eyes." Organ only.

No. 20. " He shall feed " and " Come unto Him." There is a tendency among some artists to sing these too slowly, while others want to take them too quickly. By taking them at M. 108 to 112 we strike the happy medium, avoiding "dragging " on the one hand and singing " with a lilt " on the other.

No. 21. " His yoke is easy." This used to be the Cinderella chorus of the oratorio. On account of its supposed lack of interest it has been treated with undeserved neglect, being omitted from many performances of the work. And yet this is one of the finest choruses of the whole series of masterpieces. My choir delight in it, are never weary of singing it, and if recognition from the public be any criterion of the attractiveness and power of a piece, " His yoke " stands very high, for the demands for its repetition are very frequent.

The real reasons for this neglect were the difficulties of the performance and the failure to grasp the character and possibilities of the chorus.

The principal subject with which it opens is typical of the freedom from anxiety in the contemplation of the easiness of the burden and the lightness of the yoke to be borne by the followers of the Lord Christ. Joyous religious fervour seems to permeate the whole chorus. It commences in a rather restrained manner, keeps in this mood until bar 36, where there is a marked *crescendo* to bar 38, when the whole of the choir, with orchestra and organ, burst into a glorious passage of exalted feeling which reaches its climax —and such a climax—at bar 45 in the passage :—

[NOTE.—Great breath-pressure is needed to realise the *tour de force* of this transcendent effort; but as the vowels are very favourable to easy production, the singers always rise to the occasion. By commencing the chorus rather softly and continuing the movement more or less in this manner, this chorus is not only quite contrasted with the preceding choruses, but it makes the *fortissimo* at bar 38 and forward doubly impressive, while the brilliant peroration at bar 44 to the end is really dazzling and uplifting in its effect. In the working up of this chorus regard should be had to the following hints.]

First make sure that the subject is well-mastered, especially that the dotted semiquaver and demisemiquaver be clearly defined. This has been a main cause of the avoidance of this chorus. As a pattern of how to sing the whole subject, let the full choir practise the following transposed version in unison, observing carefully the marks of expression :—

His yoke . . is ea - - - - - - - sy, His burthen is light. etc.

Note that there is only one dotted semiquaver, as at (*a*), and not two, as in some copies.

Although it may be contrary to the rhetorical accent to make a small swell on the second syllable of "burthen," as at (*b*), it is advisable to do so in this case to secure an effective point of imitation. It should be said that to sing this opening *mezzo* is so much more difficult than to sing it *forte*, that great care is necessary or the sopranos will sing it in the easier way—for which reason it is generally sung *forte*—and spoil the natural and artistic effect. After singing the first eighteen bars in a restrained manner, a welcome change is introduced by the tenors singing the subject *forte* in the telling change of key in bars 19 to 22, and the sopranos replying equally vigorously. Then at bar 23 the contraltos and basses resume *mezzo* tone till the grand climax at bar 38, when *fortissimo* and more *fortissimo* rules till the final sustained chords round off the first part of the oratorio in glorious fashion.

Part II.

No. 22. " Behold the Lamb of God." When treated in the perfunctory manner that it often receives, this chorus is most uninteresting, but when it is sung with a feeling of loving and reverential adoration, and interpreted as though, in beholding the Lamb of God, we catch a glimpse of the Holy of Holies, it is transformed into a thing of beauty and a chalice full of hallowed emotions. The problem of suggesting the solemn awe called forth by the contemplation of the sinless Lamb of God and His foreshadowed sacrifice on the Cross, to expiate the " sin of the world," is a difficult one. How I attempt to solve it is as follows.

The opening subject is treated as a *decrescendo* phrase—in this point a contrast to the other choruses—with great emotional emphasis on the

vowel "o" in "Behold." The model for all the
entries, instrumental as well as vocal, is :—

Reverential wonderment is the sentiment of the
singers in the exposition.

This chorus and the next three choruses, which
deal with the Passion of our Lord, should show
that, if skilfully treated, the swell is the basis of all
emotional expression. Therefore great care must
be taken to secure just the correct amount of
increase and decrease of sound, or the touch of
pathos or conviction will be lost. At bar 9 make a
general *crescendo* to bar 10, and *decrescendo* to bar 12.
The words "That taketh away" should be softly
sung, and then begin a *crescendo* getting to *forte* at
"of the world" (bar 15). Sing bar 16 very softly
and reflectively. On the repetition of the words in
bar 17 sing very loudly, as though you wished to call
attention to the sacred object. The next phrase is
sung :—

Note that here and in bars 22 to 26 the sopranos
sing the solo phrase very firmly, but with a tinge of
sorrow in the tone, and then shade off to *piano*, or

even to *pp*, to allow the contralto and other moving
parts to predominate, they having the principal
theme. Meanwhile the softly sustained soprano
note—which may be compared to an upper pedal—
has a soothing, glowing effect which is almost
ravishing in its appeal to the senses. The final
entry (bar 27) should be sung *forte*, then all shade
off by well-ordered *diminuendo* to *pianissimo*, taking
care that the instrumentalists play in like manner,
or the effect desired will be lost. It may be well to
remark here that, unless the wood-wind players are
very expert and can play real *pianissimo*, I shut
them off in bars 27 and 28.

No. 23. " He was despised." The chief thing
in this solo is to get sympathetic accompaniment.
In such a phrase as

the accent should be the same as in the spoken
word, there being a slight stress on the middle note,
and a shading off on the third; in fact it must
follow the rhetorical accent so as to be in perfect
sympathy with the singer.

Whenever the second part of the solo, " He gave
His back to the smiters," is sung—and it is well
worth performing—I always take the repeat from
bar 34, the unaccompanied phrase, " He was
despised." This abbreviation introduces the salient
points of the solo without prolonging it unduly, and
thereby gives a sense of satisfaction.

No. 24. " Surely He hath borne our griefs."
Commence *forte*, and let the pent-up expression of
overwrought feeling of sympathetic emotion, evoked

Q

by the recital of griefs of the " Man of Sorrows,"
be fully realised in the opening word "Surely."
Give prominence to the sibilant; swell and dwell
on the vowel and shade off softly at " -ly." More
than all, put " tears " into the utterance, as that of a
soul in pain. At the words " He hath " (bar 6),
commence *mezzo-forte*, then begin a *crescendo*, and
at bar 8 reach *fortissimo*, which sustain with full
force till the second quaver of bar 10, when
decrescendo to *piano* at the word "sorrows." In this
falling cadence a fine contrast is secured to the
rising cadence at bar 8, the whole forming a
beautiful six-bar curve of emotion. Then at bar 12
comes the distinguishing feature of this chorus,
namely, the apotheosis of the sustained note and
the glorifying of the prepared discord, two effects
which fill the picture with absolute fitness.

The following excerpt will illustrate this better
than words :—

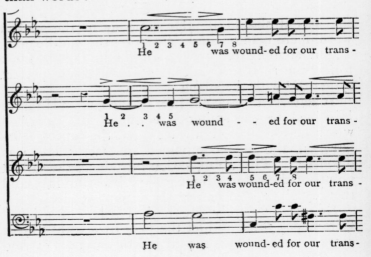

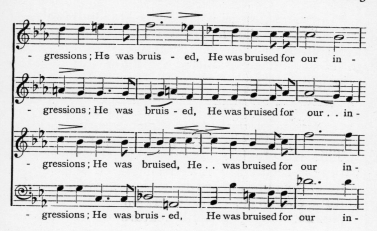

Note that at the end of either three quavers—as in the first contralto lead—or five quavers—as in sopranos and tenors—the *molto cres.* is followed by *molto dim.*, that is, as soon as the strong accents are struck. The tenors have two impressive chances at bars 20 and 21, while the contralto should emphasize the A before descending to G.

A *crescendo* by all parts should reach *fortissimo* at bars 18 and 19.

The following is the best way of treating the next phrase:—

The last two bars should be *pianissimo*.

No. 25. "And with His stripes." In this chorus try to make the listeners realise your idea of the self-abnegation of the Saviour by means of the emotional swell, as shown in the treatment of the principal subject :—

And with His stripes we are heal - ed.

This pattern is followed by all the voices, but variety is secured by louder singing as the subject is reiterated, until near the end a *decrescendo* sets in, and the chorus closes *mezzo-piano*.

No. 26. "All we like sheep." Here we have a chorus of self-condemnation. The singers, after contemplating the suffering the Holy One has undergone on their behalf, feel like the prophet of old, who cried out in agony of spirit, "Woe is me, for I am a sinful man." Their souls are stirred to the quick, and they cry out loudly that they have erred and strayed like lost sheep.

Although sung *forte*, it is possible to put an emotional swell on the words " we " and " sheep " sufficient to show a spirit distraught, not with reflective but with vociferous anguish. Sung in this way, the runs, with their turns and twists typical of a giddy, heedless throng, fit into the picture admirably. At the words "we have turned" the second syllable "-ed" must be sung rather softly, to allow the interjectory words of each incoming voice to be heard distinctly, and thus carry on the point of imitation. The three bars before the pause bar should be given *fortissimo*, and the pause chord should be the same, but should have a marked *diminuendo* just before the end to glide into the

next most impressive and moving portion, the
Adagio, which opens as follows :—

At the seventh bar (page 102, Novello's edition)
the tenors must swell on the F, and in bar 8 the
contraltos must imitate this almost spasmodic
wave-like singing of the voices, pregnant with grief
and dejection.

At bar 10 the contraltos and tenors must come in *mp*, and all parts should swell slightly on the word "Him" (bar 12); from this point a decided *diminuendo* should set in, and the close should be *pianissimo*.

To heighten the impressiveness, or rather to prevent it from being spoiled, I shut off all the wood-wind three bars from the end, and the organ also—only the strings, which can be regulated in sound, remaining.

No. 27. "All they that see Him." This short dramatic recitative aptly serves as an introduction to the jibing, derisive chorus next following.

No. 28. "He trusted in God." This chorus is usually regarded as one of the least interesting, if not the least interesting, in the oratorio, and so it is, unless it be sung with the proper spirit and atmosphere. But if the cue be taken from the preceding recitative, and it is sung with sarcastic tone and the scornful expression implied in the words, "They shoot out their lips and shake their heads," it becomes a living reality, and is such a contrast to everything that has gone before, that if encores were ever taken this chorus would, by the impression it makes, have to be repeated at every performance.

To get the desired effect it is necessary to use a very hard, nasal tone—or rather nasal twang—in each voice. To those choristers who have never sung with hard, contemptuous nasal tone it will be a difficult achievement, because they will imagine that they are exaggerating tremendously, when the probability is that they will be just on the fringe of nasality. On account of the modifying effect of the string tone more nasality is required than would otherwise be the case. The organist should only employ the reed stops in this chorus.

After the exposition the voices will naturally become more normal, but care must be taken that the jibing tone does not disappear. At the interjectory phrases " Let Him deliver Him " a strong accent must be put on the syllable " liv," and great pains be taken to sing correctly the note it is set to, as grievous errors are often made at these points. The difficulty in singing these notes firmly is one of the reasons for the unpopularity of the chorus. At the climax of the chorus (bar 50) the choir must sing as though it were a frenzied, howling mob, with unmusical tone, and at the last three bars there must again be a great excess of nasality in the tone. It is advisable to dwell on the " m " in " Him."

No. 29. " Thy rebuke "; No. 30. " Behold and see "; No. 31. " He was cut off." The Passion music calls for little remark, save that at bar 7 and forward of " Behold and see," the first violins should play as follows, the high notes having a slight pressure and shading off to silence, as though each note were a suppressed sob :—

No. 32. " But Thou didst not leave." Here the sentiment changes from one of gloom to radiant hope and victory, therefore the soloist should change the quality of tone to a bright, ringing timbre, and the solo should be sung with joyful confidence fairly quickly, at about M. 84, four crotchets in a bar.

This is twice as fast as the metronome mark, which is always disregarded.

No. 33. " Lift up your heads." The opening trio part affords a charming contrast to anything in the work, and as much as possible should be made of the antiphonal effects. It opens *piano* and maintains this for four bars, when there is a slight *crescendo*. The tenors and basses ask inquiringly (*mezzo*), " Who is the King of Glory," increasing the tone a little at each repetition. The ladies with confident ardour and pealing voices declare that " The Lord strong and mighty " is the King of Glory. At bar 19 the original theme is repeated, not, as many suppose, in the contralto, but in the tenor part, which should be sung boldly for one bar—other parts singing *piano*—after which the contraltos take the lead. At bar 26 the ladies ask the question, " Who is the King," at first very softly with *crescendo*, until at bar 28 the inquiry is insistent and should be sung as loudly as possible. From this point the chorus proceeds with a massive sweep like a grand, triumphant march heralding the power and might of " The King of Glory." The end of this chorus is, for many reasons, the most convenient place for the interval to be taken. I usually omit Nos. 34 to 37, resuming the work at No. 38— " How beautiful are the feet "—if there be a good flautist, but if not, at No. 39, " Their sound is gone out." This chorus allows a distinct treatment of its sustained notes in the first twelve bars. I regard each minim or semibreve as a point of imitation, and get each voice to *crescendo* with all the power it can on these long sounds. The effect of the voices alternately dominating and irradiating the picture with their ever-increasing sound and

culminating at the basses' top E flat seems to
suggest the brilliance of intersecting flashlights of
our warships at a naval review.

After this figurative electric - light display the
tenors take up their entry *mezzo,* and by degrees
this force is worked up to a *forte* close.

No. 40. "Why do the nations." Should be
sung with great spirit, which should be emphasized
by the contrasts of force in the accompaniments.
If possible the *réprise* should be taken a little
quicker than at the beginning. There is no *ritard.*,
the first time through, but the singer can take the
last three bars of the repeat at will.

No. 41. "Let us break." Usually there is so
much applause at the end of "Why do the
nations "—notwithstanding the announcement that
the audience must not applaud—that a consider-
able time elapses between the end of the solo and
the beginning of the chorus. The choristers should
be prepared for this, and keep the pitch of the
starting note in mind, and when absolute silence is
restored, they, at the conductor's sign, must
ejaculate, "Let us break," like the explosion of an
eighty-ton gun. This is a chorus of defiant vigour,
and all parts must be sung in this vigorous mood.
A fine contrast to everything else in the work is
afforded by the phrase :—

And cast a - way,

where the syncopations must be sung with forceful
dynamic *sforzandos,* and the runs given out like a
rushing, irresistible torrent of sound. The words,

especially at the opening and close, must be very emphatic.

No. 43. "Thou shalt break them." The only point which calls for remark relates to the way in which the solo should close. In the vocal score the voice part ends on the two low A's, but usage and tradition have sanctioned the upper octave for the last G and the penultimate A. Latterly, however, several musical critics have denounced this as "playing to the gallery," as a "departure from good taste," and as "doing violence to the written word," &c.

Personally, I do not mind which ending is given, but I prefer the upper ending because it is distinctly in the picture; it harmonizes with the spirit of the solo, and also, seven bars before, there is the identical low cadence, and to repeat it again so soon produces a sense of anticlimax.

No. 44. "Hallelujah." This *transcendent pæan* stands unique. It is a thing apart from any other composition, therefore it will be unnecessary to dwell upon its points of contrast, and better to deal with the music, so as to reflect the spirit of the words and music in a true worshipful interpretation. It should be sung majestically at about the speed indicated—M. 72, four crotchets to a bar—and not hurried, as it often is. Some conductors fail to realise that it is in the phrasing —the giving of distinction to each group of notes,— rather than in speed, that the secret of maintaining interest is to be found. They act on the principle, "When a piece seems to be falling flat increase the speed," with the result that they often entirely destroy the spirit of the composition. This happens frequently with the "Hallelujah." Really this is not necessary, as, I trust, the following scheme of performance will show.

Open majestically, glorify the first chord, the first word, and the first phrase by singing them as follows:—

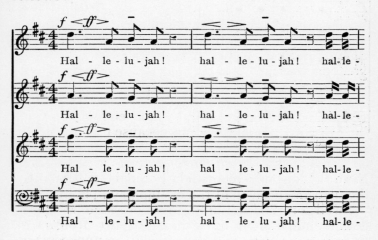

hal - le - lu - jah !

hal - le - lu - jah !

hal - le - lu - jah !

hal - le - lu - jah !

Note that the above model should be followed by the instrumentalists in the opening symphony.

Swell on " Hal " and give pressure to " lu." Although marked *forte*, by means of these swells and pressures the effect will be *fortissimo*. Besides, they give a warmth and glow to the phrase which would be absent were it sung by an unrelieved, swell-less *fortissimo*.

Similarly treat the next four bars in the *dominant*, but with more fervour on account of the pitch being more favourable to increase of tone. The next phrase, " For the Lord God omnipotent reigneth," should be taken in a broad and stately manner at about M. 60, the original *tempo* (M. 72) being resumed at the Hallelujahs. Where the contraltos, tenors, and basses sing the words " For the Lord God," the *tempo* is again slower. At bar 21, where the Hallelujahs come in, the original speed is resumed and carried on until the last beat of bar 34,

where there is a decided slackening of the time and
a diminution of force, as :—

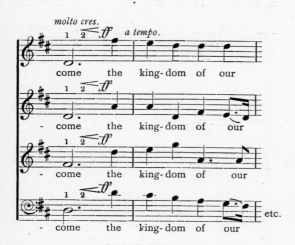

The bass lead which follows sets the pattern for
firm, clean attack. The tenors, having a vowel

favourable for nasal resonance, should give their top A with a brilliant effect, to balance which the second sopranos must join the contraltos in their lead, and to crown the series of entries the sopranos must sing with bright clarion tone without a trace of forcing or wooliness. At bar 52 a series of phrases begins, which I treat rather differently from common usage, as will be seen in the following :—

The sopranos sing " King of kings," and at bar 55 " and Lord of lords," very firmly, but immediately shade off to *piano*. This is done partly to save the voices, partly to prepare for the grand climax at bar 68, but chiefly not to obscure the effect of the " Hallelujahs " of the tenors and basses, and (later) contraltos.

The repetition phrase (bars 58 to 63) is treated similarly, but at bar 64 a change, for which the preceding has been a preparation, takes place as indicated below :—

. . King of kings, ... and Lord of lords . .

The other parts correspondingly increase their force. After the somewhat subdued sustained notes of the preceding phrases, this change comes first as a welcome surprise, then as a thrill, and finally the last two bars 68 and 69 as concentrated ecstatic emotion.

This strenuous effort of the choir calls for a short respite, therefore somewhat less strenuously they go on their even but praiseful way till bars 76 and 78, where the tenors *crescendo* as much as possible on the sustained D's to give distinction to the phrases, there being no fear of the sustained notes swamping the other parts as there was when the prolonged notes were in the soprano part.

To dispel the danger and monotony of being too metronomic, and as a concession to the emotional excitement and exaltation of spirit aroused by the foregoing, it is permissible to make a slight *accelerando* at bars 91, 92, and 93, which is corrected by the very slow majestic *fortissimo* of the final " Hallelujah."

No. 45. " I know that my Redeemer liveth." Appropriately leads the way to the chain of four choruses which follow.

No. 46. " Since by man came death " and " For as in Adam all die," are really quartets, but the immense gain in effect when well sung by the choristers has led to their being regarded as choruses. These two numbers are fine examples of the importance of the curve of sound in phrasing. The first bar of " Since by man " is begun *pianissimo*, and there is a very gradual *crescendo* to the sixth bar, when a sustained *molto dim.* brings the sound down to a whisper again (*see* page 127, *supra*).

In " For as in Adam all die " it is advisable to make the marked *crescendo* to the fourth bar at the word " Adam." From the *forte* reached at this point there is a *molto dim.* to *pianissimo*. In previous choruses I have suggested strengthening parts by other voices to get certain effects or to give prominence to a phrase, but in " Since by man " and " For as in Adam " I always do the opposite.

In the first bar of each chorus the first voices only of each part sing *ppp ;* at bar 2 the second voices join in equally softly, but the increase in numbers gives the desired increase in sound. From this point the whole choir sing the *crescendo* together till the first beat of the last bar, when the first part voices drop out and the second voices of each part finish *ppp* alone. It is perhaps worth remarking that one of the critics to be referred to later said that it was worth attending the performance, if only to hear the exquisite rendering of these two short expressive choruses (*see* page 126, *supra*).

No. 47. " By man came also the resurrection," and No. 49, " Even so in Christ," are sung in a bright, straightforward manner as foils to the slow movements.

No. 50. " Behold, I tell you a mystery," and No. 51, " The trumpet shall sound," always lead to the two final choruses—

No. 55. " Worthy is the Lamb " and its pendant, No. 56, " Amen," which so grandly crown the edifice.

After the comparatively unexciting numbers which follow the " Hallelujah " the apotheosis of the glorified Lamb comes as a welcome and fitting consummation of what has gone before.

For many years I was always dissatisfied with the opening bars of this chorus. True, they were grand and uplifting by the power and sonority of the chords, and one felt that it was a glorious outburst of praise at the word " worthy," but there seemed to me something lacking. I probed into the subject and found the reason to be that the theme was not in the soprano part, as popularly supposed, but was split up between the tenor and contralto parts. This knowledge I put to good account by getting the tenors to sing in bars 2 and 3 with the contraltos at the words " Lamb that was slain." When I first asked the tenors to do it, many shook their heads at the daring innovation, but when I explained the reason, and they, by singing it, had realised the brilliant and quite legitimate effect, they sang it afterwards *con amore*. Though this made the latter part of the theme prominent,

R

the first four notes were not definite enough to call the attention of the listeners to the leading motive. This could only be done by weakening the full sonorous notes of the sopranos and by strengthening the first four notes of the tenors. Therefore the following scheme was evolved, which utilises all the possible force of all the voices which this opening outburst requires :—

Wor - thy is the Lamb that was slain,

1st TENORS for four notes.

Wor - thy is the Lamb that was slain,

2nd SOPRANO and CONTRALTO for four notes.

Wor - thy is the Lamb that was slain,

Wor - thy is the Lamb that was slain,

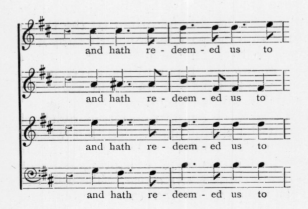

and hath re - deem - ed us to

and hath re - deem - ed us to

and hath re - deem - ed us to

and hath re - deem - ed us to

Putting it in words, it is merely the strengthening of the theme by getting the second contraltos and second sopranos to sing the first four notes of the tenor part, and then the tenors and second sopranos to sing the last four notes of the contralto part to the words " Lamb that was slain."

At bars 11, 12, and 13, where the theme appears in the sopranos, to get a corresponding prominence the first contraltos sing with the sopranos. From this point the chorus proceeds in normal fashion, care being taken, however, to give a *crescendo* in the reiterated notes, the climax being reached at the word " Him," and also to give marked definition to the syncopated notes, as in bar 26 (*see* page 108, *supra*).

The sopranos should practise bars 33 and 34 until the upward rush of the run can be given with brilliance. The contralto and bass runs in bar 65 should be mastered in the same manner. The last three bars should be given with pompous breadth, to lead into the climax of the whole oratorio, the " Amen " chorus (No. 56). The stately subject hardly foreshadows the masterly treatment which it will receive later. A few years back, before its possibilities in performance were revealed, this chorus was regarded as a sort of recessional by most of the audience, who accordingly left while it was being performed.

At the present time it is regarded as almost sacrilege to leave the hall until the last note has been sung, so potent is its spell. The basses open firmly, and the tenors follow. The contraltos cannot make much impression, and therefore the second sopranos help them for four bars and three beats. To secure a uniform following on, the sopranos should commence *mezzo-forte*, making a *crescendo* at bar 17 to bar 19 when, to crown the exposition, all parts (with full organ) should sing *fortissimo*.

The violin interlude is marked *piano* in some copies, but it is better to play it *forte*, and even then it sounds thin compared with the full-voiced choir which comes before and after. The basses, having the theme at bars 26 to 30, must be very emphatic, with rather hard tone, and the same remark applies to bars 33 to 35. From bar 37 to the end the chorus increases in power and interest, if care be taken to make manifest to the ear the close imitations which are seen in the score by the eye of an experienced musician. On page 107 (*supra*) will be found the model of how to perform bars 42 and 43. The following bars, 45 to 48, are performed exactly in the same way, except that they are a fifth lower in pitch :—

In getting a large body of singers to do anything out of the ordinary, like the striking of these notes *forte-piano*, unless what is required to be done is set forth in well-defined formulæ, confusion always arises and failure is the result. It was so with this very example, until the plan was simplified into the following statement.

In these phrases there are in each part two cases of *forte-piano*, that is, at the beginning and the first top note of the point of imitation. Then, after two beats, there is a *crescendo* with pressure marks on the next two high notes. As everything is in "twos" the singers readily grasp the idea. It should be remarked that the seeming exaggeration of the attack is modified greatly by the even tone of the organ, and unless the accents are exaggerated no effect is heard. These throbs of sound coming first in one voice and then in another arouse interest to a wonderful extent, and all sense of strong accent monotony is lost by each voice merging ultimately into a general *fortissimo*.

Here very pronounced accents cease, though the pressures are still agreeably recognizable. At bar 51 the soprano theme can take care of itself, but at bar 52 the tenor theme, being very low, is all the better with some help from the baritones. The subject in contrary motion appears in bar 55, which should be treated as follows :—

This is to prepare for similar treatment of all parts. Note at bars 63 and 64 in each case only two *fp's*

must be given, after which there are a few bars of less pronounced pressures, to secure variety and to avoid over-emphasis. There should be a *decrescendo* in bar 67 to prepare for the repetition in bars 68 and 69 of the treatment of bars 42 and 43. A fine crisis is reached in bar 71 on the first beat which precedes a short *decrescendo* to prepare for the last display of close imitation in bars 72 and 73. Special care should be taken to get these clearly defined, as they are really thrilling when well done. Up to this point the excitement of the listener has steadily increased as the wonderful close imitations have been unfolded by the splendid mastery of the voices, which, as they come surging along in ever-growing volume, sound like the voice of many waters spoken of by the Seer of Patmos. And now comes the supreme effort of all to crown not only this chorus but the whole oratorio with the glory which is its due. The full chorus moves along grandly. The sopranos at bar 75, mounting like brilliant meteors, strike with electrical effect the top A, the basses thunder out the top D, while the tenors glorify the whole with their trumpet-like top A in response to the sopranos, and the whole choir comes ecstatically to the sustained chord before the pause. This pause is held for seemingly a long time ; then every singer summons strength for the final grand " Amen," and the oratorio closes with praise and thanksgiving in the heart of every one who has listened or sung.

From the above outline of the possibilities of *The Messiah* in the way of providing diversity of treatment, it can safely be said that the charge of boredom against this and other works of Handel need not be made if only proper treatment be accorded to them. In addition to the repose, change of atmosphere, and tone-tint provided by the solos, there are many points of contrast and variety of treatment provided by the choruses. Passing these in review they may be summarised as follows :—

" And the Glory."	Bold, bright, and rhythmic.
" And He shall purify."	Reiterated notes and effective " runs."
" O Thou that tellest."	Marked entries of voices, marked contralto phrases, and very marked expression.
" For unto us."	Confident joy, fine cumulative divisions, notable solo phrases in each vocal part, and glorious climaxes.
" Glory to God."	Praiseful trio phrases with contrasted *pianissimo* phrases for tenors and basses.
" His yoke is easy."	Virtuosic treatment of the fine florid subject, and most brilliant climax to wind up Part I.
" Behold the Lamb of God."	Impressive swells and artistic dovetailing of the voices, joined to moving expression.
" Surely He hath borne."	The sob in music ; extended curves of sound ; contrasts of expression in cadences ; the glorifying of sustained sounds and prominence of the percussion of prepared discords.
" And with His stripes."	Realisation of grief of heart by emotional swell.
" All we like sheep."	The outburst of self-condemnation which ends in speechless humility of spirit.
" He trusted in God."	Hard, bitter scorn and jibing sarcasm depicted by harsh nasal tone and howling voices.

" Lift up your heads."	Charming antiphonal effects, varied expression, and triumphant vindication of the power of "The King of Glory."
" Their sound is gone out."	The rousing, illuminating and dominating effect of blazes of sustained sound in alternate voices.
" Let us break."	Fierce, forceful attack and vehement rendering of the syncopations.
" Hallelujah."	Soulful declaration of adoration and praise, each change of sentiment being appropriately met by change of *tempo* and power of voices.
" Since by man."	Example of unaccompanied voice control in negotiating long swell from *pianissimo* to *forte* and back to *pianissimo*.
" By man came also."	Bright, contrasted movement.
" For as in Adam all die."	Similar to " Since by man," but varied in length of sound-curve.
" Even so in Christ."	Confident assurance.
" Worthy is the Lamb."	Distinction of tenor and soprano parts in emphasising theme, glorious rushes of sound in each voice, imposing effect of reiterated notes and triumphant strains of a victorious army.
" Amen."	Apotheosis of choral effect as each series of close imitations rises to higher and still higher expression of ecstatic excitement, culminating in the last grand " Amen."

It will be seen from the above analysis that there is nothing in the whole interpretation which can be considered *ultra vires* or strained, but that it is in strict keeping with the spirit and letter of the oratorio; yet some critics have charged me with exaggeration. This was because I kept introducing one or two points each season, so as not to startle people too much by changing all at once the old stodgy way of performing the work. However, there is no question of the correctness of the interpretation, as there is not a single thing done simply for effect. Nevertheless many things are effective simply because they are the outcome of the spirit of the music itself.

Happily the critics referred to—each of whom has a national reputation—have gradually changed their view, and this year have fully justified the rendering, although I have emphasised more than ever every point mentioned in the foregoing analysis. The fact is that after the shock of the difference of treatment had been overcome, the reasonableness of the new interpretation became manifest even to those who clung for a while to tradition.

THE CHORAL CONDUCTOR.

In speaking of the equipment of a choral conductor, it would be easy to draw a fancy sketch of what he should be—a perfect genius in music ; a master of language and of English in particular ; an exquisite in dress ; a paragon in manner—but these things, though valuable, must give place to other and more serviceable qualifications if success is to be attained.

The first thing a conductor requires is self-reliance, born of mastery of the subject he has to conduct and confidence in himself. If he is nervous and apologetic, if, when he makes a slip, he feels crushed and would like to sink through the floor, he had better leave conducting alone. It is the confident, not-to-be-daunted man who is fit to be a leader of men. Again, the conductor who wishes to excel must be patient in two senses. In the first place he must, till near the performance, tolerate mistakes without signs of ill-temper, remembering that it is only a few amongst his choir who can do things perfectly from the start. Let him be prepared for, say, a score of errors at every rehearsal, and count any diminution from that number as so much gain. But it is the second kind of patience, *i.e.*, waiting patience, which is the more important. It is in this fight with time that most conductors fail. Whatever they do in the way of "labour" they must learn to *wait*. No greater mistake can be made by aspirants in any branch of art than to suppose that as soon as they are fit for a position the position will come. Art will have its price, and waiting is part of that price. One may be justified in believing that "a stone that is fit for the wall is not left in the road," but it is often a long time before that stone is noticed and put into its proper place. Generally speaking, it takes an artist from five to ten years to get proper recognition. In the case of a conductor it usually takes longer, because opportunities for showing his skill come so seldom. I know a number of musicians up and down the British Isles who might have been in high places, but because they were not quickly and sufficiently recognised they gave up the struggle; had they had faith in themselves and waited a little longer they would probably have realised their highest ambition. It seems hard to pass judgment on these men—some of them clever conductors—but this abandonment of the struggle through hope being deferred is perhaps a proof that they lacked the essential staying qualities which every conductor must possess. Therefore it was perhaps fortunate that they quickly retired.

PERSONAL INFLUENCE.

In addition to the cardinal virtue named above, the conductor must have power to inspire, incite, and command—a kind of personal magnetism, which makes his persuasive will law.

To get this power two things are necessary. First, he must be so thoroughly master of the work in hand that the choir have confidence in him and will follow him in everything. Second, he must be an enthusiast in his work. To be the master he must be at the service of all. His zeal must infect his followers, so that the motto *Do ut des* ("I give that you may give") is faithfully carried out. Let these personal traits be acquired, and a kind of beneficent autocracy follows as a matter of course.

THE REHEARSALS.

The conductor must take every precaution to make the rehearsals interesting. The test of a society's success is the popularity of the rehearsals, and the test of the rehearsals is the feeling that if one be not attended something in the way of enlightenment or pleasure has been missed.

Plans for making the rehearsals stimulating and for keeping up the interest have been stated in a previous chapter, but it was not mentioned that a conductor must not be dull. Even if he be ill he must keep a cheerful countenance. He must employ all sorts of legitimate devices for saving time and working to perfection, two of which will be found later under the heads of "Catch Words" and "Motto Words." In fact, thorough preparation in matter and manner for each rehearsal is the touchstone of success.

INTERPRETATION OF PIECES.

The chief function of a present-day conductor is to interpret the music rather than to conduct it. The centre of gravity has been shifted from the mechanical to the mental; from merely directing

the music to grasping and imparting the spirit
behind the notes and words. To accomplish this,
hard thinking and imagination are necessary.
Before the ideal rendering can be given, the work
must have been thoroughly studied privately.
Analysis must always precede synthesis. Through
not doing this conductors fail to give distinction to
performances, and they wonder why they fail.
Other people do not.

Having formulated the plan of interpretation,
then comes the task of transmitting it to the choir.
Remember that highly-sensitive brains are a scarce
commodity. But though this be so, and the
choralists as a body may have, artistically, a low
saturation point, they are often quick at following
a pattern, and are more enthusiastic with their two
talents than others who are blessed with five. This
is the conductor's salvation. He can pattern, they
will imitate ; he can Svengali them into enthusiastic
response.

As to the artistic technique at his disposal, the
rules already tabulated give the conductor ample
scope for every shade of expression or characterization. But every rule needs modification according
to the context of the music. Herein the skill and
individuality of the conductor are revealed. It is
in the judicious toning-down of a rule, or the carrying
to extreme lengths of an idea or principle, that the
artist is displayed. So let the conductor rejoice
that he has the chance in almost every piece
of showing the touch of a gifted soul, or at least
refinement of taste. But while never neglecting the
printed marks of expression, do not let him miss
the ideal through crossing every " t " and dotting
every " i," or he will be a musical example of the

man with the muck-rake. Finally let him remember that, like the conjurer with his inexhaustible hat, he will get out of the piece and the choir exactly what he has put in. Therefore, as the initiation of all artistic results lies with the conductor, he must sow lavishly to reap bountifully.

TACT.

The man who lacks tact is not fit to be a conductor. Tact is the lubricant that keeps the administrative machinery smoothly working when heat and friction would otherwise arise.

TACT IN REHEARSALS.

Making rehearsals enjoyable is a valuable kind of tact, but it is in the management of the mass of singers that this quality, or the lack of it, is made most manifest. One of the best methods is to turn a petty annoyance into a pleasantry, while one of the most tactless things is to be cleverly sarcastic either to the whole body or to a single person. It is so easy and self-satisfying to a conductor to square accounts with some offensive person by a crushing impromptu, that it is hard to resist the temptation. But these things must be avoided. for, boomerang-like, they always rebound.

TACT WITH MEMBERS.

A conductor should always be accessible to every member of his choir; and though it is impossible to give much time to each person, whenever a member speaks to him he should not give the impression of being either bored or in a hurry, but imply that for the time being the member is the only person in the universe. Consideration begets appreciation.

TACT WITH COMMITTEES.

This opens the question, " Is it better to work with or without a committee ? " I say it is better to work with and through a committee. Even when a conductor is supposed to work alone he has always a kind of informal committee. Further, autocracy always breaks down. Conductors should realise that a man is a committee-forming animal— with a strong bias towards being chairman. Therefore they should accept this fact of natural history cheerfully, and with a view to utilising collective brains for the furtherance of artistic purposes. By a little tact this can be done. You make the bolts, the committee shoots them. As a rule committees look to the conductor for initiative; therefore all he has to do is to propose a well-thought-out idea in a courteous manner, and they, thankful that they have got someone to formulate their wishes so admirably, carry the proposition with pleasure. Tact in dealing either with choirs or committees is simply displaying a prompt sweet reasonableness.

TACT IN CONDUCTING.

I once saw a conductor do a most tactless thing. The choir got out of hand and sang much too quickly. Instead of going with them, and by long, decided sweeps of the baton bringing them to the proper *tempo*, he went on beating as usual and gesticulating that they were beats before him. By so doing he showed the audience that there was something wrong, and spoiled the effect of the chorus. This illustrates the general principle that when a conductor is before the public he must not show by any sign of confusion or displeasure that anything is other than perfect. It is always better to go on until some favourable moment when, by a look and sign, the scattered forces can be re-united. Incidentally it should be said that if the conductor referred to had had a firm square beat instead of one of the erratic, " curly " order, the probabilities are that everything would have gone as it ought to have done. Tact in conducting includes looking pleasant, and, by a quick eye and encouraging smile, calling forth that responsive whole-hearted effort upon which, in rehearsal, I lay so much stress.

UNRESPONSIVE CHORALISTS : MALCONTENTS.

A conductor came to ask me what he should do under the following circumstances. He had succeeded a man who was worthily held in high esteem, and whose good work was often referred to by a certain few in a way which implied disparagement of himself. Further, these people were partisans of an unsuccessful candidate, and they were covertly disloyal to the new conductor. This is indeed a common trial, and one with which I could quite sympathise, for thrice I have passed through the same experience. To undergo it is heart-breaking, because you feel not only a lack of sympathetic response, but that everything you say and do is misconstrued, while the covert indifference or open rebellion is like an arctic trickle running

s

down your spine. " The silent smile of slow
disparagement " takes all the heart out of you.
Then you realise the full force of the scriptural
words, " And he did not many mighty works there,
because of their unbelief."

Still, as these conditions do exist, the question
arises " How are they to be met ? " Three plans
present themselves :

   (1) Wear the malcontents down ;
   (2) Win them over ;
   (3) Shake off the dust from your feet and retire.

Plans 1 and 2 usually work concurrently. To be
forewarned is to be forearmed, therefore, as you
know all these disloyal spirits, prepare for their
opposition by putting on the impervious cloak of
indifference to all they say and do. But while you
ignore their conduct, be as polite to them as possible.
Surprise them by your magnanimity. Make them
feel ashamed of themselves. The other members—
outsiders in the feud, but yoursiders in sympathy—
see the game and consciously or unconsciously help
you. In, say, two or three seasons the malcontents
will either have withdrawn or will have become
your ardent supporters. This has been my
experience, at least. Should this not happen, but
your opponents maintain a vendetta spirit, resign
your position, and present your pearls to those who
will appreciate them, or the worry will kill both
your reputation and yourself.

THE REWARDS OF LEADERSHIP.

Young aspirants for the conductor's baton,
reading the above, and bearing in mind what was
said about a probationary stage of five or ten years'

hard work with the choir on the technical and
artistic sides before due recognition comes, will
probably ask the question, " Is the game worth the
candle ? " To this I say decidedly " Yes." It is
true that it seems a long time to look forward to,
but the time will go whether effort be made or not,
and it will be certainly better to have acquired some
assets at the end of a decade than to talk of what
might have been.

But this ten years' waiting is not all desert.
Although a conductor may not get commensurate
reward for his time, work, and skill, he will get some
recognition. He will be having continual, if humble,
feasts by the way. It is said that to the members
of each choir there is only one perfect conductor
and that is their own. If you be that conductor, is
it nothing to have the devoted service and
enthusiastic regard of your own choir ; to have them
helping you in your ambitions ; to have the delights
of a long vista of glorious successes, although made
merely in your own little circle; to feel that each
year some progress has been made and that the
goal is nearer than it was ; to feel growing power
within you and with it an enlarged vision of what
you can do in the future ?

It is no small thing to have the delights mentioned
above to tone down the many disheartening worries
incidental to being in the wilderness. The sum
total of it all is this : The joys of the struggle are
worth the sacrifices. Therefore let the determined
aspirant " rejoice and be glad " that there are these
difficulties, because they form the testing fires which
eliminate the clever but weak, the brilliant but shifty,
the steady but stodgy, while they bring out the fine
qualities of the man of parts, power, and reliability.

HOW TO SELECT A CHOIR.

This question is often asked, and it is impossible to answer it unless the conditions and the resources of the district are known. Further, the nature of the choir, whether for a village concert, a competition, or a Musical Festival, must be considered. If it be in a district where singers are scarce, then it is a good policy to take in everybody who wishes to join the choir, and press in every singer who would otherwise stand aloof. But there are many districts where there is an abundance of singers who are only waiting for a leading spirit to gather and re-organize the remains of choral societies which, from one cause or another, have become defunct or are in a state of suspended animation.

Assuming that singers are available, what should be the basis of admission into a choir or choral society? Should it be social position, nomination, or individual examination? It will have to be one of the three. You cannot mix two or three systems together. I doubt if even music would soothe the breast of a young lady who, having passed the test for admission successfully, has insult added to injury when her neighbour gives her to understand that she (her neighbour) is a "superior person," having been introduced by nomination and not by test.

As to the social qualifications, I am convinced that, other things being equal, the better a singer has been educated the more refined are the results obtainable. But while admitting, with pleasure, that some of the most energetic and enthusiastic singers I have ever met are high in the social scale, it would be fatal to a high standard of performance to elect members upon social position alone, because so many would join and then refuse to work. This I have seen over and over again in societies. The best plan, therefore, is to insist on vocal and reading ability as being the basis of admission to a choir. This has good effects both positive and negative, for while it secures only useful members it chokes off shoals of pretentious people who never get as far as the examination room through fear of the test.

VOICE AND READING POWER.

I attach the utmost importance to reading power. I do not mean that a person without a voice at all should be admitted ; but I always prefer singers with good average voices who can read fairly well, to singers with really good voices who cannot read, or can read only indifferently. The reasons for this preference are these : With good readers of average voice I can extract every ounce of tone they have in them ; whereas one can never get half the normal power out of a body of poor readers owing to their lack of confidence, while if they should take it into their heads to " sing out " they often do more harm than good. Again, the confident singer, by hitting the note fair in the middle gets twice or thrice the amplitude of vibration, with its four-fold or nine-fold increase of intensity and loudness. Mathematically stated it stands thus :

	Power.	Attack.	Total.
The good voice (unit of power)	4	× 1	= 4
The average voice (unit of power)	3	× 2	= 6

As to the standard of the tests imposed upon candidates, these should not only be comparatively easy, but designed to show what the candidates know rather than to find out what they do not know. There should be (*a*) an easy voice-test, (*b*) a time-test, and (*c*) a tune-test. But though easy they should be accurately done, as it is this positive certainty which gives the promise of future pliability and responsiveness. Some conductors test candidates by choosing some difficult piece from an oratorio at random, and if the candidate is approximately correct he or she is accepted. This is not a good method, as it puts a premium on mere guesswork, and is no test of what a candidate is able to master.

The following are specimens of the tests used by the Sheffield Musical Union :—

(1) A sight-test in the major mode, including transitions to related keys, of moderate difficulty :

(2) A sight-test in the minor mode, about as long as the above (8 or 10 bars) ;

(3) A time-test, to be sung on one tone ;

(4) The voice-test as follows, which is required to be sung with clear articulation, and due regard to expression :

For He shall give His an - gels charge o - ver thee, that their hands shall uphold and guide thee, lest . . thou dash thy foot a- gainst a stone, they shall pro- tect . . . . thee. His mer - cies on thou - - sands fall, . . on thou - sands, on thou - - - - - - - sands fall.

For the World Tour Choir the voice-tests were:—

" Hear ye, Israel " (sopranos),
" Woe unto them " (contraltos),
" If with all your hearts " (tenors),
" Lord God of Abraham " (basses).

CHOICE OF VOICES.

The saying that " nothing beats a good old voice except a good young one " is only true when the old voice is a worn voice, and not primarily the

voice of an old singer. If I were selecting a choir
for, say, a competition, I should prefer voices of
sopranos and contraltos from twenty to forty years
of age, tenors and basses from twenty-five to
forty-five. This is only a rough average, because
some of the best choralists I know, both ladies and
gentlemen, have attained their jubilee. Certainly
the rich, mature, mellow voices of the middle age
are to be preferred to the thinner voices of the
young singers. But some one may remark, " Do
we not miss the ring of young, fresh voices in the
choir formed of older people ? " Not of necessity.
Voices are what we term fresh when they attack the
notes firmly with good ring, and are free from the
upward " scoop " and the downward " swoop " and
the harsh metallic quality which some singers
develop. As these defects more frequently occur
in old singers than in young ones we associate them
with the seniors. But really, if care be taken, old
singers can keep their voices fresh and vigorous,
while they have the advantage of fulness and
power. While making this defence of old singers I
do not undervalue young ones. Young, clear,
bright voices form the complement of the mature
voices, and should never be absent from a choir.
The ideal choir is one in which both old and young
are represented—that is, if the old singers have taken
care of their voices. If, on the other hand, they
have developed a shrill, wiry, drawling tone, drastic
measures should be taken to exclude these fossilized
voices. Therefore it would be a good thing if every
important society were to pass a rule to have a
re-examination of every one of its members once
every five years. Further consideration is given to
this subject under the heading next to be considered.

COMPETITIONS.

Although choral singing has made tremendous progress both in quantity and quality during the last fifty years, and more especially during the twentieth century, the great outstanding fact has been the astounding development of the competitive musical festival, which has now an assured place in the musical life of the British Empire.

Therefore it will not excite surprise if I state that I have received scores of letters asking for advice on matters relating to competitions, such as the choice of test-pieces, how to perform them, how to select voices and train them, balance of parts, how to maintain pitch, &c. The accumulated evidence that thousands of earnest-souled conductors are keenly interested in the varied topics connected with competitions has greatly influenced me in writing these pages.

Though designed for the choral society conductor in general, I have ever kept in mind the competitive conductor who, as a rule, likes to know the why and the wherefore of everything that affects marks at a competition. But though I have gone fairly well into details, I propose to give, in these final chapters, hints, suggestions, directions, and advice which the ordinary society conductor would think too minute, too exacting, or too elaborate for an ordinary choral society, but which conductors and choirs who delight in competitive struggles will examine carefully to find a few grains of wheat to add to the desired garner of 100 per cent.

It should be said that in the following pages nothing is suggested or recommended that has not been put to the test and found to be of advantage artistically. My apology for mentioning some apparently trivial matters is that I know that competing choirs have nothing to give away, and nothing must be overlooked which is likely to yield a point or even half that amount.

THE PENALTY OF COMPETING.

The primary fact which should be *burned* into the mind of every competitor, from the conductor to the humblest member of the choir, is that *trouble* is inevitable. This trouble may be taken before or after the event. If taken before, it assumes the form of hard work and self-sacrifice. If competitors refuse to take it in this form they get trouble all the same, only it comes after the event in the shape of disappointment and chagrin which may rankle for years. Therefore, let each competitor be prepared to take just the kind of trouble which he or she is called upon to bear, and not begin the slacker's whine that if it had only been some other kind of burden or pinch they would have borne it without a murmur. Really there should not be a murmur, because if anyone goes into a competition in the right spirit, the doing, striving, and working are the pleasant features of the whole business, just as the exhausting efforts in hockey, tennis, football, and cricket are the joy of the sport.

Therefore let the point of view be, Work with pleasure, and the outcome will be the pleasure with the work.

HOW TO ACHIEVE SUCCESS.

The heartbreaking thing about many societies is the "Come easy, go easy" attitude of a large percentage of the members.   In a competitive choir you stand on a different platform.   You can regard inertia as non-existent, and can frame your plans on fighting lines.   Therefore, as you have only to command and obedience is given, let the following be two of your working axioms :—

(*a*) Method is the secret of success ;
(*b*) Divide and conquer.

Do everything methodically in the sense that you know *why* you are doing it, and do not try to do too many things at once.   First make sure of the music, then the words, then the expression, then the blend and balance of voices, the attack and release. Of course these things will be considered together, but let the emphasis be placed on each point in turn, so that it may not be overlooked.

HOW TO MASTER THE MUSIC.

To accomplish this in the minimum of time it is essential that the conductor be absolutely familiar with every note before the rehearsals begin.   I do not know whether it be telepathy, sympathy, or what, but if a conductor knows the work, somehow the choir learns it in half the time, although he may say little and correct less frequently than if he did not know the work well.

Therefore he should obtain the music at the earliest moment and play it over—or better, get someone else to play it—a dozen times. Personally I find a score of times preferable. This is to get a subconscious grasp of the key progressions and a sense of the harmonic structure. Meanwhile he should sing each part in succession and put a circle round every difficult interval for reference at rehearsal. Specially hard or strange transitions and unusual discords should be played over and over again till they have sunk into his inner consciousness. With this equipment, and concurrent independent study of the words, he will be prepared to begin rehearsals.

THE FIRST REHEARSAL.

As an index of the earnest, thorough spirit which is to be characteristic of the whole preparation and consummation of the contest, tackle the difficulties at once by the Specializing Method (*see* pages 13, 14). Take each difficult interval seriatim, and insist upon every member putting a ring round each treacherous leap in his or her part.

THE BLUE PENCIL.

Here allow me to digress for a few words on the blue pencil. It should be a law of the Medes and Persians that every member has always a *blue* pencil to mark all instructions from the desk. Some clever ones will object to the unnecessary labour, but insist, or you will pray to be delivered from "clever but idle choristers," who are a terror to the conductor. The uses of the blue pencil are manifold. The mere re-marking of an existing mark calls attention to the composer's wishes, and supplementary signs are often needed. The marks help the singers to memorise the music more quickly by acting as guide-posts, and when used at the concert or contest the singer can see these at a glance, and they are reminders at the supreme moment of performing. Therefore insist on its use, for great is the power of the blue pencil. After this digression we will proceed with the rehearsal.

The cautionary explanations having been given, the music should be attempted and repeated until the general " hang " of the work has been realised. If errors are made, call attention to them, but do not let them delay you, as you will deal with them later.

WORDS.

As mentioned before, the words are usually the weakest part in a rendering, more marks being lost in this section than any other. Therefore, from the first, great attention should be given to the words. It would be found an admirable thing to have three minutes' lip, tongue, and mouth (facial muscles) drill at each rehearsal, going through the articulatory exercises given on page 84.

After the music has been tried, the conductor should pattern the words for the choir to imitate and memorise in the process. The plot or idea of the poem should be explained, and the meaning of obscure or unusual words should be made clear. This will prevent misconceptions and quaint questions, such as one that arose after singing the line

" O with what divers pains they met,"

when a young lady in my choir asked, " *Do* divers
have special pains ? "

The latter part of the rehearsal might be devoted
to arranging special private sectional rehearsals for
each part, the object being to perfect the knotty
points in each division. These private rehearsals
are invaluable. When the Sheffield Musical Union
had Beethoven's *Mass in D* to get up in less than a
month for the Kruse Festival performance in
Queen's Hall, London, the sopranos formed themselves into groups of about a dozen, and rehearsed
at each other's houses. The contraltos, tenors, and
basses did the same, with the result that I doubt if
ever so difficult a work was got up so well in
so short a time. This plan should be followed by
competing choirs, as it not only tends to note-
perfection, but develops that enthusiasm which is
essential to real success—a brilliant performance,
whether the prize be won or not.

THE VOICE.

The importance of the voice in all choral work,
and especially in competitions, is so manifest that
nothing need be said to emphasise this fact.

The two features which need chief attention from
a contesting point of view are, first, the selection of
the proper class of voices, and secondly, the
cultivation of homogeneity so as to secure perfect
blend. With respect to the first point, I would
strongly recommend that efforts be made to
include a certain proportion, say 15 per cent. to
20 per cent., of voices which are pure in quality
even though they may be light in quantity. This
applies especially to sopranos and tenors. These

clear, pure voices have a value far beyond their mere volume of sound. They have a carrying power which is of great importance in giving clear outline to the melody or theme, even when it appears in the lower parts. This purity of tone cuts through the less pure sounds, and the fuller but duller, sometimes rather breathy, voices seem to build round or coalesce with the clear, pure tones and make a grand compound tone, which is suffused with the radiance of the lighter, brighter voices. Therefore if you require, say, twenty-five sopranos, and you have the chance of taking that number of full, rich voices which can reach B flat with or without an effort, you would act wisely to reject five in favour of the same number of light, pure-toned sopranos. I have singers in my choir, in all parts, who are known to have light voices in solo work, but who are regarded by their colleagues as amongst the very best singers, on account of the carrying and binding effect of their voices. Some years ago the theoretical carrying power of weak but pure sounds was practically demonstrated to me. I was in the country, and heard in the distance a boy whistling. As the lumbering cart which he was driving came nearer, its noise drowned the whistling, but as it passed, the pure sound became louder and louder. This is what I have realised again and again in my choir. It is the pure voice, even when it is not powerful, that tells.

For securing quality, unity, and blending in the choir as a whole, there should be ten minutes' practice of Exercise 1 on the lines recommended on pages 22-24. Another plan which I have found very useful is to have the singers ranged round the room in a circle. The conductor, being in the

centre, is able to get to any singer and listen as he
or she sings, and give such hints as are necessary.
It puts the singers on their mettle, because a tactful
conductor commends audibly all good singers and
singing. As both the maintenance of pitch and the
development of artist tone require the same kind of
voice-production, each piece should occasionally be
hummed through, not only to cultivate these
excellences, but to promote good chording, balance,
and blend, for if these points are perfectly secured
in soft singing there is small fear of falling off in
forte passages. The phrase " Sing with your ears."
is a favourite direction, which quickens perception
both in chording and in keeping the pitch.

EXPRESSION.

After the exhaustive treatment already given to the
subject, there seems little left to say on expression ;
but there are one or two points which the conductor
would do well to consider, as I have found them
very useful. The first point is : Get steeped in,
and grasp, the atmosphere of the piece during its
frequent reiteration. Always endeavour to get
inside the subtleties of a piece. In this spirit, at
each rehearsal look out for and seize upon any
feature which will bear development in order to
produce a legitimate and striking effect. If the
word or music seems to demand a special emphasis
or shading-off that is not indicated in the printed
copy, put it to the test by getting it performed as
you suggest, and if the effect be good and " in the
picture," incorporate it in the design of expression.
This varying of expression is common enough in
concert performances, but to make any change in

a test-piece is a very debatable point, and sometimes very risky, because some adjudicators are fossilized legalists, who abide by the letter and ignore the spirit of a piece beyond what is in black and white. Fortunately the majority of adjudicators are responsive to everything that is artistically correct, and they appreciate little touches which show well-judged perception. Personally I believe there may be several correct ways of rendering a phrase, and if the rendering at the contest shows proper proportion and unity of design I give full marks, although the printed instructions may not have been strictly followed.

SINGING WITH IMPULSE FROM WITHIN.

The next point I lay stress upon is this: Inspire the choir to sing "through the impulse from within." The ideal choralist is one who learns the piece so thoroughly that he becomes a reflex of the conductor's wishes. But there is something even beyond this, viz., becoming so imbued with the spirit behind every note and nuance that the work could be sung without any guidance at all from the conductor. It is this singing from within that gives the glow of super-excellence to a performance, because the ethereal essence of the soul is thereby revealed.

PERSONIFICATION OF ABSTRACT EXPRESSION.

It is when a large body of choralists sing with this impulse from the inner consciousness that the expression seems to become personified, as though it were a living thing. Then every rise and fall of sound, every accent, pressure-note, or shading-off

T

appears to be the manifestation of a sentient being, a something quite apart and distinct from the persons who are the vehicle of the sounds.

This facility should be aimed at because when it is realised the listeners, including adjudicators, are simply carried away by its subtle effect.

SINGING FROM MEMORY. RESTS.

No singer should be allowed to sing in a competition who has not learnt the words and music by heart. It is only by this thoroughness that the best mechanical results can be obtained, to which must be added the inward impulse just mentioned. Still, notwithstanding that the choir may know the music perfectly, the singers should use the copies at the performance. A glance will remind them of critical or delicate phrases, and keep them right when there are rests. More catastrophes at performances occur through neglect of "rests" than from any other cause. The things which make me run cold when I recall them are connected with the rests. Of course what is a tragedy to one person may be a comedy to another. Once when I was adjudicating at Keighley a choir was singing finely and with triumphant swing, when an absent-minded beggar came in boldly at a rest. The conductor gave a tremendous stamp, and exclaimed " That 's done it." It was as he said. This shows (*a*) the importance of calling attention to "rests," especially where similar phrases have pauses of different lengths, as in the first chorus of *The Golden Legend* and in the " Soldiers' Chorus" from Berlioz's *Faust*, and (*b*) suggests that it is too risky to sing without occasionally glancing at the copies.

CATCH-WORDS.

There are certain errors which in every season, and almost at every rehearsal, recur over and over again with the inevitability of recurring decimals, and it becomes tiresome to have to repeat the same old reproof or caution in the same dull, prosy, matter-of-fact fashion. But if you can convey the correction in a pleasant or humorous manner, you gain your point by changing irritation into inspiration.

Whenever possible I endeavour to get a word or short phrase to embody a well-understood idea, and by its use prevent long explanations, corrections, and tiresome reproofs.

It would be impossible to tell how much time and temper have been saved by such words as " No inertia," " Make it cut," or " Cut," "Happy land," " Back again," " Thrill." These represent different ideals, and they give in few words a warning, a reproof, or stimulus, often while the choir are singing.

The word "Cut" refers to giving the supreme edge of virtuosity to vocal effort. It sprang into life at the closing rehearsals for an important musical festival. The pieces were going splendidly, but still I was not quite satisfied. Some members with strong tendencies towards inertia blurred, by their lack of quick response, the photographic clearness of the attack, release, words, or expression, which was necessary to give the desired 100 per cent. in every division. So I said to them, " You all know that in making a razor, after all the material has been prepared, the blade has to be forged, smithed, hardened, ground, glazed, and polished. In the hafting quite as many processes have to be gone through. Notwithstanding these processes and the value of the materials, the razor is useless unless it is carefully whetted—that is, given a cutting edge.

" Now if it would be foolish not to give the cutting edge to the razor after the whole of the work of preparation had been done, it would be equally foolish of you not to crown your work by putting forth the final effort of carefulness, alertness, and overcoming inertia, to give clear words, delicate shadings, massive climaxes, &c., and thus secure thrills, by making your singing ' cut.' "

After many a concert members have come to me and said, " Haven't we made it ' cut ' ! "

The phrase " Happy land " has proved very useful. It relates to the common fault of omitting the aspirates. Everybody knows that they should be given, but in singing they are frequently dropped. To call attention to the omission in a direct way might be taken as an insult; therefore I call attention to it by the words " Happy land," which arose in this way : We were rehearsing a phrase which contained several aspirates, which were not given. I did not wish to suggest that the singers did not know how to do the correct thing, so I said, "I will tell you a story and you shall apply the moral yourselves " :—

" A man was singing ' 'Appy land, 'Appy land, O is not this a 'Appy land.' His friend said ' Tom, why don't you mind your aitches,' to which Tom replied, with superior scorn, ' That shows you know nothing about music ; it only goes to G.' "

The shaft struck home, and now it is only necessary to say " 'Appy land " to correct a common and recurring error.

MOTTO WORDS.

However ardent choristers may be, there comes a time when the incessant strain of preparation becomes so irksome that a stimulus of some sort is necessary. It therefore becomes imperative for conductors to counteract this physical weariness by some mental uplift. This I have found can be supplied by any short phrase which represents an ideal for the singer. These phrases or words I call "Motto words"; their influence is somewhat similar to that of "Excelsior" in the poem.

As a practical illustration I will take the words "The unexpected" and "The impossible." When preparing for the first Sheffield Festival I told the choir that the critics would expect very good voices, but not brilliant tone; grand *fortes*, but not overpowering climaxes; delightful *pianos*, but not ethereal shadings; clear words, but not perfect diction. These unlooked-for excellences being unexpected would captivate and thrill them, therefore the point to work up to and for was— "The unexpected." The words acted like a charm, an ideal was set up, and all worked until "The unexpected" was realised.

At the following festival we had several difficult works in which real perfection was never expected, because it was thought impossible for a large body of singers to acquire the vocal technique demanded, nor could they attain the required flexibility of voice. It will be seen that to reach perfection we had to achieve "The impossible." This became our watchword, and was both a challenge and a stimulus. Could we do the "Impossible"? Well, we would try, and, as results proved, we succeeded.

Motto words should be reserved for supreme events such as musical festivals and important competitions. Let each conductor seize upon some word or ideal which arises out of the test-piece or the conditions of the competition, and then he will be able to use the Motto with electrical effect.

Let it be borne in mind that there must be an ideal, because the words used are simply a terse way of glorifying the preconceived idea.

THE EXCELLENCE OF CUMULATIVE EFFECT.

The present-day conductor must aim at excellence in every detail of every piece performed. This is a somewhat different attitude from that of old. The unimportant choruses of an oratorio were treated with scant respect, and all the trouble was devoted to the favourites. Many a time have I heard it said, " Oh, never mind this chorus going badly; wait till we give 'The Heavens are telling'"; or "It does not matter how we sing ' He trusted in God'; we'll show them 'Who is the King of Glory'"! This "in-and-out" singing must be avoided, because every time the mind of the audience is allowed to lose its grip of perfection it takes some time to get it back to an appreciative mood; whereas if a consistent level of excellence is maintained, the cumulative effect is such that the hearers pass from pleasure to excitement, ending in rapturous delight. Several festivals that I recall owe the unique impression they made to this fact. The works taken singly were not sufficient to arouse such wonderful enthusiasm; but as each one in succession was perfectly rendered, the mind was dazzled and the soul was carried away in wonder and rapture. Therefore, in competitions have no weak or doubtful phrases. " Leave no unguarded place," but " from strength to strength go on," and you will carry the adjudicators with you.

CONCENTRATION AT THE END.

In all important work care must be taken not to get stale. Always leave sufficient freshness to be able to give concentration to the final touches. At the last rehearsals I often let the choir do very little singing, but call attention to each topic seriatim, taking the more difficult points of technique first. For instance, every *sforzando* or *fp* is referred to and patterned, and perhaps imitated by the choir ; *staccatos* are referred to ; all *pianissimo* passages are sung ; the words in special places are repeated, points of imitation are tried, and a word of encouragement given. This specialization and concentration, while they rest the voice and the body, call attention to the salient points which have been already mastered, but which must be at command at the critical moment of performance.

VALUE OF PRINTED DIRECTIONS.

In the course of the preparation circumstances may arise which tend to chill or dishearten the singers. Some important member may be laid aside by illness ; others may be dissatisfied ; there may be disunion, or the work undertaken may be too great to be done in the given time. In these and similar circumstances it will be necessary to adopt some means to maintain enthusiasm, and to brace the members for the task in hand. A cheerful spirit on the part of the conductor is a great factor. But something is wanted to plead with the singer when the conductor is absent; therefore an occasional well-considered personal appeal in the form of a circular or manifesto often produces the desired results. As an ounce of example and fact is of more weight than a pound of surmise and precept, I beg to illustrate this point by circulars, &c., which I issued on one or two important occasions. These have been in such request by conductors and others that their publication may be found very acceptable (*see* Appendix II.).

Finally, I would say that although I have endeavoured to meet every problem connected with Choral Technique and Interpretation, there may be and probably are topics upon which some readers may require further information. Any queries on these topics, addressed to the writer, c/o Novello & Co., Ltd., shall have every attention.

The tabulated "Notes of Interpretation" given in Appendix I. will illustrate in part the manner in which the foregoing principles of expression can be applied. Different types of compositions have been purposely selected.

APPENDIX I

THE FOLLOWING ARE NOTES ON SOME OF THE
PIECES WHICH WERE SUNG AT QUEEN'S HALL,
LONDON, ON JUNE 1ST, 1911, IN CONNECTION WITH
THE INTERNATIONAL CONFERENCE OF MUSICIANS;
AND ON THE WORLD TOUR, 1911.

You are requested to number each bar of each piece carefully,
and to write on each copy the instructions relating to your own
part, as well as all general instructions.

The pieces chosen are of the highest class, and are worthy of
selection on account of their excellence, and also as affording
the choir full scope for their powers.

Madrigals in general are inadequately performed, either
because the proper idea of how to interpret madrigals is not
grasped, or because the singers will not be at the trouble of
mastering the difficult phrasing. What is required is that the
themes or points of imitation should be known to the singer,
and then sung in such a way as to individualise each subject
without obscuring the entry of the point of imitation in the
succeeding voices.

The following hints are given to enable this to be done.

" HOSANNA TO THE SON OF DAVID." *Gibbons.*

This contains five principal subjects :—

The first extends from bar	1 to 11.
„ second „	„	„	11 „ 21.
„ third „	„	„	21 „ 37.
„ fourth „	„	„	37 „ 40.
„ fifth „	„	„	41 „ 49.

and from bar 50 to 66 the first theme is worked up to the
final climax.

DETAILED INSTRUCTIONS.

Bar.	Beat.	Voice.	
1	1	Tenor	First Theme, given by tenors, to be phrased as follows:—

Ho - san - na *to* the Son of Da - vid

Bar.	Beat.	Voice.	
2	1	1st S.	Firm attack at " Ho."
	3	2nd C.	„ „ „
4	1	B.	Bass entry „
	3	1st C.	„
			At each succeeding entry follow this plan.
11		1st S.	Strike B flat firmly and truly, then *dim.* in all parts at word " David."
	3	T.&B.	These commence second subject at " Blessed." Emphasise first syllable.
12		1st S.	Pressure on syncopated C at " Blessed," then *dim.* to end of phrase.
12	4	1st C.	Marked pressure at " Bless."
13	2	2nd C.	„ „ „
			This pattern to be well followed in all parts.
19 and 20		C.& S.	Sing words clearly on crotchets in soprano and contralto.
21	2	1st S.	Fresh theme started in sopranos. Sing " Blessed be the " with marked entry.
22	2	2nd S.	Counter theme " Blessed be the " to be struck firmly and sung prominently for four notes. This phrasing is continued to bar 37.
26	2	2nd S.	Climax note D to be sung with jubilation.
30	2	1st S.	This phrase to be treated in same way.
37	1 and 2	T.&B.	Strike firmly, then *molto dim.* to *piano*, so as not to interfere with *p* entry of sopranos and contraltos at beat 2. Secure real *p* in each part from bar 37 to first beat of bar 41.

Bar.	Beat.	Voice.	
41	2	2nd S.	Fifth subject started; the first seven notes "and Glory in the Highest" must be emphasised.
44	2	2nd C.	Theme to be brought out, other parts subordinate.
45	3	1st C.	Subject to be well defined, „ „ „
46	4	2nd S.	Theme „ „ „ „ „ „
48	4	1st S.	„ „ „ „ „ „
49			Theme started firmly in all parts and then *dim.* on beats 3 and 4.
50			All parts *p* except 1st contralto, which begins original theme "Hosanna" very firmly and *forte.* Tenors on fourth beat bring out same theme, and other voices follow. Last eight bars to be sung as jubilantly as possible.

"As Vesta was from Latmos Hill." *Weelkes.*

"As Vesta" contains 10 themes :—

First theme is commenced by sopranos in bar 3, beat 4.

Second theme commences in bar 9, " She spied."

Third theme commences in bar 12 in the contraltos, the ascending scale-passage being the chief feature.

Fourth theme commences in bar 22 at "attended," by 1st sopranos.

Fifth theme is announced by 1st sopranos at end of bar 32, " to whom Diana's darlings."

IMPORTANT.—Sixth theme is led off by the bass on fourth beat of bar 35, "came running down amain."

Seventh theme is delicately given by the 2nd sopranos and contraltos in bar 47, "first two by two."

Eighth theme is announced by 2nd sopranos on beat 4, bar 60, "and mingling with."

Ninth theme appears in 2nd sopranos, beat 2, bar 65.

Tenth and most important theme is announced vehemently by the 2nd tenors, beat 2, bar 81, " Long live fair Oriana." At bar 85 the basses have the theme in quadruple augmentation, which on account of the length of the notes is not realised by the ear. But at bar 104 the augmented subject in the bass can be easily followed, and if the other parts will subordinate themselves to this the most impressive feature of the madrigal, a splendid result and triumphant finish will be achieved.

Bar.	Beat.	Voice.	
3	4	1st S.	This subject should be sung in all parts as follows :—
L.			*cres.* *f* *p* As Ves - ta was de -scend - ing
4	2	C.	The downward quavers should be given firmly.
11	4	C.	Pressure on " the same " and marked *cres.* on the upward scale. The whole phrase is to be sung as follows :— *f* *p* the same as - cend - - - - ing
13	4	S.	Theme to be given firmly, and 1st contraltos should join them for bars 14 and 15.
15	4		Tenor lead " the same," with emphasis on the scale-passage.
18		2nd S.	Emphasis on scale-passage.
20		1st S.	„ „ „ „
22		1st S.	„ „ " at."
23	1	All	„ „ " at."
27		1st T.	More emphasis on " at."
28		All	Very emphatic " at," especially in bass.
32	4	1st S.	" To whom Diana " delicately sung, other parts *pp*.
34	2	2nd S.	Theme brought out, but not too prominently. All parts finish *pp* end of bar 35, to allow the soft entry of the basses " came running " to be distinctly heard.
35	4	B.	Slight emphasis on " came running," then marked *dim.*
36		1st T.	Emphasis on " came run-" then *dim.*

Bar.	Beat.	Voice.	
36	2	2nd S.	Emphasis on "came run-" then *dim.*
	3	1st S.	„ „ „ „ This pattern to be followed for next 10 bars, with constant *crescendo* to bar 47, then *molto dim.*
47	4	2nd S. & C.	"First two by two," *pp* slightly *staccato ;* ditto in other voices to bar 52, then follow markings of music.
60	4	2nd S.	"And mingling with the shepherds" slightly prominent, other parts *pp*.
62	4	1st S.	Theme "And mingling" rather prominent.
65	2	2nd S.	"With mirthful" prominent.
	4	1st S.	"With mirthful tunes" prominent.
74 to 79		All	Bold, full, *sostenuto* chording.
81		All	*Dim.*
	2	2nd T.	Bold entry at "Long live." From here to the end, bar 116, emphasis must always be given to "long live." ("Oriana" being at high pitch can take care of itself.)
89		All	*Dim.* to *p*, then gradual *cres.* to bar 102, when all parts make a *decrescendo* to allow the emphatic entry of the basses at bar 104 to be heard most distinctly. From bar 104 to 110 the bass must dominate the music, and the last six bars must be in jubilant *fortissimo* in every part.

" FIRE, FIRE ! "   *Morley.*

1		All	Firm sustained *forte.* Cancel pressure mark $>$
2	2	2nd S.	Strike firmly.
	3	All	*ff* quick *molto dim.* to *piano*.
	4	1st S.	*ff* firm attack.
3	1	1st S.	*fp*.
3	3	2nd S. C.T. B.	*fp* on minim.

Bar.	Beat.	Voice.	
4			Same as bar 3.
5 and 6			Sing as marked in copy.
7	2 to 4	B.	Prominent for 4 beats, other parts *p*.
8	2 to 4	2nd S.	” ” ” ”
9 and 10	4	2nd S.	Syncopated note *fp*; pressure to be put on each quaver.
11	1	1st S.	Sing E♭ very firmly.
12 to 24		All	Sing real *pianissimo*, but preserve same relative variations of pressure on notes.
24 to 27		All	Sing as marked in copy.
28 to 33		2nd S.	Real *pianissimo* in 2nd sopranos.
28 to 33		1st S.	1st sopranos as follows:—

34	2 to 4	C.	Four notes well marked, then *p*.
35	2 to 4	1st S.	” ” ”

("Then call for help").

36 and 37		T.	Prominent $<\ >$
37 and 38	4	B.	Four notes prominent.
38 to 43	4	2nd S.	Leading voice. Sing chiefly against musical accent, as follows:—

43	2	T. B.	In each part sing the first note of the
	4	C.	point of imitation *ff*, with full
44	2	1st S.	broad vowel at the word "Fa"

Bar.	Beat.	Voice.	
45 to 49	3	2nd S.	(pronounce " Fah "), then quickly shade off to *piano*, saying all the " la's " very lightly at the tip of the tongue. This will allow the point of imitation to be heard distinctly in each part.
50	4	1st S.	
51	2	C.	
51	4	2nd S.	All these " C's " must be struck *ff* spasmodically with very quick release to *mp* (= *ff*, *mp* or *ffp*).
52	2	T.	
52	4	1st S.	
53	1	B.	
53	4	T.	
54 to 56		All	*Dim.* to *p* in all parts.
57 to end		All	Repetition of above instructions, only last phrase must be sung as *f* as possible with a good tone.

" In the Merry Spring." *Ravenscroft.*

The words of this piece must be sung very daintily. Mind contrasts of *piano* and *forte*.

2		All	Slight swell on word " spring."
8	1 and 2	S.	Pressure and clear word.
10 to 12		T.	Very vigorous *f* entry of tenors, who dominate these three bars.
16 to 19		All	Rather slower. Words with mock grief.
20		All	Original tempo.
28 to 29			Chief point of piece is in these two bars.
		All	In each voice sing the first quaver with great pressure *f*; the succeeding three quavers very lightly, with delicate vowel rather *staccato*, and the minim *ffp*.
30		S. C.	Very emphatic " No, no, no, no, not I !" In second verse sing as first verse, but repeat third and fourth bars from end bars 59 and 60.

"In Going to My Lonely Bed." *Edwards.*

(*See* pages 191-193.)

Bar.	Beat.	Voice.	
1 to 2		All	Give swell on word "In," finishing *p* at word "going."
3		T.	

lone - ly bed, As one that

Each voice must put slight pressure on "as one," then *dim.* to *piano*.

6		T.	"I heard," put pressure on each word and ^v shade off to *piano*, all other voices to follow suit.
9 to 16		All	Smoothly in all parts, as marked in copy.
17	23	T.	Marked pressure on "That would," then quickly *dim.* to *p.* All the other voices give marked entry and *cres.* to bar 21.
21 to 24		All	Smooth cantabile *pp* and *cres.* In repeat open *ppp.*
25		All	*Molto cres.* to tenor entry "She rocked" *ff.* Other voices follow suit, then *dim.*
30		B.	Gentle pressure on "Then did she." Other voices follow suit but continual *cres.* to the tenor entry. The falling out,

$$f < f\!f > mf.$$

ff entries by other voices and finish *forte.*

"The Lady Oriana." *Wilbye.*

This madrigal is unusually difficult to interpret on account of the close imitations, to get which clearly defined requires great vocal control and agility; but if the following directions be carefully marked and followed, the great charms of this delightful and clever madrigal will be unfolded to the listener.

The music consists of contrasted phrases of points of imitation, followed by plain chordal passages.

Bar.	Beat.	Voice.	
1 and 2		C.	Contralto theme to be prominent, soprano *p*, tending to *pp*.
3	3	2nd T.	Theme prominent *f*.
4 and 5	2	1st T.	*Piano, semi-staccato.*
4, 5, 6	4	1st S.	*f p fp* *cres.* *p* The .. La - dy
6, 7, 8	1	B.	Theme *f*, all other parts *p*.
9 and 10		All	Plain, smooth singing as marked in copy.
11 and 12		All	The word "all" in every part to be struck *f* and then rapid *dim.* to *p* at words "in the."
13 to 15		All	Plain chording as in copy.
16 and 17		All	As bars 11-12.
18 to 22		All	Plain, as in copy.
22	2	T.	*f p* Other voices *piano*.
23	2	1st S.	*f p*
23	4	2nd S.	*f p* A thou - sand, thou-sand
24 to 33		All	Plain chording as in copy; mind contrasts in *p* and *f*.
34 to 37		2nd S.	Melody prominent, other voices subordinate.
38 and 39		C.	Melody for six notes prominent, then *p*.
39	3	1st S.	Take up theme prominently for six notes. The high 2nd soprano must be sung *pp*.
38 to 40		T.B.	To be subordinate to the ladies' voices.

Bar.	Beat.	Voice.	
41 to 44		All	Let each voice give accent on the syllables " vir," " ed," " crown." The 1st and 2nd sopranos will have some difficulty in doing this until they have studied it carefully.
45		All	Let each part sing the first two notes loudly to the syllables "which," " Ce," then *dim.* to *p* on succeeding syllables "re," " -mony ended." By doing this in every part the imitations will be made clear.
54 to 62		All	Plain chording to be sung as in copy.
63 to end		All	Give extra accent on the word " live," whenever it occurs in any voice. Sing the quavers (half beats) forcibly. Say every word clearly. Take ample breath, and finish as loudly as possible *ff* or *fff*.

Special Note.

You will notice that in the madrigals the same instruction is repeated time after time, so that if you learn to do a certain thing once (for instance, the striking of a note *f* and the sudden decrease to *p*) you should be able to apply the principle to all similar phrases. In a way, it is a trick, but to do it well, you must practise it assiduously until you can do it subconsciously. Practise each example separately. You will then get into the way of doing it spontaneously, which is the end in view.

" Go, Song of Mine." *Elgar.*

This piece—like all Sir Edward Elgar's works—is so carefully marked for expression that it will only be necessary to give one or two cautions where there is a tendency to sing other than as the copy directs.

2	4	All	Make a real *pianissimo* for all three beats at the words " and in tears," then at " go " give slight pressure, but not overdone.

Bar.	Beat.	Voice.	
7, 8, 9		T.	Tenor melody clear and distinct with velvety tone. Shade off to *ppp* at " heart of man."
8		S.	Soprano.—It is important to sing *ppp* in this bar to avoid obscuring tenor theme.
7, 8, 9	3	A.	
11	1	S.A.B.	Slight pressure on " say," then immediately *dim.* to *pp*.
11	3	T.	Tenor marked " say," then *dim.*
16 to 19		All	As bars 7, 8, 9.
33 to 35		T.	Bring out melody in imitation of soprano.
35 and 36		S.	Lead up to brilliant B natural.
37 to 45		A.T.B.	These bars I always compare to being " bunkered," but by care and skill, distinction can be achieved by the singers. See that the rhythm be well maintained, emphasizing the triplets. Test yourselves as to keeping the true pitch.
48 to 57		S.A.T.	Realise the true meaning of *pp dolcissimo*. The low basses may sing as loudly as they can.
60		S.A.B.	Make slight swell on "go," finishing with breath to silence.

" AWAKE, AWAKE ! " *Bantock.*

2	2	S.	Brilliant G, *staccato*, at " shout."
4		C.	Contraltos prominent this bar.
5		B.	Basses prominent this bar.
9 to 10		S.	Melody prominent.
11 and 12		T.	Melody prominent, other voices *p* to *pp*.
12 and 13		S.	Commence " sunbeams " *f*, then *dim.* to *p* at " delight."
14 and 15		T.	Bring out melody *f* to *mf*.

Bar.	Beat.	Voice.	
16, 17, 18	1	S. C.	
	2	T. B.	
20		T. B.	
23 to 25			Give emphasis to "reeling" in each voice (point of imitation).
27 to 33		All	Practise this with special reference to expression and pitch.
36 to 38		S. T.	These two parts are important for these bars, the tenors replying to sopranos as follows:—
		S.	
		T.	
40		S.C.T.	*Forte.*
41			*Molto dim.* to *p* or *pp.*
43	1	S.C.T.	*mf.*
43	2	B.	Marked *f* entry.
47 and 48		B.	Emphasis on "my bride, my play-," in response to sopranos.
50 to 53		All	"The Earth holds nought to match thy love,"
60 to 65			All parts subordinate to very soft bass. Sopranos must take great care to sing last note (E flat) in tune—not flat, as is often the case.

"There Rolls the Deep." *Parry.*

The elaborate markings of this piece must be closely followed to get a beautifully poetic rendering. Bars 20 and 31 should be practised assiduously until the delicate treatment of the sentiment is realised.

"On Himalay." *Bantock.*

This piece is chiefly antiphonal, one part replying to another. This is especially so between the soprano and tenor parts. The quavers in such voices want to be slightly emphasised, with clear diction, and all sustained notes sung with smooth restraint. Follow the expression marks, but bear the above in mind.

Bar.	Beat.	Voice.	
30 and 31		S.	These bars should be practised *pp* below the proper pitch until perfection of attack of the high note is attained, then take it at the proper pitch.

"The Cruiskeen Lawn." *Bantock.*

In this setting the melody in the second and third verses is not in the soprano part, but is divided between the contralto and the tenor parts, while in the chorus it alternates between the tenor and soprano voices.

In the third verse the basses and tenors have the tune alternately.

The problem here is to get the melody well defined, without materially altering the expression as given in the copy, and without any forcing of the voices, and also without sacrificing the fulness—as distinct from *forte*—of the tone of the choir.

This can be achieved by strengthing the voice part which has the melody, by adding to it some of the voices of the next part, thus rendering the opposing force weaker, while not taking anything away from the fulness and richness of tone of the choir.

The following shows how this is to be done successfully:—

Bar.	Beat.	Voice.	
11	2	B.	*f* *dim.* s' Gra - ma - chree.
	3	T.	*f* *dim.* s' Gra - ma - chree.
12	2	B.	*mf* *dim.* s' Gra - ma - chree.
	3	C.	*f* *dim.* s' Gra - ma - chree.

Bar.	Beat.	Voice.	
17 to 26		2nd S.	2nd sopranos sing with contraltos to bar 26, then sing their own part forward.
32 to 36	4	2nd T.	2nd tenors sing with basses to third beat of bar 36, then they sing their own part to the fourth beat of bar 40, when they again sing with the basses till bar 42.
43 to 46		2nd T.	Sing bass part to the first beat of bar 46, then sing their own part to end.

" MOONLIGHT." *Faning.* (*See* page 152.)

1 to 5		T.	Tenors prominent, but with pure velvety tone ; other voices *pp*.
1	2 and 3	S. C.	At " is " slight pressure and rapid *dim.* to *pp*.
7		B.	Pressure on " A-cross."
12		B.	Pressure on bass alone ; other parts must avoid giving pressure by " sympathy."

seems   to   the eyes, (*See* page 143.)

15 and 16		S.	
15 and 16		C.T.B.	
23		T.	Tenors prominent.
25		T.	Tenors prominent.
35 and 36		All	Clear words and delicate *staccato* at the triplets.
39		B.	Basses prominent, then subordinate.
41		C.	Contraltos prominent.
42 and 43		All	Real *pianissimo* with clear delicate diction.
47 and 48		T.	Tenors prominent, then subordinate.
55 to 60			Contraltos' moving crotchets prominent.
70 and 71		All	Same as bars 15 and 16.

Bar.	Beat.	Voice.	
72 and 73		All	A "comma" breath pause after "sorrow," and commence "sad" *ppp* with *cres.* on "eyes."
74 to end			Follow copy carefully, but at bar 90 the 1st bass must give "in the land" prominently, but IN TUNE.
92		All	At "sleep" long pause, with sound vanishing into silence.

"THE ANGEL'S WHISPER." *Coward.*

This piece is so carefully marked that few additional instructions will be necessary.

9 to 15		All	These bars should be mastered very well, so as to be sung with dramatic power : especially should the tenors and basses give these bars adequate attention.
30 to 35		C.T.B.	The accompanying voices, contraltos, tenors, and basses, should study these bars till they can be sung fluently.
76 to 81		C.T.B.	Here again complete mastery of the accompanying parts is necessary.

A SONG FOR THE SEASONS." *Smart.*

9		S. C.	Sing the *staccato* delicately.
10 to 12		T.	Tenors' reply to sopranos to be prominent.
10	1	S.	*fp* gorse - flow'r
16	2 to 4	All	*Molto cres.*
17		T.	Moving crotchets figure very prominent.
18		B.	Moving crotchets figure very prominent.
18	3	S.	*f* With . . a pret - ty haste.

Bar.	Beat.	Voice.	
22 to 25		1st C.	1st contraltos sing with 2nd sopranos from bar 22 to first beat of bar 25.
23 to 26		T.	Put pressure on every note to reply in imitation to theme in 2nd sopranos.
30 and forward		All	This 2nd verse will be taken rather slower than 1st verse.
40		T.	Tenors prominent.
41 and 42		C.	Contraltos prominent.
43		T.	Tenors prominent.
44	3 and 4	C.	Contraltos prominent.
63	3 and 4		Third verse *allegro*.
72	3 and 4	C.	Bold entry of contraltos.
85		T.	Tenor reply to soprano lead to be prominent.
87		T. B.	Bold entry of tenors and basses, the words "my love" very clear.
93 to 97			These bars are a repetition of bars 22 to 26, and must be treated in the same way.
99 & 100			Make very bold finish.

"THE NIGHTS." *Challinor*.

This effective and well-marked piece calls for few observations.

21	1 and 2	T. B.	Words "and a step," very emphatic.
22		2nd T.	2nd tenors sing with the basses to first beat of bar 24, then take their own part.
25 to 39		All	The descriptive element must be very pronounced in these bars, therefore the music and words should be thoroughly mastered, especially the semiquaver points of imitation.
40 to 48		All	A cold, clear, soft tone is wanted here.
47 and 49		T. B.	Tenors and basses should be sure of true intonation in these two bars.
51 to end			Get very reposeful ending.

"THE SHEPHERD'S LAMENT." *Smart.*

Bar.	Beat.	Voice.	
10 and 11		B.	Give prominence to the words "The flocks as they " and " my dog."
14 to 19	3	All	These are critical bars, which should be practised assiduously till memorised.
			The tenors should say " Yet how I can scarcely tell " with clear, sympathetic tone and faultless diction. In bars 17 and 18 great care should be taken to sing with clear nasal resonance, or flattening will ensue, the G♮ being frequently below pitch.
			In bar 15 the sopranos, contraltos, and basses nearly always sing too loudly, and fail to say " yet how " with the crisp delicacy required.
			Let every part attend to the intonation and pitch.
28		C.	Contralto words to be very clear.
29 to 31		B.	Basses prominent, with very clear words.
33 to 39			*See* remarks, bars 14 to 19.
43 to 45		S.C.T.	Great care will be required to sing *pianissimo* and maintain the pitch.
45	2	B.	There is a marked tendency to sing B♭ (s₁) instead of B♮ (se₁). To avoid this take your note mentally from the tenor B♮ of the previous bar.
48	2	T.	Slight prominence to the words " To some."
54		C.	Give prominence to " The shepherd, O sad." Other parts short notes and *pp*.
55		T.	Tenors prominent to reply to contraltos.
56		S.	Sopranos prominent; carry point of imitation to its climax.
59		All	Put tears into the word " sad."
61		All	Shade *pp* into silence.

Notes on "Elijah" Choruses.

PART I.

No. 1.—"Help, Lord."

Bar.	Beat.	Voice.	
1		All	In addition to *fortissimo*, show anxiety in voice.
11		T.	*Crescendo* at words "summer days are gone," then *dim.* to *piano* on word "gone,"—follow this pattern in all voices. In every case get words very clear on " and yet no power."
29	3	T.	" And yet no " emphatic.
35	3	All	Letter A. Very clear words; dark, breathy tone, *pp* for two bars, then *cres.*
41	2	T.	Theme prominent from this point. Let the words " Will then the Lord " be prominent in each voice.
50	1	A.	Emphasis on " The harvest now."
50	3	T.	Emphasis on "harvest now"; see that bass C sharp is true.
52	1	B.	" Harvest now " very prominent. This to be taken up by altos, sopranos, and tenors in succession.
56		All	Breath after " yet."
57		All	Breath after " cometh."

No. 2.—"Lord, bow Thine ear."

Bring out contrasts of expression as shown in markings.

No. 5.—"Yet doth the Lord."

Bar	Beat	Voice	
1	3	B.	Show resentful discontent in voices. Rather *staccato* entry in each voice.
15	1	S.	" His curse " to be sung with a great emphasis on the " c " and "r."
21		T.	Tenor entry to be heard, if possible.
25	2	A.	Altos set pattern of saying " His wrath " fiercely with trilled " r." Give dramatic import by accentuating " curse " and "wrath " all through.

Letter C.	Metronome 60.
Letter D.	Slight *accelerando.* Marked entries of all voices at "His mercies." Last four bars *dim.* and *rall.*

No. 9.—"BLESSED ARE THE MEN."

	Gentle pressure in all voices on word "blessed," shading to *pianissimo* at "ed."
Letter A.	"Thro' darkness—" marked *cres.* to word "light" should be brilliant; *dim.* to *piano* at "right." "Through" to be clear at each entry.
Letter B.	"He is gracious," the words very clear here. Six bars from end, very sweet entry of tenors, tending to *pianissimo ;* ditto contraltos, with real *pianissimo* ending.

No. 10.—"THOU ART ELIJAH."

Letter A.	Dramatic utterance of "Thou"— forceful and sharp.
Letter B.	"And then—" breath after "then," *cres.* to "God is the Lord." 7 bars from end, "yea," get awe in voice, and breathy tone at "let him be God."

No. 11.—"BAAL WE CRY TO THEE." (*See* page 100.)

M. 60. After each *sforzando* make decided *diminuendo.*

"HEAR US, BAAL."

Bar.	Beat.	Voice.	
2		All	*Crescendo* on word "fall"; "extirpate the foe"—very savagely.
		S.	16 bars after letter C, take breath after "us"; strike "Baal" very firmly, then *dim.* to *piano.* "Hear" and "us" ditto.

"HEAR OUR CRY, O BAAL."

M. about 100. Beat two in a bar. *Presto* 6-8.

"BAAL, HEAR AND ANSWER."

Bar.	Beat.	Voice.	
			Everything in this section *marcato*, typical of frenzied earnestness. M. about 120.
		S. & C.	Pause bars—great *crescendos*.
		T. & B.	Pause bars—great sustained *crescendo* on "an-" then *molto dim.* to *pianissimo* on "-swer." Long rest as though waiting for Baal to answer, then frenzied cries for Baal.

No. 16. – "THE FIRE DESCENDS."

Letter B.	In each part very clear words and notes at " the flames consume his offering." " Upon your faces fall," dark, breathy tone, *pp*. "The Lord is God " *pianissimo;* keep same dark tone, then *crescendo*. " Take all the prophets." Mind all consonants here, and get graphic tone-colour, especially at "slay them "—let it be killing tone.

No. 19.—"OPEN THE HEAVENS." (*See* pages 126, 127.)

Commence *pp*, decided *cres.* to "relief" on the minim *molto dim.* to *pp*. " Help, help Thy servant " to be sung by 1st sopranos only, to secure very subdued effect. Same directions for " Then hear from heaven "; let 2nd sopranos alone sing " Help send," &c.

No. 20.—"THANKS BE TO GOD."

Bar	Beat	Voice	
2	1	B.	Open in grand, impressive style. M. about 90.

Letter A.	*Accel.* to M. 130. At four bars before letter C broaden out considerably to about M. 72. Five bars after C, " Thanks be to God " *tempo* for 9 bars, then M. 72 at " But the Lord."
Letter D.	*Tempo* and *accel.* to M. 144.
Letter E.	M 160. Last 10 bars "Thanks be to God " *fff* majestic. M. 70.

PART II.

No. 22.—" BE NOT AFRAID."

	Più animato. Get words " though thousands languish " very clear.
Bar 15.	Tenor entry to be made distinct.
Letter B.	Nine bars after, great emphasis on " Though thousands " in each voice in succession.
	Last 10 bars broad and sustained. M. 72.

No. 23.

Let choir sing like an excited mob, especially at the end.

No. 24.—" WOE TO HIM."

	Very marked rhythm in all voices at " Woe to him "—give full attention to *sf*.
Bar 13.	The tenor phrase "and why hath he" very emphatic.
Bar 16.	The alto crotchets *ff*.
Bar 17.	Let sopranos be the climax of this section.
Letter A.	At the words "let the guilty prophet," get very marked rhythm and hard, sinister tone-quality.
	Last 3 bars, " so go ye forth, seize on him," very clear diction, with killing tone.

No. 29.—" HE WATCHING OVER ISRAEL."

To be very calmly and sweetly sung.

Bar 11.	Bass entry with a little emphasis.
Letter A.	"Should'st thou walking in grief." Whenever this phrase occurs, begin softly and carry the *cres.* forward to "languish." Sing the crotchet loudly with marked *dim.* on the succeeding minim.
Letter B.	Four bars before. Here the two subjects are given in opposition to each other. In every voice slight emphasis on "watching," and sing the word slightly *staccato.*
	Last six bars of vocal part—carefully follow markings, and finish real *pp.*

No. 32.—" HE THAT SHALL ENDURE." (*See* pages 159-162.)

Bar 5.	The tenors sing *mf* with emphasis on first 3 beats; the sopranos, altos and basses meanwhile sing *pp* for 3 beats, then *cres.* to *f.*
Bar 11.	Altos very emphatic at "He that shall."
Bar 14.	Basses ditto.
Bar 20.	Emphasis on the two minims, next crotchets in bass "He that shall."
Bar 24.	Bass emphatic on "He that shall endure"; sopranos, altos, and tenors *pp* in same bar.
Bar 25.	Slight emphasis on "He that" in tenors and contraltos; and in next bar "He that" in sopranos.
	Last 3 bars very soft indeed, like angelic voices.

No. 34.—" BEHOLD, GOD THE LORD."

Bars 12 and 13.	Give prominence to the word "rent" in all voices, and in succeeding bars great emphasis at "break," trilling the "r."

Letter B (bars 17, 18, after).	Give prominence to words "earth" and in succeeding bars "sea."
Letter B (bars 23, 24, after).	Let the word "sea," and later the word "earth," be heard in succession in all parts.
Letter C.	A little slower for 5 bars and *pp.* "And after the earthquake—" sing with great excitement and clear enunciation of the word "fire."
Letter D.	Get words very clear at "But yet the Lord."
Letter F.	10 bars before, altos rather prominent; 2 bars later, altos sing "onward came" with emphasis shading to *pp.* Then tenors sing "onward came" with emphasis shading to *pp.* Four bars later, altos give emphasis on "onward," followed again by tenors singing "onward" prominently; sopranos and basses meanwhile sing *pp.* The end of chorus to be very softly sung.

No. 35.—" HOLY, HOLY."

Very clear words in the soft passage.

No. 36.—" GO, RETURN.

	Take breath after " go."
Bar 2.	Give emphasis on " For."
Bar 6.	*Molto cres.* to lead up to entry of ladies' voices.

No. 38.—" THEN DID ELIJAH."

	To be sung in a declamatory manner.
Letter B.	"And when the Lord" very clear and incisive, finishing *fortissimo.* At the words " Lo ! there came a fiery chariot," commence with dark, breathy tone. In " He went with a whirlwind to heaven," be sure to get notes correct and sing with great fervour *ff.*

No. 41.—"But the Lord."

Bar 6.	*Molto cres.*
Bar 15.	Bass entry emphatic, or it will not be heard. At words " The spirit of wisdom and understanding," very clear diction.
Letter C.	Slight pause before the words " and the fear of the Lord"; these words to be sung slowly. M. 72.

No. 42.—"Then shall your Light."

	Bold entry.
Bar 9.	Tenor entry, real *p*.
Bar 10.	Soprano entry, real *p*. Bass entry *mf*. These three parts keep down while altos enter *f* at bar 12 (*see* page 156).
Bar 14.	All voices *cres.* to end of that section. At words " Lord our Creator " let every voice give emphasis to those words, marking rhythm well.
14 bars from the end.	The sopranos sing with *molto cres.* to first minim of next bar, then *dim.*, as shown below :—

$$\overline{\ \textit{ff}\ }$$

A - - men.

The contraltos and tenors follow this pattern in succeeding bar. At each succeeding recurrence the sopranos, contraltos and tenors make this swell more marked, and at the fourth bar from the end the basses emphasise this feature as much as they possibly can, and thus make the oratorio finish with a blaze of glory.

APPENDIX II.

CIRCULAR TO MEMBERS OF THE WORLD TOUR CHOIR.

[NOTE.—*The following appears after instructions as to time of sailing, luggage, and list of madrigals, glees, part-songs and choruses to be sung on the tour.*]

The foregoing (160 pieces) is a long and exacting list of music to memorise, but as so much of it is already known, your daily practice and enthusiasm for the scheme will enable you to surmount all difficulties.

METHOD IS THE SECRET OF SUCCESS.

To achieve the goal of our endeavours—perfection of performance of *each* of the above pieces—we must take the motto:

"METHOD IS THE SECRET OF SUCCESS,"

as a good working axiom.

In this relation there are several instructions to be followed, which for a less important event might be considered unnecessary.

1.—It is advisable to underline in red ink the particular part you will have to sing.

2.—Please number in red ink, neatly and clearly, every bar or every third bar of every piece, as I shall issue instructions, later, stating how every bar of every piece is to be marked and sung. This will save immense time in rehearsal and lead to unity in performance.*

3.—Make special efforts to memorise the words. The most neglected part of a piece is the words. The part I lay most stress upon being perfect is—the words. To assist you in getting these perfect in articulation, pronunciation, and

---

x   * *See* pages 279-302.

characteristic diction, I have had the words of every piece printed in this booklet, so that being available in handy form they can be looked over at odd moments in arm-chair, motor, train, or tram.

4.—Practise reading aloud at least two pages of the part-song words daily. One page should be read *mf* and the next page *pp* with smart lip and tongue action.

A Plea for Constant Recapitulation.

To memorise words of music, frequent repetition is necessary. Instrumentalists who astonish us by their memory playing, learn their pieces by the frequent repetition necessary to overcome the technical difficulties. Let us take similar care, and we shall have no difficulty in memorising all the programme.

Hints on Private Practice.

1.—Practise each piece as though you had never seen it before. Even in pieces like the *Messiah* and *Elijah*, sing every bar with care until it is absolutely correct. By this means incorrect phrasings, semitones sung for full tones in the *Messiah*, runs and divisions, wrong chromatics, and many hoary errors and stereotyped mistakes will be banished from our performances.

2.—I would urge each singer to study the pieces seriatim. We are all inclined to give more attention to pieces we like than to those we rather dislike ; but as uniform excellence is demanded, please take the pieces in rotation.

3.—Practise the most difficult phrases of each piece much more than the easier portions. Put a circle round each difficult part and "grind" at it till it is mastered. This is important, because a choir gets its character from the way it surmounts difficulties. If a choir sings 99 per cent. of a piece well, and stumbles over the 1 per cent., however difficult the piece may be it suffers in prestige. Therefore take care of the difficult phrases ; the easy parts can take care of themselves.

4.—Practise five minutes each day some difficult or *pp* phrases with special reference to maintaining the pitch. Nothing "gives a choir away" more than flattening. Therefore the determination and habit of mind to keep the pitch should be cultivated. As far as possible I have avoided accepting any singer who either sang flat or showed a tendency to lose the pitch (flatten). I trust that you, by giving attention to this important point, will prove that my selection of yourself has in this respect been justified.

REHEARSALS AND REGISTRATIONS.

FULL, SECTIONAL, AND PRIVATE.

It goes without saying that every available rehearsal should be attended, due notice of which will be given.

As we shall give over 100 concerts (fancy over 100 times of thrill and delight), to ask you to average one rehearsal per concert will not be an extravagant demand. Please see that this be done either in Full or Sectional rehearsals. These latter will be arranged for privately, and called by the Local Convener.

That every member may receive full credit for all good work done, you will find at the end of this booklet a Diary in which you are requested to note day by day the full time you have devoted to the private study of the music or words of the works, as well as in Rehearsals (full and sectional). At each Full Rehearsal I hope to have the pleasure of noting your daily entries.

NECESSITY OF A HIGH IDEAL.

Some of the above requirements may seem too exacting, but we have to remember that we have the choral honour and dignity of the Motherland in our keeping. We must therefore have an exalted ideal, and must work with enthusiasm to attain it.

In addition to the above considerations, there are two very important reasons why I most strongly urge—nay, almost command—persistent work from the present moment to the 24th of March.

The first of these is : "The voice preservation aspect," which calls for our most serious thought.

By having both the words and music thoroughly mastered, you will be able to place your voice properly for each word and sound, and thus avoid vocal strain. This will enable you to keep your voice in form all through the Tour, as in Canada. Those who lack this power must expect voice failure.*

---

* *See* page 47.

The second reason is : "The pleasure preservation aspect." I am anxious that nothing preventable shall interfere with our pleasure and freedom from anxiety while on the Tour ; but the sense of inefficient preparation of any piece would be such an incubus to the whole party, that I appeal to all to accept cheerfully the drudgery of persistent practice to secure prospective pleasure, or in other words

"Take present pain
For future gain."

However, I have such confidence in the choir as a whole, that I feel I am voicing your sentiments when I say that if there be any individual member who does not regard the unique character of the Tour as calling for exceptional and determined efforts to achieve perfection, it is advisable for that member to resign at once, as none of us want any cold, half-hearted singers in our ranks.

With warmest greetings to all my colleagues in the enterprise,

Believe me,
Yours very truly,
H. COWARD.

S.M.U. WORLD TOUR.

SHEFFIELD,

DEAR SIR OR MADAM,   *February*, 1911.

Within a few weeks we embark at Liverpool upon our unique Tour Round the World. This fact suggests the importance of reviewing, revising and perfecting our preparedness for the great musical task before us. Especially would I urge upon each of you the importance of being note-perfect in the difficult phrases. Treat each passage as a solo instrumentalist does—sing it over until you have learned it subconsciously.

SINGING FROM SUBCONSCIOUS IMPULSE.—In reviewing our combined rehearsals, I have been profoundly impressed by the amount of work we have got through, and by the thoroughness shown ; but although it has collectively been wonderful that so much work should be so well done, if we had critically taken each chorus or piece separately, we should have found that the supreme finish which ought to be present in each item

was absent. Now, as each audience will judge us, not upon
the general average of 160 pieces, but upon the results shown
in a few items at each concert, it becomes imperative that we
perform each piece perfectly. Therefore we must avoid
thinking that we may sing some pieces poorly because we shall
sing other favourite pieces excellently, but bring every piece up
to the standard of perfection.

We must act on the principle of taking care of the
pence, and the pounds will take care of themselves. To do
this, may I suggest that each piece be mastered subconsciously
as most of us know the *Messiah* choruses, so that we may
sing by *the impulse from within.* It is an achievement to be able
to follow the conductor's directions, but it is a greater thing to
know and feel what the conductor wants, so as to do it
automatically, guided by *the impulse from within.* Soloists get
little assistance from conductors, because they have to depend
upon themselves. Now, as we shall have to sing occasionally
with strange conductors, I want you to realise the importance
of doing everything with reflex action of the mind, therefore
please raise your standard of learning each piece until you can
sing it with proper expression by *the impulse from within,*
irrespective of the conductor. If he should give you the proper
" leads " all the better, but learn the pieces so well that you
can be independent of direction.

MARKING OF EXPRESSION.—Owing to the absence of
some members at each rehearsal, my instructions with respect
to the marks of expression have not been entered by all the
choir. I have therefore been at the trouble of detailing the
principal points which I want to be carried out in some of the
more intricate or delicate phrases of the various numbers.*
Each singer must enter these instructions relating to his or
her part before next Saturday, as these five pieces will be
rehearsed then. Please regard all the time taken up as so
much rehearsal, and enter it in the Diary.†

---

* *See* pages 279-295.   † *See* page 305.

APPENDIX III.

SINGING WITH LATIN WORDS.

There are a few classics which it is advisable, if not imperative, to sing in Latin. To secure uniformity of pronunciation the scheme shown in the following instructions has been used with gratifying results.

The chief difficulty is to get English choralists to sing Latin with the broad Italianized vowels. It is rather difficult to give the exact vowel quantity of some of the words containing " e," " i," and " o," but the subjoined phonetic spellings give an *approximately* correct scheme for practical purposes.

In a few words the vowels are given a broader sound than strict correctness demands. But experience has shown that this broad vowel scheme is advisable because, as English choral singers have a natural tendency to favour the lighter vowel quantity, they therefore, in the few cases required, easily learn to modify the broad sounds to the conductor's pattern, which should be given in every case.

Model followed by the SHEFFIELD MUSICAL UNION, LEEDS CHORAL UNION, HUDDERSFIELD FESTIVAL CHORAL SOCIETY, and NEWCASTLE CHORAL SOCIETY.

BEETHOVEN'S MASS.
KYRIE.

Kyrie eleison,
Kee-ree-ay ay-lay-ee-*zohn
Lord, have mercy upon us,

Christe eleison.
Kree-stay ay-lay-ee-zohn.
Christ, have mercy upon us.

---

* When "s" occurs between two vowels it is usually sounded more like the English " z "

GLORIA.

Gloria in excelsis Deo, et in terra pax,
Glaw-ree-ah een ex-chel-seece Day-oh, *ait een ter-rah pahx,*
Glory be to God on high, and in earth peace,

hominibus bonae voluntatis. Laudamus te,
hoh-mee-nee-booce boh-nay vol-oon-tah-teece. Lah-oo-dah-mooce tay,
good will towards men. We praise Thee,

benedicimus te, adoramus te,
bay-nay-dee-chee-mooce tay, *ah-doh-rah-mooce tay,*
we bless Thee, we worship Thee,

glorificamus te, Gratias agimus tibi
glaw-ree-fee-kah-mooce tay, Grah-tsee-ahce ah-jee-mooce tee-be
we glorify Thee, we give thanks to Thee

propter magnam gloriam tuam, Domine Deus,
prohp-tair mahn-yahm glaw-ree-ahm too-ahm, Do-mee-nay Day-ooce
for Thy great glory, O Lord God,

Rex coelestis, Deus Pater omnipotens.
raix chay-layee-teece, *Day-ooce pah-tair (or ter) ohm-nee-poh-taince.*
heavenly King, God the Father Almighty.

Domine Fili unigenite, Jesu Christe,
Do-mee-nay Fee-lee oo-nee-jen-e-tay, Yay-zoo Kree-stay,
O Lord, the only-begotten Son Jesu Christ;

Domine Deus, Agnus Dei, Filius Patris,
Do-mee-nay Day-ooce, Ahn-yooce Day-ee, Fee-lee-ooce Pah-treece,
O Lord God, Lamb of God, Son of the Father,

Qui tollis peccata mundi, miserere nobis,
Kwee tohl-leece pek-kah-tah moon-dee, mee-zay-ray-ray noh-beece,
That takest away the sins of the world, have mercy upon us,

suscipe deprecationem nostram;
soo-shee-pay day-pray-kah-tsee-oh-naim noh-strahm;
receive our prayer;

Qui sedes ad dexteram Patris, miserere nobis.
Kwee say-dace ahd daix-tay-rahm Pah-treece, mee-zay-ray-ray noh-beece
Thou that sittest at the right hand of God the Father,
[have mercy upon us.

Quoniam   tu   solus   sanctus,   Tu solus   Dominus,
Kwo-ne-ahm   too soh-looce   sahngk-tooce,   Too soh-looce Do-mee-nooce,
For Thou only art holy,   Thou only art the Lord;

Tu   solus   altissimus,   Jesu   Christe,
Too   soh-looce   ahl-teece-see-mooce,   Yay-zoo   Kree-stay,
Thou only art most high,   Jesus   Christ,

cum   Sancto   spiritu   in   gloria   Dei   Patris.
koom   Sahngk-toh   spee-ree-too   een   glaw-ree-ah   Day-ee Pah-treece.
with the Holy Ghost   in the glory of God the Father.

Amen.
Ah-main.

CREDO.

Credo   in   unum   Deum,   Patrem   omnipotentem,
Kray-doh   een   oon-oom   Day-oom   Pah-traim om-nee-poh-tain-taim,
I believe in one God,   the Father Almighty,

factorem   coeli   et   terrae,   visibilium   omnium
fahk-toh-raim   chay-lee ait   tair-ray,   vee-zee-bee-lee-oom   om-nee-oom
Maker of heaven and earth,   And of all things visible

et   invisibilium.   Credo   in   unum   Dominum
ait   een-vee-zee-bee-lee-oom.   Kray-doh   een   oo-noom   Do-mee-noom
and invisible.   I believe in one Lord

Jesum   Christum,   Filium   Dei   unigenitum,
Yay-zoom   Kree-stoom,   Fee-lee-oom   Day-ee   oo-nee-jen-e-toom,
Jesus   Christ,   the only-begotten Son of God,

et   ex   Patre   natum   ante   omnia   saecula:
ait   aix   Pah-tray   nah-toom   ahn-tay   om-nee-ah   say-koo-lah:
Begotten of His Father   before all worlds,

Deum   de   Deo;   lumen   de   lumine;
Day-oom   day   Day-oh;   loo-main   day   loo-mee-nay;
God of God,   Light of Light,

Deum   verum   de   Deo   vero;   genitum
Day-oom   vay-room   day   Day-oh   vay-roh;   jen-e-toom
Very God of Very God,   Begotten,

non   factum;   consubstantialem   Patri,
nohn   fahk-toom;   kohn-soob-stahn-tsee-ah-laim   Pah-tree,
not made,   Being of one substance with the Father;

per   quem   omnia   facta   sunt.
pair   *kwaim*   *om-nee-ah*   *fahk-tah*   *soont.*
By   whom   all things were made :

Qui   propter   nos   homines,
Kwee   *prohp-tair*   *noce*   *hoh-mee-nace,*
Who for us men,

et   propter   nostram   salutem,
ait   *prohp-tair*   *noh-strahm*   *sah-loo-taim,*
and for our salvation,

descendit   de   coelis,
day-shain-dit   *day*   *chay-leece (or lis),*
came down from heaven,

Et   incarnatus   est   de   Spiritu   Sancto,
Ait   *een-kar-nah-tooce*   *aist*   *day*   *Spee-ree-too*   *Sahngk-toh,*
And was incarnate   by the Holy Ghost

ex   Maria   Virgine,   Et   homo   factus   est,
aix   *Mah-ree-ah*   *Veer-jee-nay,*   *Ait*   *hoh-moh*   *fahk-tooce*   *aist,*
of the Virgin Mary,   And was made man,

Crucifixus   etiam   pro nobis,   sub Pontio   Pilato ;
Kroo-chee-feex-ooce ait-ee-ahm pro noh-beece, soob Pont-see-oh Pee-lah-toh;
Was crucified also for us   under Pontius Pilate;

passus   et   sepultus   est,
pahce-sooce   *ait*   *say-pool-tooce*   *aist,*
He suffered   and   was buried,

Et   resurrexit   tertiâ   die   secundum   Scripturas,
Ait ray-zoor-raix-eet tair-tsee-ah dee-ay say-koon-doom Screep-too-rahce,
And rose again   the third day   according to the Scriptures,

Et   ascendit   in coelum,   sedet   ad dexteram   Patris ;
Ait ah-shen-deet een chay-loom, say-dait ahd daix-tay-rahm Pah-treece ;
And ascended into heaven,   And sitteth at the right hand of the
                                              [Father.

et   iterum   venturus   est   cum   gloria,
ait   *ee-tay-room*   *vain-too-rooce*   *aist*   *koom*   *glaw-ree-ah,*
And He shall come again   with glory

Judicare   vivos   et   mortuos ;
Yoo-dee-kah-ray   *vee-voce*   *ait*   *mohr-too-ohce ;*
to judge   both the quick and the dead :

cujus regni non erit finis.
koo-yooce *rain-yee* *nohn* *ay-reet* *fee-neece.*
Whose kingdom shall have no end.

Credo in Spiritum Sanctum,
Kray-doh *een* *Spee-ree-toom* *Sahngk-toom,*
I believe in the Holy Ghost,

Dominum et vivificantem,
Do-mee-noom *ait* *vee-vee-fee-kahn-taim,*
the Lord and Giver of life,

qui ex Patre Filioque procedit ;
kwee *aix* *Pah-tray* *Fee-lee-oh-kway* *proh-chay-dit ;*
Who proceedeth from the Father and the Son,

qui cum Patre et Filio
kwee *koom* *Pah-tray* *ait* *Fee-lee-oh*
Who with the Father and the Son

simul adoratur et conglorificatur ;
see-mool *ah-doh-rah-toor* *ait* *kohn-gloh-ree-fee-cah-toor ;*
together is worshipped and glorified,

qui locutus est per prophetas.
kwee *loh-koo-tooce* *aist* *pair* *proh-fay-tahce.*
Who spake by the Prophets.

Credo in unam sanctam Catholicam
Kray-doh *een* *oo-nahm* *sahngk-tahm* *Kah-toh-lee-kahm*
I believe in one holy Catholic

et Apostolicam Ecclesiam.
ait *Ah-poh-stoh-lee-kahm* *Aik-klay-zee-ahm.*
and Apostolic Church.

Confiteor unum Baptisma
Kohn-fee-tay-ohr *oo-noom* *Bahp-teece-mah*
I acknowledge one Baptism

in remissionem peccatorum.
een *ray-meece-see-oh-naim* *pek-kah-toh-room.*
for the remission of sins.

Et expecto Resurrectionem mortuorum,
Ait *aix-paik-toh* *Ray-zoor-raik-tsee-oh-naim* *mor-too-or-oom,*
And I look for the Resurrection of the dead,

et	vitam	venturi	saeculi.	Amen.
ait	*vee-tahm*	*vain-too-ree*	*say-koo-lee.*	*Ah-main.*
and the life of the world to come.				Amen.

SANCTUS.

Sanctus	Dominus	Deus	Sabaoth.
Sahngk-tooce	*Do-mee-nooce*	*Day-ooce*	*Sah-bah-oht.*
Holy, Lord God of hosts,			

Pleni	sunt	coeli	et	terra	gloria	Tua,
Play-nee	*soont*	*chay-lee*	*ait*	*tair-rah*	*glaw-ree-ah*	*Too-ah,*
heaven and earth are full of Thy glory :						

Osanna	in	excelsis.
O-zahn-nah	*een*	*ex-chel-sis.*
Hosanna in the highest.		

Benedictus	qui	venit	in	nomine	Domini.
Bay-nay-deek-tooce	*kwee*	*vay-neet*	*een*	*no-mee-nay*	*Do-mee-nee.*
Blessed is he that cometh in the name of the Lord.					

AGNUS DEI.

Agnus	Dei,	qui	tollis	peccata	mundi,
Ahn-yooce	*Day-ee*	*kwee*	*tohl-leece*	*pek-kah-tah*	*moon-dee,*
O Lamb of God,		that takest away the sins of the world,			

miserere	nobis.	Dona	nobis	pacem.
mee-zay-ray-ray	*noh-beece.*	*Doh-nah*	*noh-beece*	*pah-chaim.*
have mercy upon us.		Grant us Thy peace.		

BACH'S MASS IN B MINOR.

Nos. 1 and 3.

Kyrie	eleison.
Kee-ree-ay	*ay-lay-ee-zohn.*

No. 4.

Gloria	in	excelsis	Deo,	et	in	terra
Glaw-ree-ah	*een*	*ex-chel-seece*	*Day-oh,*	*ait*	*een*	*ter-rah*

pax,	hominibus	bonae	voluntatis.
pahx,	*ho-mee-nee-booce*	*boh-nay*	*vo-loon-tah-teece.*

No. 6.

Gratias	agimus	tibi	propter	magnam
Grah-tsee-ahce	*ah-jee-mooce*	*tee-be*	*prohp-tair*	*mahn-yahm*

gloriam	tuam.
glaw-ree-ahm	*too-ahm.*

No. 8.

Qui	tollis	peccata	mundi,	miserere	nobis,
Kuee	*tohl-leece*	*pek-kah-tah*	*moon-dee,*	*mee-zay-ray-ray*	*noh-beece,*

suscipe	deprecationem	nostram.
soo-shee-pay	*day-pray-kah-tsee-oh-naim*	*noh-strahm.*

No. 11.

Cum	Sancto	spiritu	in	gloria	Dei
Koom	*Sahngk-toh*	*spee-ree-too*	*een*	*glaw-ree-ah*	*Day-ee*

Patris,	Amen.
Pah-treece.	*Ah-main.*

No. 12.

Credo	in	unum	Deum.
Kray-doh	*een*	*oo-noom*	*Day-oom.*

No. 13.

Patrem	omnipotentem,	factorem	coeli	et
Pah-traim	*om-nee-poh-tain-taim,*	*fahk-toh-raim*	*chay-lee*	*ait*

terrae,	visibilium	omnium	et
tair-ray,	*vee-zee-bee-lee-oom*	*om-nee-oom*	*ait*

invisibilium.
een-vee-zee-bee-lee-oom.

No. 15.

Et	incarnatus	est	de	Spiritu	Sancto,	ex
Ait	*een-kar-nah-tooce*	*aist*	*day*	*Spee-ree-too*	*Sahngk-toh,*	*aix*

Maria	Virgine,	Et	homo	factus	est.
Mah-ree-ah	*Veer-jee-nay,*	*Ait*	*hoh-moh*	*fahk-tooce*	*aist.*

No. 16.

Crucifixus	etiam	pro nobis,	sub Pontio
Kroo-chee-feex-ooce	*ait-ee-ahm*	*pro noh-beece,*	*soob Pont-see-oh*

Pilato;   passus   et   sepultus   est.
Pee-lah-toh ; pahce-sooce ait say-pool-tooce aist.

No. 17.

Et   resurrexit   tertiâ   die   secundum
Ait   ray-zoor-raix-eet tair-tsee-ah dee-ay say-koon-doom

Scripturas,   Et   ascendit   in   coelum,   sedet
Screep-too-rahce ; Ait ah-shen-deet een chay-loom, say-dait

ad   dexteram   Dei   Patris;   et   iterum   ven-
ahd daix-tay-rahm Day-ee Pah-treece ; ait ee-tay-room vain-

turus   est   cum   gloria,   Judicare   vivos   et
too-rooce aist koom glaw-ree-ah, Yoo-dee-kah-ray vee-voce ait

mortuos;   cujus   regni   non   erit   finis.
mohr-too-ohce ; koo-yooce rain-yee nohn ay-eet fee-neece.

No. 19.

Confiteor   unum   Baptisma   in   remissionem
Kohn-fee-tay-ohr oo-noom Bahp-teece-mah een ray-meece-see-oh-naim

peccatorum.   Et   expecto   Resurrectionem
pek-kah-toh-room. Ait aix-paik-toh Ray-zoor-vaik-tsee-oh-naim

mortuorum,   et   vitam   venturi   saeculi.   Amen.
mor-too-or-oom. ait vee-tahm vain-too-ree say-koo-lee. Ah-main.

No. 20.

Sanctus   Dominus   Deus   Sabaoth.
Sahngk-tooce Do-mee-nooce Day-ooce Sah-bah-oht.

Pleni   sunt   coeli   et   terra   gloria   ejus.
Play-nee soont chay-lee ait tair-rah glaw-ree-ah ay-yoos.

No. 21.

Hosanna   in   excelsis.
Hoh-zahn-nah een ex-chel-sis.

No. 24.

Dona   nobis   pacem.
Doh-nah noh-beece pah-chaim.

VERDI'S " REQUIEM."

Requiem   aeternam   dona   eis   Domine;
Rek-wee-em   ay-tair-nahm   doh-nah   ay-eece   Do-mee-nay;

et lux perpetua   luceat   eis!   Te decet
ait loox pair-pay-too-ah loo-chay-aht ay-eece! Tay day-chayt

hymnus,   Deus, in Sion,   et Tibi reddetur
heem-nooce, Day-ooce, een See-on, ait tee-bee rayd-day-toor

vo-tum in Jerusalem: exaudi   orationem
voh-toom een Yay-roo-sah-laim: aix-ow-dee oh-rah-tsee-oh-naim

meam,   ad te omnis   caro   veniet.
may-ahm, ahd tay ohm-neece cah-roh vay-nee-ait.

Kyrie   eleison,   Christe   eleison.
Kee-ree-ay ay-lay-ee-zohn, Krees-tay ay-lay-ee-zohn.

Dies irae, dies illa, Solvet saeclum in
Dee-ayce ee-ray, dee-ayce eel-lah Sohl-vait say-kloom een

favilla, Teste David cum Sybilla. Quantus
fah-veel-lah Tais-tai Dah-veed coom See-beel-lah. Quahn-tooce

tremor est futurus, Quando Judex est
tray-mohr aist foo-too-rooce, Quahn-doh Yoo-daix aist

venturus, Cuncta stricte discussurus.
vain-too-rooce, Koongk-tah streek-tay dees-koos-soo-rooce.

Tuba mirum spargens sonum, Per sepulchra
Too-bah mee-room spar-jayns soh-noom, Pair say-pool-krah

regionum, Coget omnes ante thronum.
ray-jee-oh-noom, Koh-jait omnaice ahn-tay troh-noom.

Rex tremendae majestatis, Qui salvandos
Raix tray-main-day mah-yais-tah-teece, Quee sahl-van-doce

salvas gratis, Salva me, fons pietatis.
sahl-vahce grah-teece, Sahl-vah may, fohnce pee-ay-tah-teece.

Huic ergo parce Deus: Lacrymosa dies
Hoo-eek air-goh par-chay Day-ooce Lah-kree-moh-sah dee-ayce

illa,   Qua   resurget   ex   favilla,   judicandus
eel-lah,   *Quah*   *ray-soor-jayt*   *aix*   *fah-veel-lah,*   *yoo-dee-kahn-dooce*

homo   reus.   Pie   Jesu   Domine,   Dona
hoh-moh   *ray-ooce.*   *Pee-ay*   *Yai-zoo*   *Do-mee-nay,*   *Doh-nah*

eis   requiem.   Amen.
'y-eece   *ray-quee-aim.*   *Ah-main.*

Sanctus   Dominus   Deus   Sabaoth :   Pleni
Sahngk-tooce   *Do-mee-nooce*   *Day-ooce*   *Sah-bah-oht :*   *Play-nee*

sunt   coeli   et   terra   gloria   Tua.   Hosanna
soont   *chay-lee*   *ait*   *ter-rah*   *glaw-ree-ah*   *Too-ah.*   *Hoh-zahn-nah*

in   excelsis.   Benedictus   qui   venit   in
een   *ex-chel-sis.*   *Bay-nay-deek-tooce*   *kwee*   *vay-neet*   *een*

nomine   Domini.
no-mee-nay   *Do-mee-nee.*

Agnus   Dei,   qui   tollis   peccata   mundi,
Ahn-yooce   *Day-ee*   *kwee*   *tohl-leece*   *pek-kah-tah*   *moon-dee,*

dona   eis   requiem   sempiternam.
doh-nah   *ay-eece*   *rek-wee-em*   *saym-pee-tayr-nahm.*

Libera   me,   Domine,   de   morte   aeterna,   in
Lee-bay-rah   *may,*   *Do-mee-nay,*   *day*   *mor-tay*   *ay-tair-nah*   *een*

dies   illa   tremenda :   quando   coeli
dee-ayce   *eel-lah*   *tray-mayn-dah :*   *kwan-doh*   *chay-lee*

movendi   sunt   et   terra.   Dies   irae,   Dies
moh-vayn-dee   *soont*   *ait*   *ter-rah.*   *Dee-ayce*   *ee-ray,*   *Dee-ayce*

illa   calamitatis   et   miseriae :   Dies
eel-lah   *kah-lah-mee-tah-tees*   *ait*   *mees-ay-ree-ay :*   *Dee-ayce*

magna   et   amara   valde   Dum   veneris
mahn-yah   *ait*   *ah-mah-rah*   *vahl-day*   *Doom*   *vay-nay-rees*

judicare   saeculum   per   ignem.
yoo-dee-kah-ray   *say-koo-loom*   *pair*   *een-yaim.*

DVOŘÁK'S "STABAT MATER."

No. 1. CHORUS.

Stabat   Mater   dolorosa,
Stah-baht   Mah-tair (or *ter*)   *doh-lo-roh-sah,*

Juxta   crucem   lacrymosa,
Yook-stah   kroo-chem   la-kree-moh-sah,

Dum   pendebat   Filius.
Doom   pen-day-baht   Fee-lee-ooce.

O   quam   tristis   et   afflicta
O   quam   treece-teece ait   af-fleek-tah

Fuit   illa   benedicta
Foo-eet   eel-la   ben-ay-deek-tah

Mater   Unigeniti!
Mahter   Oo-ne-jen-e-tee!

Quae   moerebat   et   dolebat.
Quay   may-ray-baht   ayt   doh-lay-baht.

Pia   Mater   cum   videbat
Pee-ah   Mah-tair   koom   vee-day-baht

Nati   poenas   inclyti.
Nah-tee   pay-nahce   eeng-klee-tee.

Et   tremebat   cum   videbat
Ayt   tray-may-baht   koom   vee-day-baht

Nati   poenas   incliti.
Nah-tee   pay-nahce   eeng-klee-tee.

No. 3. CHORUS.

Eia   Mater,   fons   amoris,
Ay-ya   mah-tair   fohnce   ah-moh-reece

Me   sentire   vim   doloris
May   sain-tee-ray   veem   doh-loh-reece

Fac   ut   tecum   lugeam.
Fac   oot   tay-koom   loo-jay-am.

No. 4. Chorus.

Sancta   Mater,   istud   agas,
Sanc-ta   Mah-tair   ee-stood   ah-gahce

Crucifixi   fige   plagas
Kroo-chee-feek-see   fee-jay   plah-gahce

Cordi   meo   valide.
Kohr-dee   may-oh   vah-lee-day.

No. 5. Chorus.

Tui   Nati   vulnerati,
Too-ee   nah-tee   vool-nay-rah-tee

Tam   dignati   pro   me   pati,
Tahm   deen-yah-tee   pro   may   pah-tee

Poenas   mecum   divide.
Pay-nahce   may-koom   dee-vee-day.

No. 6. Chorus.

Fac   me   vere   tecum   flere,
Fahk   may   vay-ray   tay-koom   flay-ray,

Crucifixo   condolere,
Kroo-chee-feek-soh   kon-doh-lay-ray,

Donec   ergo   vixero.
Doh-nek   ayr-go   veek-say-roh.

Te   libenter   sociare
Tay   lee-bain-tair   soh-chee-ah-ray

In   planctu   desidero.
Een   plangk-too   day-see-day-roh.

No. 7. Chorus.

Virgo   virginum   praeclara,
Veer-goh   veer-jee-noom   pray-klah-rah,

Y

Mihi   jam   non   sis   amara,
Mee-hee   yam   non   seece   ah-mah-rah,

Fac   me   tecum   plangere.
Fac   may   tay-coom   plahn-jay-ray.

No. 10.   Chorus.

Quando   corpus   morietur
Quan-doh   cor-pooce   mo-ree-ay-toor

Fac   ut   animus   donetur
Fac   oot   ahn-ee-moos   doh-nay-toor

Paridisi   gloria.
Pah-rah-dee-see   glaw-ree-ah.

Amen.
Ah-main.

Berlioz's " Faust " (Novello).

Requiescat   in   pace. (p. 79.)
Rek-we-ais-kaht   een   pah-chay.

Students' Song (p. 67).

Jam   nox   stellata   velamina   pandit ;   nunc
Yam   nox   stayl-lah-tah   vay-lah-mee-nah   pahn-deet ; noonk

bibendum   et   amandum   est.   Vita   brevis
bee-bain-doom   ait   ah-mahn-doom   aist.   Vee-tah   bray-veece

fugax que   voluptas.   Gaudeamus   igitur.
foo-gahx kway   voh-loop-tahs.   Gow-day-ah-moos   ee-gee-toor.

Nobis   sub   ridente   luna   per   urbem   quae-
Noh-beece   soob   ree-dain-tay   loo-nah   pair   oor-baim   kway-

rentes   puellas   eamus !   Ut   cras   fortunati
rain-tayce   poo-ail-lahce   ay-ah-mooce !   Oot   krahce   for-too-nah-tee

Caesares   dicamus ;   veni,   vidi,   vici. (p. 140.)
Chay-sah-race   dee-cah-mooce ;   vee-nee,   vee-dee,   vee-chee.

WOMEN'S CHORUS.

Sancta	Maria,	ora	pro	nobis,	Magdale-
Sahngk-tah	*Mah-ree-ah,*	*oh-rah*	*pro*	*noh-bees.*	*Mahg-dah-lay-*

na.	Margarita,	ah !
nah.	*Mar-gah-ree-tah,*	*ah !*

DEMONS' CHORUS.

Irimiru	Karabrao,	Has. (p. 150.)
E-re-me-roo	*Kah-rah-brah-oh*	*Hass.*

Tradioun	Marexil	firtrudinxe	burrudixe
Trah-dee-oon	*Mah-rayx-eel*	*fer-troo-deenk-sai*	*boor-roo-deex-ee*

fory	my	dinkorlitz	O	merikahriu !
fo-ri	*mee*	*deen-kor-leetz*	*Oh*	*may-ree-kah-ree-oo !*

O	mevixe	Merikariba,	O	mindara
O	*may-veex-ay*	*May-ree-kah-ree-bah*	*O*	*meen-dah-rah*

caraibo	lakinda,	merondor	dinkorlitz,
cah-rah-ee-boh	*lah-keen-dah*	*may-ron-dor*	*deen-kor-leetz,*

Tradioun	marexil,	burudixe.	Fir	ome
Trah-dee-oon	*mah-rayx-eel*	*boo-roo-deex-ay.*	*Feer*	*oh-may*

vixe.	Trudinxe	caraibo.	Fir	ome
veex-ay.	*Troo-deenx-ay*	*cah-rah-ee-boh.*	*Feer*	*oh-may*

vixe	merondor.	Mit	aysko, oh !	Diff	Has.	Satan
veex-ay	*may-ron-dor.*	*meet*	*ays-koh-oh !*	*Diff*	*hass.*	*Sah-tan*

Belphegor,	Mephisto,	Kroix,	Astaroth,	Belzebuth,
Bel-fay-gor,	*Mef-ees-toh,*	*Kroh-eex,*	*As-tah-roht,*	*Bel-zee-boot,*

sat	rayk	irkimour.	Irimine	Karabrao.
sat	*ra-eek*	*eer-kee-moor.*	*E-re-me-nay*	*Kah-rah-brah-oh.*

INDEX

MUSICAL ILLUSTRATIONS